THE SECOND COMING

Tough Questions Answered

THE SECOND COMING

Tough Questions Answered

KEN & AGNES MACDONALD

The Second Coming: Tough Questions Answered
Ken and Agnes Macdonald

Printed in the United States of America
ISBN 0-962-6490-0-7
Library of Congress Catalog Card Number 90-091544

Scripture quotations are from the *King James Version* of the Bible.
The authors have italicized certain words for emphasis.

Dedication

This book is dedicated to the glory of God and to many earnest inquirers whom we've met in our ministry around the world. Their hunger to know the truth of God's Word spurred us on to seek answers to their many questions.

Contents

List of Charts

Preface

After serving in pastoral ministry in the United States for fifteen years, my wife and I experienced a fresh work of the Holy Spirit in our lives. Not only were we revived in our personal walk with Jesus, but God expanded our vision for His kingdom. Soon we sensed His call to go into all the world and preach the gospel. Enthusiasm gripped us as God opened door after door for our missionary-evangelistic ministry. After taking us to six continents, God has focused much of our overseas ministry in Africa.

The African people are especially inquisitive. Hours of lively discussion with our African friends filled our waking hours. In fact, many of their questions on the Second Coming have been included in this book. Because our inquirers had been affected by the "secret rapture" teaching, their questions, as well as others we've added, provide a good basis to answer the big question: Will the Church go through the Great Tribulation?

This book, which began as a personal research project, soon snowballed in size and scope. At first, it started as a study entitled, *Fourteen Reasons Why We Believe the Church Will Go Through the Tribulation.* We soon realized, however, that it was insufficient because of the teaching that certain portions of Scripture concerning the end-time and the Second Coming pertain to Israel, not to the Church. Consequently, we've included two chapters that address this very topic. With the help of the Lord, we also tackled the question, "Will all Israel be saved?"

Our research in the Scriptures also enabled us to find answers to related questions such as, "Who are the two witnesses?" and "Who are the 144,000?" Many people asked how a millennium after the return of Christ would be possible in light of the gospels and epistles. As a result, we added chapters twenty to twenty-three, "Heaven," "The Final Battle," and "A Literal Millennium?"

Some chapters are divided into two categories: Questions Answered and Objections Answered. We include many extra scripture references so the serious Bible student may pursue the various issues in depth. The questions and answers can be used easily for both personal research and Bible classes. We trust this book will spur you on to be like the Bereans who "searched the Scriptures daily, to see whether these things were so" (Acts 17:11).

The following pages will challenge your end-time theology. The message of this book cuts against the grain of some popular teaching on the Second Coming. It may even offend your long held personal beliefs on certain doctrines. But none of those reasons should deter the serious Bible student from examining what he believes about the Second Coming. Jesus promised that "the Spirit of truth . . . will guide you into all truth" (John 16:13). May you rely on the Holy Spirit for insight as you diligently search God's Word.

Introduction

The Bible speaks of an approaching day of "great tribulation, such as was not since the beginning of the world to this time, no, nor ever shall be" (Matt. 24:21); a time when the man of sin shall be revealed "whose coming is after the working of Satan with all power and signs and lying wonders" (2 Thess. 2:3,9); a time when "no man might buy or sell, save he that [have] the mark, or the name of the beast, or the number of his name" (666) (Rev. 13:17,18). Many ask when Christ will come to gather His Church—before or after this time of great tribulation? The question is not *whether* Christ will return, but *when*? Will the Church go through the Great Tribulation?

As young Christians we were taught, as perhaps you were, that Christ would come to gather His Church in a "secret rapture" before the Tribulation and the revelation of the man of sin. That is, that the Second Coming will be in two phases: the first phase when only believers will see Jesus as He comes in the air to gather them secretly before the Tribulation; the second phase, seven years later, when every eye will see Jesus as He returns to earth with His saints, after the Tribulation.

Scripture, however, troubled us because it didn't support this scenario. "Now we beseech you, brethren, by *the coming* of our Lord Jesus Christ, and by *our gathering* together unto him, that ye be not soon shaken in mind, or be troubled, neither by spirit, nor by word, nor by letter as from us, as that *the day of Christ* is at hand. Let no man deceive you by any means: for *that day shall not come, except there come a falling away first, and that man of sin be revealed*, the son of perdition" (2 Thess. 2:1-3).

This one passage made us reconsider what we had been taught. Perhaps the body of Christ might not be caught away in a secret rapture before the man of sin is revealed and the Tribulation runs its destructive course.

We began to study the Scripture diligently for ourselves and discovered, to our amazement, that not a single verse in the entire Bible actually supports the secret rapture teaching. Moreover, the scriptures commonly used to support this idea actually teach a very different timetable when taken in context. Much confusion in end-time teaching results from interpreting verses out of their setting. Scripture must be interpreted in context, and the interpretation should be reasonable—not weird. Since the Word of God is unified and does not contradict itself, every interpretation of Scripture should harmonize with "all the counsel of God" (Acts 20:27).

When we discovered that Jesus will come to gather His Church *after* the Great Tribulation, the Scripture began to take on new significance. We realized what a blessed hope we really do have. We became aware of how glorious and awesome the Lord's coming will be—glorious for the Church, but awesome and dreadful for the world.

Many assume that if a doctrine is taught by popular preachers and large denominations, it must be right. This assumption is not necessarily true, however, because Jesus warns that in the last days "many false prophets shall rise, and shall deceive many" (Matt. 24:11). In addition, God hides His truths from "the wise and prudent" and reveals them to "babes [the humble]" (Matt. 11:25); to those who love him (1 Cor. 2:9); and to those who seek His wisdom as men seek for silver and search for hidden treasures (Pro. 2:3,4).

Inasmuch as the Second Coming is the consummation of our salvation, we should know what we believe about it. A blurred understanding of a truth as vital as the Second Coming can be spiritually fatal. To neglect the Word of God is to neglect the salvation of our souls: "Therefore we ought to give the more earnest heed to the things which we have heard, lest at any time we should let them slip. . . . How shall we escape, if we neglect so great salvation?" (Heb. 2:1,3).

We do not pretend this book to be exhaustive concerning end-time issues. We offer it in humility and in the sincere hope that it will serve as a springboard for your personal study. May the truths offered here bless and enrich your life as they have blessed and enriched ours. Most of all, may this book help us to prepare for what is just on the horizon.

Ken and Agnes Macdonald

1

Why Study the Second Coming?

Why is it important to know what the Bible teaches about the Second Coming?

The coming of our Lord Jesus Christ is tremendously important because it will finalize history and usher in eternity. The prophets and every New Testament writer speak about the Second Coming. The New Testament alone lists over three hundred references on the subject.

The Second Coming also places other truths in their right perspective, namely, the resurrection of the just and the unjust, the Day of the Lord, the battle of Armageddon, the Day of Judgment, the end of the world, and the new heaven and earth. These end-time truths can revive us with new incentive:

To watch and pray always—"But the end of all things is at hand: be ye therefore sober, and watch unto prayer" (1 Pet. 4:7). See also Joel 1:13-15; Matt. 24:42; 25:13; Mark 13:33-37; Luke 11:2; 18:1-8; 21:36; Eph. 6:12,13,18; Phil. 4:5,6; 1 Thess. 5:6,17, 23; 2 Thess. 1:10-12; Rev. 5:8; 6:9-11; 8:3-5; 22:20.

To serve God with reverence and godly fear—"Wherefore we receiving a kingdom which cannot be moved, let us have grace, whereby we may serve God acceptably with reverence and godly fear: For our God is a consuming fire" (Heb. 12:28). See also Phil. 2:12,16; 1 Pet. 1:17; Rev. 11:18; 14:7; 15:4; 19:5.

To live a holy life with brotherly kindness—"Be ye also patient; stablish your hearts: for the coming of the Lord draweth nigh. Grudge not one against another, brethren, lest ye be condemned: behold, the judge standeth before the door" (James 5:8,9). See also 1 Cor. 4:5; 6:1-10; Eph. 5:25-27; Phil. 1:10,11; Col. 3:4-25; 1 Thess. 3:12,13; 5:21-23; Titus 2:11-13; 1 Pet. 1:13-17; 2 Pet. 1:5-11; 3:11-14; 1 John 2:28; 3:2,3.

To endure persecution and to rejoice in hope of the resurrection—"But rejoice, inasmuch as ye are partakers of Christ's sufferings;

that, when his glory shall be revealed, ye may be glad also with exceeding joy" (1 Pet. 4:13). See also John 16:22; 17:24; 1 Cor. 15:30-32; 1 Thess. 4:13; 5:10,11; 2 Thess. 1:4-10; 3:1-5; 2 Tim. 1:12; Heb.10:34-37; 11:35; 13:13-15; 1 Pet. 1:6,7.

To warn men and women to repent because Judgment Day is coming—"God . . . commandeth all men everywhere to repent: Because he hath appointed a day, in the which he will judge the world in righteousness" (Acts 17:30,31). See also Matt. 3:7,8; Rom. 2:4-8; 2 Cor. 5:10,11; 2 Pet. 3:9,10; Jude 1:14,15,22-24.

To live the crucified life, free from the love of money and earthly things—"If any man will come after me, let him deny himself, and take up his cross, and follow me. . . . For what is a man profited, if he shall gain the whole world, and lose his own soul? or what shall a man give in exchange for his soul? For the Son of man shall come in the glory of his Father with his angels; and then he shall reward every man according to his works" (Matt. 16:24-27). See also Matt. 19:27-29; Luke 12:32-40; 17:31-33; 21:34; Phil. 3:10,11,17-21; Col. 3:1-5; 1 Tim. 6:8-14; Heb. 11:7, 10,13,16.

To be zealous to know the Word and to preach it to the ends of the earth—"I charge thee therefore before God, and the Lord Jesus Christ, who shall judge the quick and the dead at his appearing and his kingdom; Preach the word; be instant in season, out of season; reprove, rebuke, exhort with all longsuffering and doctrine" (2 Tim. 4:1,2). "And this gospel of the kingdom shall be preached in all the world for a witness unto all nations; and then shall the end come" (Matt. 24:14). See also 2 Tim. 4:7,8; Matt. 28:19,20; Mark 8:38; Luke 12:8,9; 19:13; Acts 1:6-11; 1 Cor. 15:57,58; 1 Thess. 2:19; James 5:7.

What is the relevance of the Second Coming to other themes of the Bible?

Many themes of the Bible are linked to our Lord's return and are affected by a proper understanding of it. Consider the following scriptural themes:

Faith—"Let not your heart be troubled: ye believe in God, believe also in me. . . . I will come again, and receive you unto myself" (John 14:1,3).

Purity—"And every man that hath this hope in him purifieth himself, even as he is pure" (1 John 3:3).

The Holy Spirit—"Howbeit when he, the Spirit of truth, is come . . . he will shew you things to come" (John 16:13).

The Lord's supper—"For as often as ye eat this bread, and drink this cup, ye do shew the Lord's death till he come" (1 Cor. 11:26).

Church attendance—"Not forsaking the assembling of ourselves . . . but exhorting one another: and so much the more, as ye see the day approaching" (Heb. 10:25).

Faithfulness—"That thou keep this commandment without spot, unrebukeable, until the appearing of our Lord Jesus Christ" (1 Tim. 6:14).

Comfort—"The coming of the Lord. . . . Wherefore comfort one another with these words" (1 Thess. 4:15,18).

The grace of God—"For the grace of God that bringeth salvation hath appeared to all men, teaching us that, denying ungodliness and worldly lusts, we should live soberly, righteously, and godly, in this present world; looking for that blessed hope, and the glorious appearing of the great God and our Saviour Jesus Christ" (Titus 2:11-13).

Why should I be concerned about *when* Jesus is coming since He said in Matthew 24:36 that no man knows the day or the hour of His coming?

Although no one knows the exact day or hour of His coming, Jesus specifically told *when* He was coming, "immediately after the tribulation" (Matt. 24:29,30). Jesus spoke of future events so we would know the signs of His coming and of the end of the world: "So likewise ye, when ye shall see all these things, know that it is near, even at the doors" (Matt. 24:33).

What emphases did Jesus and the apostles place on knowing the truth about the Second Coming?

With respect to the Church and the Great Tribulation, some have the attitude, "Only time will tell!" Jesus and the apostles, however, did not take such a careless attitude. They took great care to make sure that the saints understood perfectly the doctrine of the Second Coming.

Jesus said, "But take ye heed: behold, I have foretold you all things" (Mark 13:23) and "It is given unto you *to know* the mysteries of the kingdom of heaven" (Matt. 13:11). He further indicated the seriousness of knowing by reproving the Sadducees who were in error concerning the resurrection because of their "*not knowing the scriptures*, nor the power of God" (Matt. 22:29).

Peter also earnestly desired that the Church would know about the coming of our Lord. Even though they were established in this truth, he felt compelled to remind them constantly of it. He wrote, "Wherefore I will not be negligent to put you *always in remembrance* of these things, though *ye know them*, and *be established in the present truth.* Yea, I think it meet, as long as I am in this tabernacle, to stir you up by putting you in *remembrance* . . . . Moreover I will endeavour that ye may be able after my decease to have these things *always in remembrance.* For we have not followed cunningly devised fables, when we made *known* unto you the power and coming of our Lord Jesus Christ, but were eyewitnesses of his majesty" (2 Pet. 1:12,13,15,16).

Before depicting the great events of the Second Coming, Peter further emphasized the importance of knowing these truths: "I stir up your pure minds by way of *remembrance*: That ye may be *mindful* of the words which were spoken before by the holy prophets, and of the commandment of us the apostles of the Lord and Saviour" (2 Pet. 3:1,2).

He also exhorted every believer to "be ready always to give an answer to every man that asketh you a reason of *the hope* that is in you with meekness and fear" (1 Pet. 3:15). Since the coming of our Lord is the blessed hope of the Church (the word "hope" is used at least twenty times in the New Testament with reference to the resurrection and the Second Coming), every born-again believer has the responsibility to know what the Bible says about this very important subject and to share it with others.

Every believer should also take to heart Peter's solemn warning as he summed up his great teaching on the Second Coming: "Beware lest ye also, being led away with the error of the wicked, fall from your own stedfastness. But grow in grace, and *in the knowledge* of our Lord and Saviour Jesus Christ" (2 Pet. 3:17,18).

Paul also placed great emphasis on knowing the truth about the Second Coming. He wrote about it in "all his epistles" (2 Pet.

3:15,16) and in every chapter of First and Second Thessalonians. In fact, Paul's emphasis on the doctrine of the Second Coming to the Church at Thessalonica is a fine example of its importance.

The Church at Thessalonica started when Paul and Silas preached there for about three weeks before being driven away because of unbelieving Jews who stirred up persecution against them. (See Acts 17:1-10.) Afterwards, Paul sent Timothy to establish and to comfort them in their faith. Then, when writing his first letter to these new converts, he mentioned the Second Coming in every chapter and declared, "But of the times and the seasons, brethren, ye have *no need that I write unto you.* For yourselves *know perfectly* that the day of the Lord so cometh as a thief in the night" (1 Thess. 5:1,2). How interesting that Paul could write to newly converted Gentiles, who had turned from their idols, "ye have no need that I write unto you. For yourselves know perfectly that the day of the Lord so cometh. . . ."

In Second Thessalonians, Paul devoted almost the entire letter to the Second Coming and reminded the believers about his teaching concerning the man of sin. "Remember ye not, that, when I was yet with you, I told you these things? And now *ye know* what withholdeth that he might be revealed in his time" (2 Thess. 2:5,6).

There's a clear reason why Paul placed such emphasis on this key doctrine—he was preaching the gospel of our Lord Jesus Christ. Throughout the gospels Christ teaches about the Second Coming. The subject is treated at length in Matthew 24 and 25; Mark 13; Luke 12, 17, and 21; as well as in a third of His parables.

Many of us have attended church most of our lives. We possess complete Bibles and concordances, which these new converts did not have, and suffer comparatively no persecution. Yet, what do we know about the Day of the Lord and the man of sin? The emphasis that Jesus and the apostles placed on the Second Coming indicates that it can and ought to be understood by all converts, even new believers.

What are the benefits of understanding biblical prophecy?

The benefits of understanding prophecy include faith and spiritual direction. Prophecy inspires faith when we understand it correctly. Jesus said, "I have told you before it come to pass, that, when it is come to pass, ye might *believe*" (John 14:29); and "Now I tell you before it come, that, when it is come to pass, ye may *believe* that I am he" (John 13:19). Faith in the end-time is vital because it is the victory that overcomes the world (1 John 5:4), persecution (Rev. 13:10; 14:12), tribulation (1 Pet. 1:7,8), and Satan's fiery darts, so we can stand in the evil day (Eph. 6:13,16).

Faith is also vital to readiness for our Lord's return. Noah was ready when the flood came because he understood the prophetic warning of God and by faith prepared an ark. "By *faith* Noah, being warned of God of things not seen as yet, moved with fear, prepared an ark to the saving of his house; by the which he condemned the world, and became heir of the righteousness which is by *faith*" (Heb. 11:7). Jesus asked, "Nevertheless when the Son of man cometh, shall he find *faith* on the earth?" (Luke 18:8).

Prophecy also gives spiritual direction. Peter wrote, "We have also a more sure word of prophecy; whereunto ye do well that ye take heed, as unto *a light that shineth in a dark place*, until the day dawn, and the day star arise in your hearts" (2 Pet. 1:19). First Chronicles 12:32 states that "the children of Issachar . . . had understanding of the times, to know what Israel ought to do." Believers need a clear understanding of end-time prophecy to know what to do and what to expect in the future.

Simeon and Anna are two saints who had light in a dark day because they heeded the word of prophecy given in the Old Testament. Four hundred years had passed since Malachi, the last Old Testament prophet, recorded his prophecy. Since then Israel had lived in spiritual darkness. It seemed God had forgotten His promise to bring a Savior to His people.

Simeon, a devout man waiting for the consolation of Israel, had the revelation of the Holy Spirit that he would not die "before he had seen the Lord's Christ" (Luke 2:26). Anna was a widow who "departed not from the temple, but served God with fastings and prayers night and day" (Luke 2:37). When Joseph and Mary presented Jesus in the temple at Jerusalem, the aged Simeon took "him up in his arms, and blessed God," and prophesied concerning Him (Luke 2:28). And Anna "coming in that instant gave thanks likewise unto the Lord, and spake of him to all them that looked for redemption in Jerusalem" (Luke 2:38).

Why were Simeon and Anna prepared to tell others about the coming Messiah? They were ready because they had searched the prophetic Word of God and knew the Scripture.

Darker days are coming on the earth. As believers, we must heed the prophetic Word of God and be ready for Christ's Second Coming. Then, in the dark days of great tribulation, the Word will be a light that shines with guidance, comfort, and hope.

Why is it important to know that the Bible does not teach a pre-tribulation, secret rapture?

Some say that it doesn't really matter what one believes about the Lord's return as long as one's heart is right with God. There are, however, a number of dangers in believing that the Church will be gathered secretly before the Great Tribulation.

1. There's the danger of becoming spiritually "soft." It is necessary to have one's heart right with God in preparation for His coming, but one should not overlook Jesus' forewarning the Church of great tribulation. He warned that the Church would be hated by all nations for His name's sake. Believers will not be ready to suffer for their faith if they believe they will escape tribulation by way of a secret rapture instead of enduring to the end. This unscriptural teaching with its smooth, easy way leads to carelessness and worldliness.

Notice how Paul linked faulty teaching with faulty living: "If any man teach otherwise, and consent not to wholesome words, even the words of our Lord Jesus Christ, and to the doctrine which is according to godliness; he is proud, knowing nothing, but doting about questions and strifes of words, whereof cometh envy, strife, railings, evil surmisings. Perverse disputings of men of corrupt minds, and destitute of the truth, supposing that gain is godliness: from such withdraw thyself" (1 Tim. 6:3-5). See also 2 Tim. 2:16,23; 3:1-7; Titus 1:14-16.

2. There's the danger of being unprepared for our Lord's return. One cannot be ready if he does not know what to be ready for, namely Christ's coming. Jesus and the apostles link readiness with knowing the times and seasons of His coming (Matt. 24:32, 33; Luke 21:28-31; 1 Thess. 5:1-6).

To be ready, one's mind must be armed with truth. Peter wrote, "Wherefore gird up the loins of your mind, be sober, and hope to the end for the grace that is to be brought unto you at the revelation of Jesus Christ" (1 Pet. 1:13). See also Pro. 24:5,6; Luke 12:35-40; Rom. 15:4; Eph. 6:13,14. Since the secret rapture theory does not teach to hope until the end, it hinders Christians from being prepared for the coming of our Lord.

3. There's the danger of following "cunningly devised fables" (2 Pet. 1:16). Peter didn't mention a secret rapture, but he did speak of our Lord's revelation at the end of the world (1 Pet. 1:13). Also, he implied that contrary teachings are cunningly devised fables. "For we have not followed cunningly devised fables, when we made known unto you the power and coming of our Lord Jesus Christ, but were eyewitnesses of his majesty" (2 Pet. 1:16).

Similarly, when speaking of our Lord's appearing (2 Tim. 4:1 and 8), Paul warned that "the time will come when they will not endure sound doctrine; but after their own lusts shall they heap to themselves teachers, having itching ears. And they shall turn away their ears from the truth, and shall be *turned unto fables*" (2 Tim. 4:3,4).

We know from Scripture that the secret rapture teaching is a "cunningly devised fable." This false doctrine, fabricated by twisting scriptures out of context, has been repeated so often that many accept it as biblically true without studying it for themselves. With respect to our Lord's return, Peter warned that "they that are unlearned and unstable wrest [twist], as they do also the other scriptures, unto their own destruction" (2 Pet. 3:16).

4. There's the danger of having our faith overthrown. According to the apostle Paul, faulty doctrine, particularly about the resurrection, can cause one's faith to be overthrown. "Hymenaeus and Philetus; who concerning the truth have erred, saying that the resurrection is past already; and *overthrow the faith* of some" (2 Tim. 2:17,18). Demonstrating how dangerous he thought their doctrine was, Paul wrote that "their word will eat as doth a canker [gangrene]" (2 Tim. 2:17). He also delivered Hymenaeus and Philetus to Satan, "that they may learn not to blaspheme" (1 Tim. 1:20).

We are living in perilous times when false teaching about the resurrection (Second Coming) is overthrowing the faith of many. Evil men and seducers are waxing "worse and worse, deceiving, and being deceived" (2 Tim. 3:13). Let's be careful, therefore, to heed Paul's exhortation: "Study to shew thyself approved unto God, a workman that needeth not to be ashamed, rightly dividing the word of truth. But shun profane and vain babblings: for they will increase unto more ungodliness" (2 Tim. 2:15,16). See also 1 Tim. 4:1,2,13-16.

5. *There's the danger of making the Bible seem overly complicated.* To support the secret rapture teaching and to hide the plain truth of the Second Coming, many false teachings have been spread. These teachings state that there will be two future comings of our Lord (one for the saints at a secret rapture and the other with the saints), up to seven resurrections, four to seven judgments, and two chosen peoples. As a result of such confusion, many Christians think they can't know anything for certain about these doctrines.

We must call the Church back to the simple, clear, and uniform teaching of the Bible. Accurately dividing the Word of God reveals one Second Coming (without two phases or a split rapture), one resurrection of the just and the unjust, one judgment day, and one elect people of God.

6. *There's the danger of obscuring related events.* The Lord's coming in judgment, "in flaming fire taking vengeance on them that know not God, and that obey not the gospel of our Lord Jesus Christ" is an aspect of His coming as much as when He comes in the "glory of his power . . . to be glorified in his saints" (2 Thess. 1:8-10). Because of the secret rapture teaching, however, we hear comparatively little about this aspect of our Lord's return. As a result, many are totally unaware of the coming Day of Judgment; there is little fear of God in the world; and iniquity increases.

An ever-increasing number of Christians are being deceived into looking for a new age here on this earth instead of looking for "new heavens and a new earth, wherein dwelleth righteousness" (2 Pet. 3:13). The secret rapture teaching blinds them to the fact that when Jesus comes to gather His Church, this world will burn with fire.

7. *There's the danger of thinking anyone can be saved after the Church has been "caught up" (1 Thess. 4:17).* Paul clearly declared that when the Church is caught up, "sudden destruction" will

come on the wicked and "they shall not escape" (1 Thess. 4:17, 5:3). Jesus added that now is the time to "strive to enter in at the strait gate" because in that day "many . . . will seek to enter in, and shall not be able. When once the master of the house is risen up, and hath shut to the door, and ye begin to stand without, and to knock at the door, saying, Lord, Lord, open unto us; and he shall answer and say unto you, I know you not whence ye are" (Luke 13:24,25).

Those who believe that there will be opportunity to be saved after the Lord has come and shut the door are in as much danger as the ungodly in Noah's day who believed that there was hope for them to be saved after he had entered the ark and the door was shut!

8. There's the danger of holding to or preaching "another gospel" (Gal. 1:8,9). Paul had zeal for keeping the Church free from unscriptural doctrines. He admonished, "But though we, or an angel from heaven, preach any other gospel unto you than that which we have preached unto you, let him be accursed. As we said before, so say I now again, if any man preach any other gospel unto you than that ye have received, let him be accursed" (Gal. 1:8,9). See also 1 Tim. 1:3,4.

Paul stressed the doctrine of the Second Coming as a cardinal doctrine of the gospel of Christ—speaking of it "in all his epistles" (2 Pet. 3:15,16). Like Jesus, Paul emphasized two truths:

- The Lord Jesus will not come until the Day of the Lord, which is after the Tribulation. (Compare 1 Thess. 4:17 and 5:2 with Matt. 24:29-31 and Acts 2:20.)
- The Church should be looking for "the coming [Greek, manifestation] of our Lord Jesus Christ" (1 Cor. 1:7), or for His "glorious appearing" (Titus 2:13), not for a "secret rapture."

In the light of Paul's admonition in Galatians 1, to proclaim the Second Coming differently from his epistles is to put ourselves in the dangerous position of being "accursed." This may seem like a severe warning; nevertheless, it is the Word of God. We are only safe when our beliefs correspond with the gospel that the apostles received from the Lord Jesus Christ.

9. There's the danger of accepting the "man of sin." The Lord will not come to gather His Church until after the man of sin is revealed (2 Thess. 2:1-3). Will believers who are convinced they will be caught up in a secret rapture before the Tribulation and the revelation of the man of sin be prepared for such an eventuality? Undoubtedly, the erroneous notion of a secret rapture diverts the Church's attention from the glorious appearing of our Lord to an unrealistic, hoped-for escape that keeps many believers ignorant of what to expect. As a result, they are unprepared for the events of the last days. Many will be taken by surprise. Being caught off guard, many will face bewilderment and fall away from the faith.

10. There's the grave danger of believing a lie and being damned. "Even him, whose coming is after the working of Satan with all power and signs and lying wonders, and with all deceivableness of unrighteousness in them that perish; because they received not the love of the truth, that they might be saved. And for this cause God shall send them strong delusion, that they should *believe a lie: That they all might be damned* who believed not the truth, but had pleasure in unrighteousness" (2 Thess. 2:9-12).

We will escape the deception of the Antichrist by receiving the love of the truth. To assume that God will unconditionally keep us from all deception is not enough. Jesus and the apostles repeatedly warned, "Take heed that no man deceive you" (Matt. 24:4); "Be not deceived" (Luke 21:8); "Let no man deceive himself" (1 Cor. 3:18); and "Let no man deceive you by any means" (2 Thess. 2:3). We need the entrance of God's Word in our minds and spirits to receive light (Psa. 119:130), warning (Psa. 19:11), wisdom (Psa. 19:7), faith (Rom. 10:17), and hope (Rom. 15:4). Only as we love and know the truth can we avoid being deceived by the Antichrist.

How can we know whether we have received the love of the truth? We can know we love the truth if we search for it (Pro. 2:1-4), delight in it (Psa. 119:47), meditate on it (Psa. 119:97), believe it (2 Thess. 2:13), and obey it (Psa. 119:167). The Bereans are good examples of receiving and searching the truth. "They received the word with all readiness of mind, and searched the scriptures daily, whether those things were so" (Acts 17:11).

In summary, here are the dangers of believing that the Church will be gathered secretly before the Great Tribulation:

1. The danger of becoming spiritually "soft."
2. The danger of being unprepared for our Lord's return.

3. The danger of following "cunningly devised fables" (2 Pet. 1:16).

4. The danger of having our faith overthrown.

5. The danger of making the Bible seem overly complicated.

6. The danger of obscuring related events.

7. The danger of thinking anyone can be saved after the Church has been "caught up" (1 Thess. 4:17).

8. The danger of holding to or preaching "another gospel" (Gal. 1:8).

9. The danger of accepting the man of sin.

10. The danger of believing a lie and being damned.

Why should we study the Second Coming? An incorrect view of this doctrine will have grave eternal consequences for us and for those who hear us (1 Tim. 4:16). The dangers and risks are too high. We must know this truth for ourselves. To build upon a teaching not based on the Bible is like building on sand. In tribulation, the house shall fall, and great shall be the fall of it (Matt. 7:26,27).

2

The Great Tribulation

How does the Bible describe the Great Tribulation?

It will be a time when sin will increase. "And because iniquity shall abound, and the love of many shall wax cold" (Matt. 24:12).

"This know also, that in the last days perilous times shall come. For men shall be lovers of their own selves, covetous, boasters, proud, blasphemers, disobedient to parents, unthankful, unholy, without natural affection, trucebreakers, false accusers, incontinent, fierce, despisers of those that are good, traitors, heady, highminded, lovers of pleasures more than lovers of God; having a form of godliness, but denying the power thereof: from such turn away" (2 Tim. 3:1-5).

"There should be mockers in the last time, who should walk after their own ungodly lusts" (Jude 1:18).

It will be a time when witchcraft, drugs, and idolatry will abound. "And the rest of the men . . . repented not of the works of their hands, that they should not worship devils, and idols of gold, and silver, and brass, and stone, and of wood: which neither can see, nor hear, nor walk: neither repented they of their murders, nor of their sorcery [drugs], nor of their fornication, nor of their thefts" (Rev. 9:20,21). See also Rev. 16:13,14; 18:23.

It will be a time of great apostasy. "Now the Spirit speaketh expressly, that in the latter times some shall depart from the faith, giving heed to seducing spirits, and doctrines of devils; speaking lies in hypocrisy; having their conscience seared with a hot iron" (1 Tim. 4:1,2). See also 2 Thess. 2:3; 2 Tim. 4:3,4.

It will be a time when many will say, "Peace and safety." "For when they shall say, Peace and safety; then sudden destruction cometh upon them, as travail upon a woman with child; and they shall not escape" (1 Thess. 5:3).

It will be a time when the man of sin, the son of perdition shall be revealed, "who opposeth and exalteth himself above all that is called God, or that is worshipped. . . . Even him, whose coming is after the working of Satan with all power and signs and lying wonders" (2 Thess. 2:3,4,9).

It will be a time when false prophets will work lying wonders. "For there shall arise false Christs, and false prophets, and shall shew great signs and wonders; insomuch that, if it were possible, they shall deceive the very elect" (Matt. 24:24).

"And he [the false prophet] doeth great wonders, so that he maketh fire [to] come down from heaven on the earth in the sight of men" (Rev. 13:13).

It will be a time when Satan and the man of sin will be worshiped. "And they worshipped the dragon [Satan] . . . And they worshipped the beast [the man of sin], saying, Who is like unto the beast? who is able to make war with him?" (Rev. 13:4).

"And all that dwell upon the earth shall worship him [the beast], whose names are not written in the book of life of the Lamb slain from the foundation of the world" (Rev. 13:8).

It will be a time when the Church will be hated by all nations and the beast. "Then shall they deliver you up to be afflicted, and shall kill you: and ye shall be hated of all nations for my name's sake" (Matt. 24:9).

"And it was given unto him [the beast] to make war with the saints, and to overcome them: and power was given him over all kindreds, and tongues, and nations" (Rev. 13:7).

It will be a time when the deceived will make an image to the beast. "And deceiveth them that dwell on the earth by the means of those miracles which he had power to do in the sight of the beast; saying to them that dwell on the earth, that they should make an image to the beast, which had the wound by a sword, and did live" (Rev. 13:14).

It will be a time when all who do not worship the image will be killed. "And he had power to give life unto the image of the beast, that the image of the beast should both speak, and cause that as many as would not worship the image of the beast should be killed" (Rev. 13:15).

It will be a time when no man will be able to buy or sell without a mark (666) in his right hand, or in his forehead. "And he causeth all, both small and great, rich and poor, free and bond, to receive a mark in their right hand, or in their foreheads: and that no man might buy or sell, save he that had the mark, or the name of the beast, or the number of his name. . . . And his number is Six hundred three-score and six" (666) (Rev. 13:16-18).

The Bible warns, "If any man worship the beast and his image, and receive his mark in his forehead, or in his hand, the same shall drink of the wine of the wrath of God, which is poured out without mixture into the cup of his indignation; and he shall be tormented with fire and brimstone in the presence of the holy angels, and in the presence of the Lamb: And the smoke of their torment ascendeth up for ever and ever: and they have no rest day nor night, who worship the beast and his image, and whosoever receiveth the mark of his name" (Rev. 14:9-11).

It will be a time of such great tribulation that God will shorten those days for the sake of the Church. "And except those days should be shortened, there should no flesh be saved: but for the elect's sake those days shall be shortened" (Matt. 24:22).

It will be a time followed by the coming of the Lord Jesus Christ to gather His Church. "Immediately after the tribulation of those days shall the sun be darkened, and the moon shall not give her light, and the stars shall fall from heaven, and the powers of the heavens shall be shaken: And then shall appear the sign of the Son of man in heaven: and then shall all the tribes of the earth mourn, and they shall see the Son of man coming in the clouds of heaven with power and great glory. And he shall send his angels with a great sound of a trumpet, and they shall gather together his elect from the four winds, from one end of heaven to the other" (Matt. 24:29-31). See also Mark 13:24-27; Luke 21:25-28.

The Church will be gathered "immediately after the tribulation." What exactly is meant by the term "Church"?

The true Church is not a church building or organized religion. It consists of people who have received salvation through "repentance toward God and faith toward our Lord Jesus Christ" (Acts 20:21,28).

When will the Great Tribulation take place?

The Great Tribulation is the last period in history preceding the return of our Lord Jesus Christ (Matt. 24:21-31).

How can we be certain that the Great Tribulation will be on earth just prior to the coming of the Lord Jesus to gather His Church?

Jesus foretold that the days of great tribulation will be shortened for the sake of the Church (Matt. 24:21,22; Mark 13:20-22). This would be unnecessary if the Church had already been gathered. Without the Church there would be no need to shorten those days. Jesus also said that the Church will be gathered "immediately *after* the tribulation of those days" (Matt. 24:29-31). He also asked, "When the Son of Man cometh, shall he find faith on the earth?" (Luke 18:8). This implies that the situation on earth would become dark before His coming.

Paul also indicated that tribulation will occur just prior to the Second Coming when he wrote, "we which are *alive and remain* unto the coming of the Lord" (1 Thess. 4:15,17). "Alive and remain" appears twice in this passage. According to *Strong's Concordance*, the word "remain" may be translated "survive." In other words, Paul spoke of those who are "alive and survive." Survival evidently refers to the great persecution of the Church that will occur before the coming of the Lord. Moreover, Paul wrote that the Church will be gathered *after* the man of sin is revealed and that Christ will destroy him with the brightness of His coming (2 Thess. 2:1-3,8).

The Book of Revelation describes the reign of the Antichrist and persecution against the Church right up until the time of our Lord's coming. For example, when the fifth seal was opened, John saw "the souls of them that were slain for the word of God. . . . And it was said unto them, that they should rest yet for a little season, until their fellow servants also and their brethren, that should be killed as they were, should be fulfilled" (Rev. 6:9,11). Immediately afterwards, when the sixth seal was opened, John foresaw the coming of Christ and the saints who came out of great tribulation (Rev. 6:12-17; 7:14,15).

Will the Great Tribulation affect the Church or only the Jews?

The Great Tribulation will affect the whole world. The Bible says, "And power was given him [the beast] over *all* kindreds, and tongues, and nations. And *all* that dwell upon the earth shall worship him, whose names are not written in the book of life of the Lamb slain from the foundation of the world" (Rev. 13:7,8).

"And he [the false prophet] causeth *all*, both small and great, rich and poor, free and bond, to receive a mark in their right hand, or in their foreheads" (Rev. 13:16).

The Church, however, will be affected primarily by persecution. She will "keep the commandments of God, and the faith of Jesus" and refuse to worship the man of sin and his image, and to receive his mark or the number of his name, 666 (Rev. 14:9-12; 15:2; 20:4). The beast will make war with the saints (Rev. 13:7), and all nations will hate them (Matt. 24:9).

Why will the Church be hated by all nations?

There are many reasons why men hate: envy (Gen. 37:4); pride (Psa. 83:2; Pro. 13:10); covetousness (Luke 16:14); selfishness (Psa. 44:10; 2 Tim. 3:2,3); a wicked heart (Pro. 26:24,25); spiritual blindness (1 John 2:9,11); and because they themselves have not experienced the love of God (John 5:18,42; 8:40,42,47; 16:2,3).

If we follow Jesus, we will be hated for the same reasons men hated Him—He was not of this world (John 15:18-20; 17:14); He spoke the truth of God (John 8:40); and He testified against the evil of the world (John 7:7). Indeed, He was hated "without a cause" (John 15:25). The apostles remind us, "Marvel not, my brethren, if the world hate you" (1 John 3:13); "Yea, and all that will live godly in Christ Jesus shall suffer persecution" (2 Tim. 3:12).

How will this hatred be manifested?

The Church will experience the same hatred that Jesus, the prophets, the apostles, and the early church received from their contemporaries. They were falsely accused, rewarded evil for good, cast out, reproached, beaten, tortured, imprisoned, driven from city to city, betrayed, and killed.

This hatred will affect all relationships. Jesus said, "And ye shall be betrayed both by *parents*, and *brethren*, and *kinsfolks*, and *friends*; and some of you shall they cause to be put to death. And ye shall be hated of all men for my name's sake" (Luke 21:16,17); "And a man's foes shall be they of his own household. He that loveth father or mother more than me is not worthy of me: and he that loveth son or daughter more than me is not worthy of me" (Matt. 10:36,37).

What should I do when I'm hated and persecuted for righteousness' sake?

Remember that your persecutors are persecuting the Lord Jesus Christ, not you. Jesus said, "The world cannot hate you; but me it hateth, because I testify of it, that the works thereof are evil" (John 7:7). See also Zech. 2:8; Acts 5:39; 9:4.

Do good. "Ye have heard that it hath been said, Thou shalt love thy neighbour, and hate thine enemy. But I say unto you, Love your enemies, bless them that curse you, do good to them that hate you, and pray for them which despitefully use you, and persecute you: That ye may be the children of your Father which is in heaven: for he maketh his sun to rise on the evil and on the good, and sendeth rain on the just and on the unjust" (Matt. 5:43-45). See also Gen. 50:19-21; Ex. 23:4,5; Job 31:28-30; Luke 6:27-30; Rom. 12:14-21; 1 Pet. 3:9.

Exhibit patience. "Being reviled, we bless; being persecuted, we suffer it" (1 Cor. 4:12).

Let God fight your battles. "He sent from above, he took me, he drew me out of many waters. He delivered me from my strong enemy, and from them which hated me: for they were too strong for me" (Psa. 18:16,17). See also Psa. 44:4-8; 106:10,11; Luke 1:70,71.

Believe God! "So Daniel was taken up out of the den, and no manner of hurt was found upon him, because he believed in his God" (Dan. 6:23).

Rejoice! Your reward is great in heaven! "Blessed are ye, when men shall hate you, and when they shall separate you from their company, and shall reproach you, and cast out your name as evil, for the Son of man's sake. Rejoice ye in that day, and leap for joy: for, behold, your reward is great in heaven: for in the like manner did their fathers unto the prophets" (Luke 6:22,23). See also Isa. 60:14,15; 66:5,6; Matt. 5:12; 2 Cor. 12:10; 1 Pet. 4:12,13,16.

Do not fear! Jesus said, "Ye shall be hated of all men for my name's sake" (Matt. 10:22), and gave three reasons not to fear:

1. "Fear them not . . . for there is nothing covered, that shall not be revealed; and hid, that shall not be known" (10:26).

2. "Fear not them which kill the body, but are not able to kill the soul: but rather fear him which is able to destroy both soul and body in hell" (10:28).

3. "Fear ye not . . . ye are of more value than many sparrows" (10:31). Not one sparrow falls to the ground without our heavenly Father knowing it (10:29). How much more He must care for us! See also John 14:27; Phil. 1:28,29; Isa. 35:4; Joel 2:21,22.

Be able to stand alone. Individuals must know God and His Word so that they are able to trust Him and to stand alone. The apostle Paul testified, "At my first answer no man stood with me, but all men forsook me. . . . Notwithstanding the Lord stood with me, and strengthened me" (2 Tim. 4:16,17). He also admonished, "Wherefore take unto you the whole armour of God, that ye may be able to withstand in the evil day, and having done all, *to stand*" (Eph. 6:13).

The prophet Elijah stood alone against four hundred and fifty prophets of Baal. "Then said Elijah unto the people, I, even I only, remain a prophet of the Lord; but Baal's prophets are four hundred and fifty men" (1 Kings 18:22).

Don't be surprised if persecution comes from lukewarm Christians. David said, "For it was not an enemy that reproached me; then I could have borne it: neither was it he that hated me that did magnify himself against me; then I would have hid myself from him: But it was thou, a man mine equal, my guide, and mine acquaintance. We took sweet counsel together, and walked unto the house of God in company" (Psa. 55:12-14).

Jesus and the early church were persecuted by the chief priests and elders (Matt. 27:1,2; John 18:3; Acts 23:12-15); the high priest (John 18:19-24,28); and the scribes and the Pharisees (Luke 11:53,54).

Although the world may hate us, *Jesus loves us.* He has promised to love us to the end. When we walk after the Spirit, nothing can separate us from His love (Rom. 8:35-39). Let us be strong, therefore, to suffer gladly with Jesus, to pray for our enemies, to show patience, to let God fight our battles, to believe in God, to always rejoice, to fear not, and not to be surprised if persecution should come from lukewarm Christians. "If God be for us, who can be against us?" (Rom. 8:31).

Objection Answered

Isn't the Great Tribulation a time of "Jacob's trouble" (Jer. 30:6,7) when Israel will be tested and persecuted, but not the Church?

Some propagate this teaching, but there is no evidence to prove that "the time of Jacob's trouble" is the Great Tribulation. "Ask ye now, and see whether a man doth travail with child? Wherefore do I see every man with his hands on his loins, as a woman in travail, and all faces are turned into paleness? Alas! for that day is great, so that none is like it: it is even the time of Jacob's trouble; but he shall be saved out of it" (Jer. 30:6,7).

More likely, these two verses fit the description of the Day of the Lord, which *follows* the Great Tribulation. This truth may be seen by comparing the events of "the time of Jacob's trouble" with those of the Day of the Lord:

The Events of the Time of Jacob's Trouble	The Events of the Day of the Lord
As a women in travail—Jer. 30:6.	The day of the Lord. . . . as travail upon a woman—1 Thess. 5:2,3. See also Isa. 13:8,9; Psa. 48:6.
Alas! for that day is great—Jer. 30:7.	That great and notable day of the Lord—Acts 2:20. See also Joel 1:15; 2:11,31; Zeph. 1:14; Mal. 4:5; Rev. 6:17.
So that none is like it—Jer. 30:7.	The day of the Lord. . . . there hath not been ever the like—Joel 2:1,2. The great day of God Almighty. . . . such as was not since men were upon the earth—Rev. 16:14,18.
That day—Jer. 30:7.	The day of the Lord. . . . that day—1 Thess. 5:2,4. See also Luke 21:34; 2 Thess. 2:2,3.

3

Appointed to Tribulation, Not to Wrath

Will the Church suffer the wrath of God?

Most definitely not! The wrath of God is for the "children of disobedience," not for the children of God (Eph. 5:6; Rom. 1:17,18; 2:5-8). The Church will face the Great Tribulation, but not the great day of God's wrath. God gives many promises that His people will be saved from His wrath:

"Much more then, being now justified by his blood, we shall be saved from wrath through him" (Rom. 5:9).

"And to wait for his Son from heaven, whom he raised from the dead, even Jesus, which delivered us from the wrath to come" (1 Thess. 1:10).

"For God hath not appointed us to wrath, but to obtain salvation by our Lord Jesus Christ" (1 Thess. 5:9).

In the context of the preceding verse, the apostle Paul shows that the Church will be "caught up" on the day of the Lord's wrath before "sudden destruction cometh" on the ungodly (1 Thess. 4:16-18; 5:2-9). See also 2 Thess. 1:7-10.

As Noah was saved from the flood and Lot from fire, so the Church will be saved from the wrath of God (Luke 17:26-30; 2 Pet. 3:5-7,13). See Chapter Four.

What is the difference between the Great Tribulation and the Great Day of God's Wrath?

A vast difference separates these two events. We must not confuse the two. The Great Tribulation is that period *before* the Second Coming (Matt. 24:21-24); the Great Day of God's Wrath is the time or day of the Second Coming (Matt. 24:29-31; Rev. 6:12-17). Let's contrast these distinct events.

During the Great Tribulation, the man of sin will reign (2

Thess. 2:3,4); on the Great Day of God's Wrath, he will be destroyed (2 Thess. 2:8; Rev. 19:15-20).

During the Great Tribulation, the Church will be present (Matt. 24:21-24); on the Great Day of God's Wrath, she will be "caught up . . . to meet the Lord in the air" before the final judgment (1 Thess. 4:16-18; 5:1-3).

During the Great Tribulation, the false prophet will make "fire come down from heaven" to deceive (Rev. 13:13,14); on the Great Day of God's Wrath, Jesus will come "in flaming fire taking vengeance on them that know not God, and that obey not the gospel" (2 Thess. 1:8).

During the Great Tribulation, the ungodly will rejoice over the suffering of the saints (Rev. 11:9,10); on the Great Day of God's Wrath, they will cry to the mountains and rocks, "Fall on us, and hide us from the face of him that sitteth on the throne, and from the wrath of the Lamb: For *the great day of his wrath is come*; and who shall be able to stand?" (Rev. 6:16,17).

If the Church is on earth during the Great Tribulation, how will she escape the seven vials of the wrath of God (Revelation 16)?

The Church will face hatred and persecution, but not the wrath of God. Scripture expressly states that these vials of God's wrath will be poured on:

1. "men which had the mark of the beast, and upon them which worshipped his image" (Rev. 16:2)
2. "the sea" (Rev. 16:3)
3. those who "have shed the blood of saints and prophets" (Rev. 16:6)
4. those who in rebellion blaspheme "the name of God" (Rev. 16:8,9)
5. "the seat of the beast" (Rev. 16:10)
6. "the great river Euphrates," which prepares the way for the final conflict (Rev. 16:12-14)
7. all the ungodly

The seventh vial will be poured out on the Great Day of God's Wrath when Jesus gathers His Church before destroying all men—even "the remnant" at Armageddon. (Compare Rev. 16:14, 16 with 19:7-9,18-21.)

Notice our Lord's exhortation to the Church just before His coming (between the sixth and seventh vial): "Behold, I come as a thief. Blessed is he that watcheth, and keepeth his garments, lest he walk naked, and they see his shame" (Rev. 16:15). This encouragement would be unnecessary if the Church had already been gathered before the Great Tribulation.

Moreover, the Church is *sealed* by the blood of the Lord Jesus (Ex. 12:13; Heb. 11:27,28), by faith (Rom. 4:11), and by the Spirit of God (Eph. 1:13). See also 2 Cor. 1:22; Eph. 4:30; 2 Tim. 2:19; Rev. 3:12; 9:4; 14:1; 22:4.

Nothing can hurt the saints unless God allows it. "Hurt not the earth, neither the sea, nor the trees, till we have sealed the servants of our God in their foreheads" (Rev. 7:3); "If any man will hurt them [the two witnesses], fire proceedeth out of their mouth, and devoureth their enemies: and if any man will hurt them, he must in this manner be killed" (Rev. 11:5).

God will shelter His people from His wrath just as He sheltered the Israelites living in Egypt from the ten plagues (Ex. 12:13), and as He protected them who had the burden of the Lord when judgment came to the house of Israel and Judah (Ezek. 9:4).

Why would God allow the Church to be present during the tribulation of the last days?

Although not appointed to wrath, the Church is appointed to tribulation. Consider the words of the apostle Paul: "No man should be moved by these afflictions [tribulations]: for yourselves know that *we are appointed thereunto.* For verily, when we were with you, we told you before that we should suffer *tribulation*" (1 Thess. 3:3,4). "Afflictions" and "tribulation" are used interchangeably, which is further seen by comparing Mark 13:19 with Matthew 24:21: "For in those days shall be affliction" and "for then shall be great tribulation."

The Greek word for tribulation is *thlipsis.* The *King James Version* of the Bible also translates this as "affliction," "persecution," "anguish," "burden," or "trouble." Of the fifty-five times in the New Testament that *thlipsis* occurs, it is used forty-seven times with reference to the saints' enduring tribulation. Truly, tribulation belongs to the Church.

Other scriptures also make it clear that the Church is appointed to tribulation:

"In the world ye shall have tribulation" (John 16:33).

"We must through much tribulation enter into the kingdom of God" (Acts 14:22).

"For unto you it is given in the behalf of Christ, not only to believe on him, but also to suffer for his sake" (Phil. 1:29).

"The servant is not greater than his lord" (John 15:20), Jesus said, and He suffered great persecution.

"But he that shall endure unto the end, the same shall be saved" (Matt. 24:13).

"Who shall separate us from the love of Christ? shall tribulation, or distress, or persecution, or famine, or nakedness, or peril, or sword? As it is written, For thy sake we are killed all the day long; we are accounted as sheep for the slaughter. Nay, in all these things we are more than conquerors through him that loved us. For I am persuaded, that neither death, nor life, nor angels, nor principalities, nor powers, nor things present, nor things to come, nor height, nor depth, nor any other creature, shall be able to separate us from the love of God, which is in Christ Jesus our Lord" (Rom. 8:35-39).

There are many blessings of tribulation and persecution, such as having fellowship with Christ in His sufferings (Phil. 3:10; 1 Pet. 4:13) and someday reigning with Him (2 Tim. 2:12). Also, "tribulation worketh patience; and patience, experience; and experience, hope; and hope maketh not ashamed; because the love of God is shed abroad in our hearts by the Holy Ghost which is given unto us" (Rom. 5:3-5).

When writing to persecuted saints at Thessalonica, the apostle Paul mentioned added blessings: "That ye may be counted worthy of the kingdom of God, for which ye also suffer," and "It is a righteous thing with God to recompense tribulation to them that trouble you" (2 Thess. 1:5,6).

Peter mentioned yet another blessing: "That the trial of your faith, being much more precious than of gold that perisheth, though it be tried with fire, might be found unto praise and honour and glory at the appearing of Jesus Christ" (1 Pet. 1:7).

Are there other blessings of enduring persecution for Christ's sake?

Yes, the Bible describes other blessings:

- Persecution makes a distinction between true and false Christians (2 Tim. 1:15-18; John 6:66-69).
- Persecution unites saints (Acts 4:23; 14:19,20).
- Persecution brings happiness because the glorious Spirit of God rests on you (1 Pet. 4:14; Acts 6:15; 7:55,56; 16:23-25).
- Persecution advances the gospel (Acts 8:1-4; 14:5-7).
- Persecution draws us closer to God in prayer (Acts 4:24-31; 12:5,12).
- Persecution gives us boldness in the Holy Spirit (Matt. 10:16-20; Acts 4:6-13,29; 5:28,29; 7:51; Eph. 6:20; Phil. 1:14).
- Persecution gives a greater longing for our Lord's return (Rev. 6:9-11).
- Persecution causes faith, love, and patience to grow exceedingly (2 Thess. 1:3,4).
- Persecution strengthens the saints to comfort others (2 Cor. 1:4,5).
- Persecution causes either the conversion or the damnation of our persecutors (Acts 8:1 with 9:1-6; 13:45,46; 1 Thess. 2:15,16).
- Persecution makes the Word of God come alive (Acts 4:25, 26).
- Persecution demands perseverance, which produces godly character (Matt. 24:13; Acts 13:43; 14:22; 20:23,24; 1 Cor. 15:57,58; 16:13; Eph. 6:18-20; Phil. 1:28-30; Heb. 10:32-39; 1 Pet. 3:14; Rev. 2:10,25).
- Persecution works together with all things for our good and through Christ makes us more than conquerors (Rom. 8:28-39).
- Persecution brings great reward in heaven (Matt. 5:10-12).

Will it be fair to those who will be persecuted during the Great Tribulation that believers who lived previously did not have to suffer such persecution?

The Bible illustrates that believers backslide as much as, if not more, in times of peace and prosperity as in persecution and hardship. The apostle Paul wrote to Timothy, "Demas hath forsaken me, having loved this present world" (2 Tim. 4:10). Affluence often leads to forgetting the Lord (Deut. 8:13,14), to pride (Ezek. 28:5), to denying God (Pro. 30:8,9), to rebelling against Him (Neh. 9:25,26), to falling into temptation and a snare (1 Tim. 6:9,10), and to erring from the faith (1 Tim. 6:10).

On the other hand, suffering for Christ usually leads to rejoicing (Acts 5:40,41), to glorifying God (1 Pet. 4:16), to praying and singing (Acts 16:25), to preaching with boldness (Acts 5:17-20), to furthering the gospel (Phil. 1:12-14), and to conforming to the image of Christ (Rom. 8:28,29).

Scripture promises, "Yea, and all that will live godly in Christ Jesus shall suffer persecution" (2 Tim. 3:12). In Bible times and throughout church history, many Christians have suffered untold tribulation (Heb. 11:33-38). Remember that "God is faithful, who will not suffer you to be tempted above that ye are able; but will with the temptation also make a way to escape, that ye may be able to bear it" (1 Cor. 10:13). See also Rev. 2:10.

The Church is appointed to tribulation. Peace and worldly prosperity are more dangerous to her than times of bloody persecution and affliction.

Are there other reassuring scriptures for believers in tribulation?

Several of the following passages are found in the context of the end-time and the Second Coming. That the Word of God abounds with these comforting scriptures confirms once again that His people are appointed to tribulation, but not to the wrath of God.

- Let not your heart be troubled (John 14:1-3).
- Greater is He that is in you, than he that is in the world (1 John 4:4).
- The Lord is a refuge from the storm (Isa. 25:4).
- The Lord is our confidence (Pro. 3:21-26).
- God's grace is sufficient (2 Cor. 9:8; 12:9,10).
- The Lord is with us until the end of the world (Matt. 28:20; Phil. 1:6).
- The Lord gives power over all the power of the enemy (Luke 10:19).
- We can do all things through Christ who strengthens us (Phil. 4:13).

• The sufferings are not worthy to be compared with the glory (Rom. 8:17,18; 2 Cor. 4:17; Heb. 11:25-27).

• God gives assurance that He has everything under control (Psa. 37:18,23-25; Matt. 16:18; Rev. 6:9-11; 10:7; 17:17).

• God promises a glorious deliverance on the Day of the Lord (Psa. 66:9-12; Mal. 3:15-18 with 4:1-3; Matt. 24:29-31).

• We look for heaven (2 Pet. 3:12,13).

4

Will Believers Escape the Great Tribulation?

Does First Thessalonians 5:9, "For God hath not appointed us to wrath," teach that the Church is exempt from the Great Tribulation?

The Church is exempt from the Day of the Lord, not from the tribulation period. Confusion exists over this verse when verses 4:13 through 5:9 are not viewed as one event. The Bible was first divided into chapters about 1228 A. D. Sometimes a chapter division breaks the continuity of thought, as in this case. We should not forget that this is one complete passage.

The following four proofs show that First Thessalonians 5:9 refers to escaping the Day of the Lord, not the Great Tribulation:

1. First Thessalonians 4:16,17 is the same post-tribulation description of the Second Coming that is given in Matthew 24:30 and 31: the Lord descending from heaven, the clouds, the angels, the trumpet, and the gathering of the saints.

2. Saints who have survived the Great Tribulation will be among those "caught up." "Then we which are alive and *remain* shall be caught up together with them in the clouds" (1 Thess. 4:17). As stated earlier, the Greek word translated "remain" also means "to survive." Since Paul says "alive" and also "remain," he implies that those believers who are alive at the coming of the Lord are those who have survived the persecution of the Great Tribulation.

3. The gathering of the Church occurs on the Day of the Lord, not before the Tribulation. (Compare 4:16,17 with 5:2.)

4. The promise, "For God hath not appointed us to wrath" (5:9), considered in context, is given with reference to the "sudden destruction" that Paul described in verse three, not to the Great Tribulation.

Clearly, then, First Thessalonians 5:9 promises that the saints will be spared the wrath of God that is poured out on the Day of the Lord when Jesus comes to gather the Church and to judge the world. It's not a promise the Church will escape the Great Tribulation.

Is Luke 21:34-36 a promise that the Church will escape the Great Tribulation?

No. As we examine these verses in context, we see that God has not promised the Church an escape (a secret rapture) before the Tribulation. "And take heed to yourselves, lest at any time your hearts be overcharged with surfeiting, and drunkenness, and cares of this life, and so *that day* come upon you unawares. For as a snare shall it come on all them that dwell on the face of the whole earth. Watch ye therefore, and pray always, that ye may be accounted worthy to escape *all these things* that shall come to pass, and to stand before the Son of man" (Luke 21:34-36).

Is Jesus referring to escaping the Great Tribulation (the events of verses 8 through 24) or escaping His wrath upon the ungodly when He comes to gather His Church on the Day of the Lord (the events of verses 25 and 26)? Since Christ's coming is *after* the events of verses 8 through 24, without even the slightest hint of His coming before then, we must conclude that He is referring to escaping the events of verses 25 and 26. In other words, Jesus was not promising an escape from the Great Tribulation but from His wrath when He comes on the Day of the Lord.

It is important to remember that the Day of the Lord, which Jesus commonly called "that day," is not the time of the Great Tribulation. The Day of the Lord comes "immediately after the tribulation" (Matt. 24:29; compare with Acts 2:20). Throughout the Bible, the Day of the Lord is referred to as the great day of His wrath, not the Great Tribulation. See Chapter Ten.

By comparing the events of Luke 21:25-36 with related scriptures (in the following chart), one can see that Jesus referred to an escape from the catastrophic events and the final outpouring of His wrath that will occur at His coming, on the Day of the Lord, not an escape from the Great Tribulation.

The Events of Luke 21:25-36	**The Events of the Day of the Lord**
And there shall be signs in the sun, and in the moon, and in the stars—Luke 21:25.	The sun shall be turned into darkness, and the moon into blood, . . . day of the Lord—Joel 2:31.
And upon the earth distress—Luke 21:25.	The great day of the Lord. . . . a day of trouble and distress—Zeph. 1:14-17.
The sea and the waves roaring—Luke 21:25.	That great day of God. . . . every island fled away, and the mountains were not found—Rev. 16:14,20.
Men's hearts failing them for fear—Luke 21:26.	The day of the Lord. . . . every man's heart shall melt—Isa. 13:6,7.
For the powers of heaven shall be shaken—Luke 21:26.	The heavens shall tremble. . . . the day of the Lord—Joel 2:10,11.
And then shall they see the Son of man coming in a cloud with power and great glory—Luke 21:27.	The Lord . . . shall descend. . . . in the clouds. . . . the day of the Lord—1 Thess. 4:16,17; 5:2.
Your redemption draweth nigh—Luke 21:28.	The day of redemption is the Day of the Lord; on that day He will be glorified in His saints—2 Thess. 1:10; Rom. 8:17-23; Eph. 4:30.
Heaven and earth shall pass away—Luke 21:33.	The day of the Lord . . . the heavens shall pass away . . . the earth also—2 Pet. 3:10.
Lest . . . that day come upon you unawares. For as a snare shall it come—Luke 21:34,35.	The day of the Lord will come as a a thief—2 Pet. 3:10. As a snare, the thief comes suddenly with destruction upon the unprepared.
On all them that dwell on the face of the whole earth—Luke 21:35.	The day of the Lord's wrath . . . a speedy riddance of all them that dwell in the land—Zeph. 1:18.
Watch ye therefore, and pray always—Luke 21:36.	The day of the Lord. . . . let us watch—1 Thess. 5:2,6.
That ye may be accounted worthy—Luke 21:36.	That ye may be accounted worthy. . . . in that day—2 Thess. 1:5-10.
To escape all these things that shall come to pass, and to stand before the Son of man—Luke 21:36.	The great day of his wrath. . . . A great multitude . . . stood before . . . the Lamb—Rev. 6:16, 7:9.

Does Revelation 3:10 teach that the Church will not go through the Great Tribulation?

Revelation 3:10, addressed to the church at Philadelphia, states, "Because thou hast kept the word of my patience, I also will keep thee from the hour of temptation, which shall come upon all the world, to try them that dwell upon the earth." Some believe "the hour of temptation" is the Great Tribulation, and this verse promises the Church deliverance before then if she faithfully serves the Lord. But this belief is inconsistent with Scripture for several reasons:

First, the Great Tribulation is never called "an hour." The Day of the Lord, however, is called "an hour" at least sixteen times. See Matt. 24:36,42,44,50; 25:13; Mark 13:32; Luke 12:39,40,46; John 5:28; Rev. 3:3; 11:13; 14:7; 18:10,17,19. Also note that Jesus said, "the hour of temptation"—not seven, or three and one-half years of temptation as some believe.

Second, the phrase, "*which shall come upon all the world,*" is used throughout the Bible to describe the Day of the Lord's wrath. Consider the following verses:

"Behold, the day of the Lord. . . . I will *punish the world* for their evil" (Isa. 13:9,11).

"The day of the Lord's wrath . . . *The whole land* shall be devoured" (Zeph. 1:18).

"That day. . . . As a snare shall it come on all them that dwell on the face of *the whole earth*" (Luke 21:34,35).

"The day of the Lord . . . *the earth also and the works* that are therein shall be burned up" (2 Pet. 3:10).

Finally, other churches besides the church at Philadelphia kept the "word of his patience." No promise of deliverance was given to them other than the Lord's return after the Great Tribulation—

The church at Smyrna. "I know thy works, and tribulation, and poverty. . . . Fear none of those things which thou shalt suffer: behold, the devil shall cast some of you into prison, that ye may be tried; and ye shall have tribulation ten days: be thou faithful unto death, and I will give thee a crown of life" (Rev. 2:9,10).

The church at Thyatira. "*I know . . . thy patience. . . .* Hold fast till I come. And he that overcometh, and keepeth my works unto the end, to him will I give power over the nations" (Rev. 2:19,25,26). Would Jesus expect these saints to overcome and keep His works to the *end*, while promising the saints at Philadelphia an escape *before* the end? No.

In fact, Jesus exhorted each of the seven churches in Revelation chapters two and three to overcome. Overcoming includes having victory in suffering, conflict, and even martyrdom. This truth is exemplified by the saints in Revelation 12:11: "And they overcame him by the blood of the Lamb, and by the word of their testimony; and they loved not their lives unto the death." All believers are expected to be overcomers and, with patience, keep the works of Jesus to the end. Consider further examples from the Word of God:

The church at Thessalonica. "We ourselves glory in you . . . for your *patience* and faith in all your persecutions and tribulations that ye endure" (2 Thess. 1:4). Since her beginning, this church had been suffering patiently for the sake of the Word of God (1 Thess. 1:6). Although Paul commended these saints for their patience, he didn't say it would keep them from the Great Tribulation. Instead, he consoled them by telling why God allowed them to suffer, and he exhorted them to rest—not until a secret rapture, but until "the Lord Jesus shall be revealed from heaven" (2 Thess. 1:7). In other words, although these saints were suffering and keeping the Word of God patiently, Paul did not give any promise of deliverance from persecution and tribulation until the Lord would be revealed.

The believers referred to in Hebrews 11:33-35. They are another example of those who kept the "word of his patience." These heroes of faith "subdued kingdoms, wrought righteousness, obtained promises, stopped the mouths of lions, quenched the violence of fire, escaped the edge of the sword, out of weakness were made strong, waxed valiant in fight, turned to flight the armies of the aliens. Women received their dead raised to life again: and others were tortured, not accepting deliverance; that they might obtain a better resurrection." This has been the hope of all saints down through the ages—a better resurrection, not a deliverance before then.

The Church in the end-time. Contrary to promising an escape, Jesus prophesied that the Church will go through the Great Tribulation (Matt. 24:21,22). *Patience*, according to Jesus, will *not* exempt the Church from tribulation, but is needed to go through it: "In your patience possess ye your souls" (Luke 21:19).

"He that leadeth into captivity shall go into captivity: he that killeth with the sword must be killed with the sword. Here is the *patience* and the faith of the saints" (Rev. 13:10).

"And the third angel followed them, saying with a loud voice, If any man worship the beast and his image. . . . The same shall drink of the wine of the wrath of God. . . . Here is the *patience* of the saints: here are they that keep the commandments of God and the faith of Jesus" (Rev. 14:9,10,12).

What are the implications of the phrase "my patience" (Rev. 3:10)?

This phrase speaks of the patience of our Lord Jesus Christ. Consider the following passage: "Be *patient* therefore, brethren, unto the coming of the Lord. Behold, the husbandman waiteth for the precious fruit of the earth, and hath *long patience* for it, until he receive the early and latter rain. Be ye also *patient*; stablish your hearts: for the coming of the Lord draweth nigh. Grudge not one against another, brethren, lest ye be condemned: behold, the judge standeth before the door. Take, my brethren, the prophets, who have spoken in the name of the Lord, for an example of suffering affliction, and of *patience*. Behold, we count them happy which endure. Ye have heard of the *patience* of Job, and have seen the end of the Lord; that the Lord is very pitiful, and of tender mercy" (James 5:7-11).

In the above passage, the word *patience* is used five times for emphasis. It speaks of our Lord's patience in waiting for the precious fruit of the earth. It also encourages the Church to be patient for the coming of the Lord. Then, with direct reference to His coming, it links patience with suffering, affliction, and endurance. But how long will the Lord patiently wait for the precious fruit of the earth before He comes again? The answer is clear: "The harvest is the end of the world" (Matt. 13:39).

Peter affirmed this truth: "The Lord . . . is *longsuffering* to usward, not willing that any should perish, but that all should come to repentance. But *the day of the Lord* will come as a thief in the night; in the which the heavens shall pass away with a great noise" (2 Pet. 3:9,10). Therefore, when the Lord speaks of keeping "the word of my patience," He is speaking of patience to the end, when He comes on the Day of the Lord.

Revelation 3:10, then, does not promise that the saints will be gathered before the Great Tribulation. But it does promise that on the Day of the Lord when "sudden destruction cometh," the Church will be kept from that "hour of temptation" because she will first be "caught up" to meet the Lord in the air (1 Thess. 4:16,17; 5:1-2).

Does Revelation 3:11 give further evidence that Revelation 3:10 does not promise deliverance before the Great Tribulation?

Yes. Consider the phrase "Behold, I come quickly: hold that fast which thou hast" (Rev. 3:11). How long must we hold fast? Until a supposed secret rapture or until the end? The Bible says to hold fast until the end—until Jesus comes to judge the nations. Let us not forget His words to the church at Thyatira: "But that which ye have already hold fast till I come. And he that overcometh, and keepeth my works *unto the end*, to him will I give power over the nations" (Rev. 2:25,26).

Consider also the phrase "That no man take thy crown" (Rev. 3:11). To the church at Smyrna, the Lord also spoke of a crown (Rev. 2:10). Surely He wouldn't promise the church at Smyrna a crown of life for their suffering, imprisonment, tribulation, and even faithfulness unto death and then promise the church at Philadelphia deliverance from all suffering and tribulation, and give them a crown as well.

James 1:12 states, "Blessed is the man that endureth temptation: for when he is tried, he shall receive the *crown of life*, which the Lord hath promised to them that love him." The apostles taught that the saints would be crowned at our Lord's appearing, not before (2 Tim. 4:8; 1 Pet. 5:4).

Can Isaiah 26:20 be interpreted as God's promise that the Church will be withdrawn before the Great Tribulation?

Isaiah 26:20 states, "Come, my people, enter thou into thy chambers, and shut thy doors about thee: hide thyself as it were for a little moment, until the indignation be overpast."

This verse refers to the saints' escaping the wrath of God that will be poured out when Jesus comes to gather the Church "after the tribulation" on the "day of the Lord," not to escaping the Great Tribulation itself. The following comparison of the events of Isaiah chapters 24 to 26 with the same events as taught in the gospels and in the epistles shows that they occur after the Tribulation, on the Day of the Lord.

The Events of Isaiah chapters 24-26	**When These Events Will Occur as Taught in the Gospels**	**in the Epistles**
The Lord's coming as a snare—thief Isa. 24:17,18	After the tribulation—Compare Matt. 24:29, 30 with 24:43; Luke 21:35.	Day of the Lord—1 Thess. 5:2; 2 Pet. 3:10.
Cataclysmic events Isa. 24:18-23	After the tribulation—Matt. 24:29.	Day of the Lord—2 Pet. 3:10; Rev. 6:12-17.
The resurrection Isa. 26:19.	After the tribulation—Matt. 24:29-31.	Day of the Lord—1 Thess. 4:16-18; 5:2.
Door shut—saints safe from wrath Isa. 26:20	After the tribulation—Compare Matt. 24:29-31 with 25:10,34.	Day of the Lord—1 Thess. 4:15-18; 5:2,3.
Death swallowed up in victory and tears wiped away Isa. 25:8	After the tribulation—Compare Matt. 24:29; 25:46 with Rev. 20:14; 21:4.	Day of the Lord—1 Thess. 4:16; 5:2; 1 Cor. 15:52-55.
The wicked burned Isa. 24:6	After the tribulation—Matt. 24:29-31; 25:41.	Day of the Lord—2 Pet. 3:7,10.
Earth is dissolved Isa. 24:3-6,19	After the tribulation—Matt. 24:29-35.	Day of the Lord—2 Pet. 3:10-12.
The Lord reigns Isa. 24:23	After the tribulation—Matt. 24:29; 25:31.	The end—1 Cor. 15:23-25; Rev. 11:15; 19:6.

In summary, First Thessalonians 5:9, Luke 21:34-36, Revelation 3:10, and Isaiah 26:20 are *not* promises that the Church will escape the Great Tribulation. The Church will escape the wrath of God that will be poured out on the whole earth when Jesus comes to gather the Church and to judge the world.

5

Written to the Church or to the Jews? (Part I)

Do the gospel of Matthew, chapters four through nineteen of Revelation, and the end-time prophecies of Daniel pertain to the Church or to the Jews?

They pertain to the Church. Most Christians believe that the gospels, as well as the epistles, apply to them. They also associate Daniel with Revelation in that they contain the same prophetic message about the Church in the end-time. Yet, there is a widespread teaching that these portions of Scripture are not primarily for or about the Church, but about Israel. It is necessary to show that these passages pertain to the Church; otherwise, all evidence from them that the Church will go through the Great Tribulation will be irrelevant.

This chapter (Part I) discusses the gospel of Matthew. The next chapter (Part II) discusses chapters four through nineteen of Revelation and the end-time prophecies of Daniel.

How do we know Matthew's gospel concerns the Church and not primarily the Jews?

It is significant that the word "church" is recorded three times in Matthew's gospel (16:18; 18:17), yet not once in the other gospels—which is unusual if it, among the gospels, were intended primarily for the Jews.

The gospel of Matthew is meant for "whosoever," not for any select nationality. The words "whoso" and "whosoever" are emphasized more in this book than in any of the other gospels (forty-two times). Jesus said, "*Whosoever* heareth these sayings of mine, and doeth them, I will liken him unto a wise man, which built his house upon a rock" (7:24). In addition, He frequently used the words "every one," "any one," "any man," "all," and "every man." Jesus meant the entire Book of Matthew to be for everyone, which includes chapters twenty-four and twenty-five on the end-time: "*Whoso* readeth, let him understand" (24:15).

Furthermore, all the sayings of Jesus in the gospels and His teachings as reflected in the epistles are not treated piecemeal. For example, the apostles preached "the words of our Lord Jesus Christ" (1 Tim. 6:3) and "the message which we have heard of him, and declare unto you" (1 John 1:5) without making any distinction between the gospel of Matthew and the other three gospels.

Moreover, "*all* things" written in Matthew's gospel are meant for "*all* nations," not for Jews only. Notice that this gospel ends with Christ's command to go and teach all nations to observe all things He has commanded (28:20). Jesus told His followers that the Holy Spirit shall bring "*all* things" to your remembrance, "whatsoever I have said unto you" (John 14:26). "All things," all Jesus' teaching, surely includes His sayings in the Book of Matthew.

Finally, Matthew's gospel harmonizes perfectly with Mark, Luke, and John. The gospel of Matthew records more than one hundred and twenty events of Christ's ministry. At least thirty of these are recorded in all four gospels. In addition, eighty-five of these events are recorded in at least one of the other gospels, which include major themes such as the ministry of John the Baptist, the Sermon on the Mount, *Christ's discourse on the Second Coming*, His teaching on the Holy Spirit, about eight of the parables, the betrayal of Jesus by Judas, the denial by Peter, the trial, crucifixion and resurrection of our Lord Jesus Christ, and the Great Commission. Because Matthew's gospel also includes these major themes, we should not single it out as pertaining to the Jews in particular. The sayings of Jesus are unified, whether they are found in Matthew or the other three gospels. They are for all, Jew or Gentile.

Do Matthew 24 and 25 pertain to Israel but not to the Church?

The argument that these chapters concern only the Jews is not valid for three reasons:

1. Matthew 24 and 25 were not addressed to the Jews, but to

the disciples, the foundation of the Church. In the preceding chapters, the Jews reject Christ; therefore, He sorrowfully rejects them. Three parables bear out this fact: the parable of the two sons (21:28-32); the parable of the householder (21:33-46); and the parable of the marriage feast (22:1-14). Then, in the near context of these parables, Jesus solemnly states, "O Jerusalem, Jerusalem. . . . Behold, your house is left unto you desolate" (23:37,38). He does not later revoke these words.

Immediately after making this pronouncement against the Jews, "Jesus went out, and *departed* from the temple [the Jews]: and his disciples came to him. . . ." (Matt. 24:1). Thus, Jesus was addressing His disciples about His coming and the end of the world; He was not addressing the Jews as a nation. Although He foretold that the buildings of the temple would be destroyed (which took place during the destruction of Jerusalem in 70 A. D.), this is no reason to conclude that His teaching about the Second Coming and the end of the world applies only to the Jews and has nothing to do with the Church. (See Matt. 24:2.)

2. Jesus' discourse in Matthew 24 and 25 agrees with the epistles, which are clearly written to the Church. It is also recorded in the gospels of Mark and Luke.

3. In Matthew 24 and 25, Jesus refers to the Church at least seven times, without using the word "church." It is dangerous to assume that since the word "church" is not mentioned, these chapters pertain to Israel. After all, the words "Israel" and "Jew" do not appear either. In fact, the word "church" is not found in Mark, Luke, John, Second Peter, First and Second John, and Jude, which are clearly written for the Church's edification. The writers simply use other terms, which is also true of Matthew.

How is the Church represented in Matthew 24 and 25?

By carefully comparing these chapters with other scriptures, we see the Church referred to as:

His disciples (24:1)—They are described as the foundation of the Church in Ephesians 2:20. They will preach the gospel in all the world (Matt. 24:14).

"His elect" (24:31)—These are Christ's elect, His Church, which is composed of both Jew and Gentile believers. "And he shall send his angels with a great sound of a trumpet, and they

shall gather together *his elect. . . .*" (Matt. 24:31). If "his elect" is the nation or a remnant of Israel, as some claim, then we would have to assume there will be a special coming of Christ for "Jews only," which even some of those who equate the elect with Israel are not willing to admit. In the New Testament the Church is designated as God's "elect" (Col. 3:12). See Chapter Eleven.

They who are commanded "to watch" (24:42,43; 25:13)—Throughout the New Testament, the command "to watch" is given to the Church, not to Israel.

They who will go "out to meet him" (25:6)—According to Paul, they who "meet the Lord" are those who are "in Christ," the Church (1 Thess. 4:16,17). The five wise virgins represent the Bride, the Lamb's wife, the glorious Church without spot or wrinkle (Matt. 9:15; 2 Cor. 11:2; Eph. 5:25,27; Rev. 19:7).

In the parable of the marriage feast (Matt. 22:1-14), the nation of Israel had been invited to the wedding, but "would not come" (v. 3). It had the opportunity to be the Bride of Christ, but refused. The invitation was then given to all (vs. 8,9). Jesus concluded this parable with the words, "For many are called, but few are chosen" (v. 14). The called are those who were invited to the wedding feast; the chosen are those who accepted the invitation, the Church. She will go out to meet her Bridegroom when He comes. See also Matt. 8:10-12; Luke 13:24-30; 14:15-24; John 1:11,12.

The "good and faithful servant" (25:21)—This servant represents the Church; those who are ready for their Lord. Jesus contrasted His servants and the Jews who were ready to crucify Him. "Jesus answered, My kingdom is not of this world: if my kingdom were of this world, then would *my servants* fight, that I should not be delivered to *the Jews*" (John 18:36). See also Isa. 65:12-15; John 12:26; Rev. 22:3.

"The sheep" who inherit the kingdom and enter life eternal (25:33,34,46)—Only to His Church would the Lord Jesus say, "Come, ye blessed of my Father, inherit the kingdom prepared for you from the foundation of the world" (25:34). See also 1 Pet. 1:4; Rev. 21:7. The sheep represent the Church because they follow Christ and hear His voice. To unbelieving Jews, Jesus said, "But ye believe not, *because ye are not of my sheep*, as I said unto you. *My sheep* hear my voice, and I know them, and they follow

me: And I give unto them eternal life" (John 10:26-28). See also Matt. 10:5-15. Repentance and believing the gospel is the only way for individual Jews to be saved (Mark 1:15).

"My brethren" (25:40)—Jesus declared in Matthew's gospel that His brethren are they who do the will of His Father (12:50), and He identified the brethren with His Church (18:15-17). The term "brethren" is synonymous with the saints (Col. 1:2), the elect (1 Thess. 1:4), and the Church (1 Thess. 1:1,4; Heb. 2:11,12). Moreover, Jesus made a distinction between His brethren and the Jews: "Jesus saith unto her . . . go to my brethren. . . . The disciples were assembled [behind shut doors] for fear of the Jews" (John 20:17,19). See also Acts 14:2; 17:5,6; 1 Thess. 2:14-17. The truth of Matthew 25:40 is also illustrated by Matthew 10:11-15,40-42 and Hebrews 6:10. See Chapter Twelve.

In summary, the Church, in Matthew 24 and 25, is represented as Christ's disciples, His elect, they who are commanded to watch, the five wise virgins, the good and faithful servant, the sheep, and His brothers.

In Matthew 24:24, is the use of the Jewish term "Christ" or "Messiah" an indication that the events of this chapter pertain to Israel and not to the Church?

Not at all! The same warning of false Christs and false prophets is given to the Church.

"Even him [the man of sin], whose coming is after the working of Satan with all power and signs and lying wonders" (2 Thess. 2:9).

"And he [the false prophet] doeth great wonders, so that he maketh fire come down from heaven on the earth in the sight of men, and deceiveth them that dwell on the earth by the means of those miracles which he had power to do in the sight of the beast" (Rev. 13:13,14).

Does the term "kingdom of heaven" mark Matthew's gospel as being exclusively for the Jews?

Although the phrase "kingdom of heaven" is found only in Matthew's gospel (thirty times), this by no means establishes that this gospel applies exclusively to the Jews. In fact, the terms "kingdom of heaven" and "kingdom of God" mean the same thing. They are used interchangeably, not distinctively, as illustrated in the following chart:

Descriptions of the Kingdom	**Kingdom of Heaven**	**Kingdom of God**
Relates to the Church	Matt. 16:18,19	Acts 14:22,23
Was taken away from Israel	Matt. 22:2-8	Matt. 21:43
Is eternal	Matt. 19:16 with 23	Matt. 19:16,24
Is universal	Matt. 8:11	Luke 13:29
Is for "whosoever"	Matt. 5:19; 18:4	Mark 10:15
Is at hand	Matt. 4:17	Mark 1:15
Contains "mysteries"	Matt. 13:11	Luke 8:10
Is present	Matt. 23:13	Luke 17:20,21
Is future	Matt. 7:21-23	Mark 14:25
Has qualifications for greatness	Matt. 11:11	Luke 7:28
Pertains even to little children	Matt. 19:14	Mark 10:14
Comes with healing and peace	Matt. 10:7,8,13	Luke 9:1,2
Has a Holy Spirit baptism	Matt. 3:2,11	Acts 1:3-5,8
Requires true righteousness	Matt. 5:20	1 Cor. 6:9,10
Is associated with joy	Matt. 13:44	Rom. 14:17
Rewards the persecuted	Matt. 5:10	2 Thess. 1:5,10
Comes not with open show	Matt. 13:11,31,44	Luke 17:20,21
Is coming with glory	Matt. 25:14 with 31	Luke 21:27,31
Shuts door on the unprepared	Matt. 25:1,10,11	Luke 13:25,28
Will be purged of the wicked	Matt. 13:24,40-42	Luke 13:28
The kingdom's terms of entrance are:		
Repentance and faith	Matt. 4:17	Mark 1:15
The new birth	Matt. 18:3	John 3:3,5
Conversion with childlike humility	Matt. 18:3	Luke 18:17
Poverty of spirit	Matt. 5:3	Luke 6:20
Keeping the commandments	Matt. 19:17,23	Luke 18:19-25
Doing the will of the Father	Matt. 7:21	Matt. 21:31,32
Trusting in God, not in riches	Matt. 19:23	Matt. 19:24

In addition, Scripture records more than seventeen different terms for God's kingdom that include, for example, "My Father's kingdom," "My kingdom," and "the kingdom of Christ and of God." Obviously, there are not seventeen different kingdoms of God! Moreover, when speaking to the rich young ruler, Jesus used the terms "kingdom of heaven, "kingdom of God," "eternal life," "life," "heaven," and "everlasting life" (Matt. 19:16-29). He also used the various terms when he spoke with Nicodemus:

"kingdom of God," "heaven," "eternal life," and "everlasting life" (John 3:5-16).

Clearly, the "kingdom of heaven" and the "kingdom of God" are the same eternal kingdom. It is the eternal inheritance of all true believers. The phrase "kingdom of heaven" cannot be used to suggest that Matthew is a gospel to the Jews.

Objections Answered

Won't 144,000 Jews be converted during the Tribulation and preach "this gospel of the kingdom" (Matt. 24:14) with regard to a future millennium?

Not one scripture indicates that 144,000 Jews will be converted during the Tribulation, nor that there will be a future millennium after Christ's return. The following five reasons show that Jesus ordained the Church, consisting of Jews and Gentiles, to preach the gospel of the kingdom until His return at the end of the world:

1. The kingdom and its mysteries are given to the Church, not to Israel (Matt. 13:10-15). Israel rejected the gospel; therefore, Christ took the kingdom from Israel and gave it to the Church—"a nation bringing forth the fruits thereof" (Matt. 21:41,43). The mysteries of the kingdom are hidden from the nation of Israel in fulfillment of Isaiah's prophecy (Isa. 6:9; Mark 4:11,12; Col. 1:26,27). See also John 15:16; 1 Pet. 2:9; Matt. 13:11,12; 16:18,19; 18:18; Luke 12:31,32; Acts 13:44-46; 28:23-28; Isa. 65:1-16.

2. Jesus commissioned the Church to preach the gospel to the end of the age (Matt. 28:19,20).

3. Jesus sent His Holy Spirit to empower the Church to witness His gospel and to seal the Church "unto the day of redemption," which is the day of His coming. See also Luke 24:48,49; John 15:16,27; Acts 1:8; 4:33; 5:32; 10:39,41; 13:31,32; 22:14,15; 23:11; 26:16,22; 1 Pet. 5:1; 1 John 1:2.

4. The Church, not Israel, is Christ's fruit-bearing branch. Jesus said, "I am the vine, ye are the branches: He that abideth in me, and I in him, the same bringeth forth much fruit: for without me ye can do nothing" (John 15:5).

5. The Church is responsible to patiently preach the gospel until Christ's return because He delays His coming for the sake of the unsaved. "Be patient therefore, *brethren*, unto the coming of the Lord. Behold, the husbandman waiteth for the precious fruit of the earth" (James 5:7). The Father is waiting for His gospel to be spread "in all the world for a witness unto all nations; and then shall the end come" (Matt. 24:14). The Lord will not come until the harvest, which is the end of the world (Matt. 13:30,39; 2 Pet. 3:9,10).

Doesn't the "gospel of the kingdom" (Matt. 24:14) differ from the "gospel of the grace of God" (Acts 20:24)?

There is absolutely no difference between the "gospel of the kingdom" and the "gospel of the grace of God." They are the same. The "gospel of the kingdom," in simple terms, is the "gospel of Jesus Christ" that calls men and women to repentance and faith. It is the same "gospel of the grace of God" that Paul "received of the Lord Jesus" and testified of "both to the Jews, and also to the Greeks" (Acts 20:24,21). This is seen in the following comparison of the preaching of Jesus and of Paul:

Jesus	**Paul**
"The gospel of Jesus Christ"	"The gospel of the grace of God"
"Preaching the gospel of the kingdom"	"Preaching the kingdom"
"Repent . . . and believe"	"Repentance . . . and faith"
(Mark 1:1,14,15)	(Acts 20:24,25,21)

Just as there are many biblical terms for God's kingdom, so there are many terms for the gospel, such as "the gospel of peace" (Rom. 10:15), "the gospel of your salvation" (Eph. 1:13), "the glorious gospel of Christ" (2 Cor. 4:4), "the gospel of the grace of God" (Acts 20:24), "the everlasting gospel" (Rev. 14:6), "this gospel of the kingdom of God" (Mark 1:14), and many more. Yet we know there is only one gospel of our Lord Jesus Christ. The apostle Paul strongly affirmed this truth not once but twice: "But though we, or an angel from heaven, preach any other gospel unto you than that which we have preached unto you, let him be accursed. As we said before, so say I now again, if any man preach any other gospel unto you than that ye have received, let him be accursed" (Gal. 1:8,9).

Isn't "this gospel of the kingdom" (Matt. 24:14) about a future earthly kingdom?

"This gospel of the kingdom" is *not* about a future earthly kingdom for the following three reasons:

First, in this discourse (Matthew 24 and 25), Jesus showed that "this gospel of the kingdom" is the gospel of a heavenly kingdom, not a future, earthly one. Just as the righteous "inherit the kingdom prepared . . . from the foundation of the world" (25:34), so the unprepared go "into everlasting fire" (25:41). It may seem in the following first three instances that the righteous will be rewarded in an earthly kingdom, but when comparing them to the eternal punishments and to related scriptures, we see that Jesus spoke of a future eternal kingdom—heaven.

Eternal Reward in Heaven	Eternal Punishment in Hell
He shall make him ruler over all his goods—Matt. 24:47.	Cut him asunder, and appoint him his portion with the hypocrites: there shall be weeping and gnashing of teeth—Matt. 24:51.
And they that were ready went in with him to the marriage: and the door was shut—Matt. 25:10.	Lord, Lord, open to us. But he answered and said, Verily I say unto you, I know you not—Matt. 25: 11,12.
I will make thee ruler over many things: enter thou into the joy of thy lord—Matt. 25:21,23.	And cast ye the unprofitable servant into outer darkness: there shall be weeping and gnashing of teeth—Matt. 25:30.
Then shall the King say unto them on his right hand, Come, ye blessed of my Father, inherit the kingdom prepared for you from the foundation of the world—Matt. 25:34.	Then shall he say also unto them on the left hand, Depart from me, ye cursed, into everlasting fire, prepared for the devil and his angels—Matt. 25:41.
The righteous into life eternal—Matt. 25:46.	And these shall go away unto everlasting punishment—Matt. 25:46.

Second, throughout the New Testament, the hope of the gospel is identified with a heavenly kingdom:

"We preached unto you *the gospel of God. . . .* his *kingdom and glory*" (1 Thess. 2:9,12).

"The Lord stood with me . . . that by me the *preaching* might be fully known. . . . and will preserve me unto his *heavenly kingdom*" (2 Tim. 4:17,18).

"*The everlasting kingdom* of our Lord and Saviour Jesus Christ. . . . be established in this present *truth*" (2 Pet. 1:11,12).

"The hope which is laid up for you in *heaven . . . the gospel*" (Col. 1:5).

Finally, everything about this glorious gospel is heavenly. It prepares people's hearts so they might live an abundant life in Christ here on earth and inherit the kingdom of heaven for eternity.

The gospel has come because our Lord Jesus Christ "came down from heaven" (John 3:13).

The gospel is preached with "the Holy Ghost sent down from heaven" (1 Pet. 1:12).

The gospel message is repentance. When heeded, there is "joy in the presence of the angels" in heaven (Luke 15:7,10).

The gospel gives faith, which is necessary for entrance into "the kingdom of heaven" (Matt. 8:10,11).

The gospel, when obeyed, will cause men's names to be "written in heaven" (Luke 10:20).

The gospel, when disobeyed, will exclude men from heaven (2 Thess. 1:7-9; Rev. 22:14,15).

The gospel motivates us to "give thanks" to God, our Father in heaven (1 Thess. 1:1-5).

The gospel demands sacrifice, but great will be our "reward in heaven" (Mark 10:21,29,30; Heb. 10:34,35).

The gospel also gives "hope which is laid up for you in heaven" (Col. 1:5).

There should be no doubt that "this gospel of the kingdom" refers to a heavenly, eternal kingdom, not to a future earthly one.

6

Written to the Church or to the Jews? (Part II)

Is it true that Revelation chapter four to nineteen refers to Israel and, therefore, these chapters do not apply to the Church?

There is no basis for this assertion. Revelation begins and ends with references to the grace of our Lord Jesus Christ (1:4; 22:21), just as almost all the epistles to the Church. We can see that the entire Book of Revelation applies to the Church in the following verses:

"The Revelation of Jesus Christ, which God gave unto him, to shew unto his servants things which must shortly come to pass" (1:1; 22:6). "The Revelation of Jesus Christ" means the *complete* book is meant for His servants, not just certain chapters.

"I Jesus have sent mine angel to testify unto you these things *in the churches*" (22:16). Again, the *entire* Book of Revelation is to be read in the churches, not just part of it.

Furthermore, Christ commanded John to prophesy not primarily to Israel, but "before many peoples, and nations, and tongues, and kings" (10:11).

In chapters four to nineteen, we see a vivid picture of the Church keeping the faith of Jesus in spite of persecution from the beast, but we do not find anything about the beast persecuting Israel. Moreover, the events of these chapters coincide precisely with events described in the gospels and the epistles. (See the chart at the close of this chapter.) There are also at least thirty-seven references to the Church, employing terms such as "brethren," "the faithful," "his wife" "saints," etc. In fact, almost every chapter in Revelation 4-19 refers to the Church:

Chapter 5:8,9—"The prayers of the saints." The redeemed "out of every kindred, and tongue, and people, and nation."

Chapter 6:11—"Fellow servants" and "brethren."

Chapter 7:9—"A great multitude, which no man could number, of *all* nations, and kindreds, and people, and tongues."

Chapter 8:4—"The prayers of the saints."

Chapter 9:4—Those who have "the seal of God in their foreheads" are protected.

Chapter 11:3,18—The "two witnesses." "The saints, and them that fear thy name."

Chapter 12:11,17—Overcomers "by the blood of the Lamb." They who "keep the commandments of God, and have the testimony of Jesus."

Chapter 13:7,10—"War with the saints." "The patience and faith of the saints."

Chapter 14:12,13—"The patience of the saints . . . they that keep the commandments of God and the faith of Jesus." "The dead" who "die in the Lord."

Chapter 15:2—Those who have "victory over the beast."

Chapter 16:15—"He that watcheth, and keepeth his garments."

Chapter 17:14—The "called and chosen [the elect], and faithful."

Chapter 18:4—"My people."

Chapter 19:7,8—"His wife—saints."

We even read a warning to the Church: "Behold, I come as a thief. Blessed is he that watcheth, and keepeth his garments, lest he walk naked, and they see his shame" (Rev. 16:15). Jesus gave an admonition in Revelation 13:9 that is similar to the Word He gave to each of the seven churches in chapters two and three: "If any man have an ear, let him hear."

From beginning to end, the Book of Revelation is not only for the Church, but it is clearly *about* the Church. Its message, therefore, is most vital to the Church. This is why Satan opposes it. Is there any wonder that out of sixty-six books of the Bible it is in Revelation that God pronounces blessings to those who read and keep it, and cursing to those who add or take away from it?

"Blessed is he that readeth, and they that hear the words of this prophecy, and keep those things which are written therein: for the time is at hand" (1:3; 22:7).

"For I testify unto every man that heareth the words of the prophecy of this book, if any man shall add unto these things,

God shall add unto him the plagues that are written in this book" (22:18).

"And if any man shall take away from the words of the book of this prophecy, God shall take away his part out of the book of life, and out of the holy city, and from the things which are written in this book" (22:19).

In saying that Revelation four through nineteen does not apply to the Church, we should beware that we do not "take away from the words of the book of this prophecy."

Can the Book of Revelation be understood?

Absolutely! God would not promise a blessing for reading it if He didn't intend for us to understand it. The sayings of the prophecy of this book are *revealed*, not *sealed* (22:10). God Himself will show "unto his servants things which must shortly come to pass" (1:1). But humility and holiness of heart are essential for those who read Revelation and want to understand it. It's impossible to live contrary to the Bible and at the same time have spiritual insight into the revelations of God. "The secret of the Lord is with them that fear him; and he will shew them his covenant" (Psa. 25:14). Jesus said, "I thank thee, O Father, Lord of heaven and earth, because thou hast hid these things from the wise and prudent, and hast revealed them unto babes" (Matt. 11:25).

To understand Revelation, at least three things must be kept in mind:

1. Much of Revelation is written in figurative speech—the four beasts, a great red dragon, the woman with two wings of a great eagle, the serpent, the beast with two horns like a lamb which speaks as a dragon, etc. Therefore, it should be interpreted in the light of the books that we understand such as the gospels and the epistles.

2. The events in chapters four through twenty are *not* written in chronological order; they repeat themselves at least four times. Events describing the Second Coming, for example, are repeated in chapters 6, 11, 14, 16, and 20. The seal, trumpet, and bowl judgments are more or less parallel descriptions of the same events, each ending with the coming of our Lord Jesus Christ.

3. We must determine by comparing with the context and

other scriptures whether a particular passage is present or future—"The things which are" or "the things which shall be hereafter" (Rev. 1:19).

Does Revelation 4:1 depict the gathering of the Church before the Tribulation?

No, not at all. Revelation 4:1 states, "After this I looked, and, behold, a door was opened in heaven: and the first voice which I heard was as it were of a trumpet talking with me; which said, Come up hither, and I will shew thee things which must be hereafter." This verse refers to *John*, not the *Church*—"*I* looked," "*I* heard," "talking with *me*," "shew *thee* things which must be hereafter."

Moreover, according to his other writings in the gospel and the epistles of John, the gathering of the Church will occur *after* the Tribulation: "When he [Jesus] shall *appear*" (1 John 2:28; 3:2); "in the day of judgment" (1 John 4:17); "at the last day" (John 6:39,40,44,54).

Are there other indications in Revelation that the Church will go through the Tribulation?

Yes, many:

- The foretelling of the rise of the beast and the false prophet and of the number of the beast (666), which the Church will resist taking (chapter 13; 15:2).
- The prophecies of fierce persecution from the beast against the Church (6:9-11; 7:14; 13:7-10; 14:12; 20:4).
- The mention of God's protection upon the Church (3:12; 7:2,3; 9:4; 14:1; 22:4).
- A warning to the faithful of the consequences of worshiping the beast and his image, and of receiving his mark (14:9-12).
- Encouragements to the Church, such as, "Behold, I come as a thief, Blessed is he that watcheth, and keepeth his garments" (16:15). See also Rev. 2:25; 3:11; 14:13; 22:7,12,20.
- Assurances to the Church that she will have ultimate victory in her conflict with the powers of darkness at the glorious return of her Lord Jesus Christ (15:2,3; 17:14; 19:11-20; 20:4; 21:3-7).

In Revelation 13:7, the beast makes war with the saints. Can you prove that "the saints" refers to the Church and not to Jews, as many teach?

The word "saints," meaning holy ones, occurs thirteen times in Revelation. In the rest of the New Testament, the word "saints" is found at least forty-seven times with reference to the Church, but not once to Israel. There is no reason to believe this usage is changed in Revelation. Also, the saints in Revelation 19:8 are described in verses 7 and 9 as "his wife" who is called to "the marriage supper of the Lamb." Clearly, the Bride of Christ is the Church.

In addition, the description of the saints in Revelation fits the description of the saints in the epistles:

The Saints	In the Epistles	In Revelation
Are redeemed by Jesus' blood	Eph. 1:1 with 1:7	Rev. 5:8,9
Will judge the world	1 Cor. 6:1,2	Rev. 20:4,9
Are the called	1 Cor. 1:2,24	Rev. 17:14
Are the chosen	Eph. 1:1 with 1:4	Rev. 17:14
Are the faithful	Eph. 1:1	Rev. 17:14
Are out of every nation	Rom. 1:5 with 1:7	Rev. 5:8,9
Are holy	Col. 1:2 with 3:12	Rev. 20:6,9
Are a praying people	Eph. 1:1 with 1:16	Rev. 5:8; 8:3,4
Have faith and patience	2 Thess. 1:4 with 1:10	Rev. 13:10
Are the wife of Christ	2 Cor. 1:1 with 11:2	Rev. 19:7,8
Are called "God's servants"	Rom. 1:7 with 6:22	Rev. 19:2,5,8
Are overcomers	Rom. 1:7 with 12:21	Rev. 15:2,3
Keep the commandments of God	1 Cor. 1:2 with 7:19	Rev. 14:12
Die in the Lord	2 Cor. 1:1 with 5:8	Rev. 14:12,13
Fear God	Phil. 1:1 with 2:12	Rev. 11:18
Are resurrected	2 Thess. 1:10	Rev. 19:6-9
See their enemies judged	2 Thess. 1:5-10	Rev. 19:8,17,18
Are rewarded	Heb. 6:10	Rev. 11:18
Are God's covenant people	Eph. 2:12-19; Heb. 8:10	Rev. 21:7
Are recorded in the book of life	Phil. 1:1 with 4:3	Rev. 13:7,8

In what other ways does the Book of Revelation relate to the Church?

Revelation particularly relates to the Church because it contains Christ's message of repentance and revival. He comes to the

Church to encourage, to warn, and to rebuke in love that she might repent and receive new life to overcome and walk in righteousness (chapters 2 and 3). If there were ever a time the Church needed this message, it's today!

Also, it relates to the Church because it is "the Revelation of Jesus Christ," which the Church needs to overcome the world. Jesus Christ is revealed as the *Lamb* of God twenty-eight times. The saints have their robes washed "white in the blood of the *Lamb*" (7:14), their names written in the "book of life of the *Lamb*" (13:8; 21:27), and they have power to overcome Satan "by the blood of the *Lamb*" (12:11).

As a result, the saved will have "victory over the beast, and over his image, and over his mark, and over the number of his name, [and] stand on the sea of glass, having the harps of God" and singing "the song of the *Lamb*" (15:2,3).

What a day of rejoicing that will be! "Let us be glad and rejoice, and give honour to him: for the marriage of the *Lamb* is come, and his wife hath made herself ready . . . Blessed are they which are called unto the marriage supper of the *Lamb*" (19:7,9).

The revelation of Christ is a tremendous source of strength and courage to the Church. He is revealed as:

- The Almighty (1:8)
- Alpha and Omega (1:8)
- Amen (3:14)
- Beginning of the creation of God (3:14)
- Bright and morning star (22:16)
- Faithful and true witness (3:14)
- First and last (1:17; 2:8; 22:13)
- First begotten of the dead (1:5)
- King of saints (15:3)
- King of kings (17:14; 19:16)
- Lion of the tribe of Judah (5:5)
- Lord of lords (17:14 19:16)
- Lord God Almighty (11:17; 15:3)
- Offspring of David (22:16)
- Root of David (5:5; 22:16)
- Prince of the kings of the earth (1:5)

In contrast, Satan is portrayed as the great red dragon (12:3);

that old serpent (12:9); the devil (2:10; 12:9); the accuser of our brethren (12:10); and the deceiver of all nations through the beast and the false prophet (19:19,20; 20:3,8).

Revelation also reveals the holiness of God and of all that pertains to Him: the Lord holy and true (3:7; 4:8; 6:10; 15:4); the holy angels (14:10); the holy apostles and prophets (18:20; 22:6); and the holy city for a holy people (21:2,10,27). In these last days when iniquity abounds and the love of many is waxing cold, this message of holiness of heart should be preached and insisted upon in the Church. Without holiness, no man shall see the Lord (Heb. 12:14; Matt. 5:8).

Revelation thunders warning about the wrath of Almighty God and His judgments on "the men which had the mark of the beast, and on them which worshipped his image" (14:9-11; 16:2); them who "have shed the blood of saints and prophets" (16:6); them who "blasphemed the name of God" and "repented not" (16:9); "Babylon" (14:8; 16:19); Satan, the beast, and the false prophet (16:10; 19:20; 20:10); and on whoever "was not found written in the book of life" (20:15; 21:8).

These truths must be preached in order for men and women to fear God and repent. It is the responsibility of the Church to warn perishing souls to flee the wrath of God to come. If we fail to do so, their blood will be on our hands (Ezek. 3:18,19).

Finally, the Book of Revelation applies to the Church in its example to her of our Lord's tender love and compassion for the backslider and for whoever will come to Him. "Behold, I stand at the door, and knock: if any man hear my voice, and open the door, I will come in to him, and will sup with him, and he with me" (3:20). "And the Spirit and the bride say, Come. And let him that heareth say, Come. And let him that is athirst come. And whosoever will, let him take the water of life freely" (22:17).

According to the Book of Revelation, who is "blessed"?

In Revelation, the following seven beatitudes occur:

1. "Blessed is he that readeth, and they that hear the words of this prophecy, and keep those things which are written therein: for the time is at hand" (1:3; 22:7).

2. "Blessed are the dead which die in the Lord from hence-

forth: Yea, saith the Spirit, that they may rest from their labours; and their works do follow them" (14:13).

3. "Blessed is he that watcheth, and keepeth his garments, lest he walk naked, and they see his shame" (16:15).

4. "Blessed are they which are called unto the marriage supper of the Lamb" (19:9).

5. "Blessed and holy is he that hath part in the first resurrection: on such the second death hath no power, but they shall be priests of God and of Christ, and shall reign with him a thousand years" (20:6).

6. "Blessed is he that keepeth the sayings of the prophecy of this book" (22:7).

7. "Blessed are they that do his commandments, that they may have right to the tree of life, and may enter in through the gates into the city" (22:14).

Is the Church represented in the end-time prophecies of Daniel?

Yes. In Daniel, the Church is represented as "the saints," "the mighty and holy people," "the people that do know their God," "thy people, written in the book," "they who awake to everlasting life," and "they that be wise." A comparison of these scriptures with parallel verses from the New Testament shows clearly that these prophecies in Daniel refer to the Church.

The Church in Daniel's Prophecies	The Church in Parallel N. T. Verses
The saints	
But the saints of the most High shall take the kingdom, and possess the kingdom for ever, even for ever and ever—Dan. 7:18.	The kingdoms of this world are become the kingdoms of our Lord, and his Christ; and he shall reign for ever and ever—Rev. 11:15.
I beheld, and the same horn made war with the saints, and prevailed against them—Dan. 7:21.	And it was given unto him to make war with the saints, and to overcome them—Rev. 13:7.
Judgment was given to the saints of the most High—Dan. 7:22.	Do ye not know that the saints shall judge the world?—1 Cor. 6:2.
And he shall speak great words against the most High, and shall	And he opened his mouth in blasphemy against God, to blaspheme his

The Church in Daniel's Prophecies	The Church in Parallel N. T. Verses
wear out the saints of the most High—Dan. 7:25.	name, and his tabernacle [the Church, Eph.2:21,22]—Rev. 13:6.
The mighty and holy people And his power shall be mighty, but not by his own power: . . . and shall destroy the mighty and the holy people—Dan. 8:24.	And it was given unto him to make war with the saints [holy ones], and to overcome them—Rev. 13:7.
The people that know their God And such as do wickedly against the covenant shall be corrupt by flatteries: but the people that do know their God shall be strong, and do exploits—Dan. 11:32.	He that believeth on me, the works that I do shall he do also; and greater works that these shall he do; because I go unto my Father—John 14:12; 17:3.
Thy people, written in the book And at that time thy people shall be delivered, every one that shall be found written in the book—Dan. 12:1.	And there shall in no wise enter into it any thing that defileth . . . but they which are written in the Lamb's book of life—Rev. 21:27.
They who awake "to everlasting life" And many of them that sleep in the dust of the earth shall awake, some to everlasting life, and some to shame and everlasting contempt—Dan. 12:2.	All that are in the graves shall hear his voice, and shall come forth; they that have done good, unto the resurrection of life; and they that have done evil, unto the resurrection of damnation—John 5:28,29.
They that be wise And they that be wise shall shine as the brightness of the firmament—Dan. 12:3.	Then shall the righteous shine forth as the sun in the kingdom of their Father—Matt. 13:43.

Is the message of Matthew 24 and 25, Revelation 4-19, and Daniel 7-12 for the Church as much as the message in Mark, Luke, Acts, and the epistles?

Yes, because their events are in harmony, which may be seen on the chart below:

End-Time Events of Matthew 24 and 25, Revelation 4-19, and Daniel 7-12
Compared with the Same in Mark, Luke, Acts, and the Epistles

Events	Matt. 24-25	Rev. 4-19	Dan. 7-12	Mark-Luke	Acts-Epistles
Many deceivers	Matt. 24:4, 5,11,24,26	Rev. 18:23; 19:20	Dan. 11:23	Mark 13:22, Luke 21:8	2 Thess. 2:3, 4,9-12
Church persecuted	Matt. 24:9, 10,13,22	Rev. 6:9-11; 13:6,7,10	Dan. 7:21, 25; 8:24	Mark 13:20; Luke 18:7,8	1 Thess. 3:4; 2 Thess. 1:4
Iniquity abounding	Matt. 24:12	Rev. 9:20, 21; 13:5,6	Dan. 11:32; 12:10		2 Thess. 2:7; Jude 1:17-19
Apostasy	Matt. 24:5, 10,12	Rev. 13:3,8, 16; 18:3	Dan. 11:32	Luke 13: 25-27	2 Thess. 2:3; 1 Tim. 4:1
The end	Matt. 24:3, 13,14	Rev. 14:14, 15 with Matt. 13:39	Dan. 7:26; 8:19; 11:27; 12:9,13	Mark 13:7, 13; Luke 21:9	1 Cor. 1:8; 15:24; 1 Pet. 1:13
Gospel preached	Matt. 24:14	Rev. 11:3; 14:6	Dan. 12:3	Mark 13:10	Col. 1:5; 2 Pet.3:9, 10
Coming in glory for His Church	Matt. 24:30, 31	Rev. 6:12-17 with 7:9-17; 14:14-20	Dan. 7:9-14	Mark 8:38; 14:62; Luke 21:27	Col. 3:41
Judgment	Matt. 25:31, 34,41,46	Rev. 6:16; 20:11,15; 21:7,8	Dan. 7:9,10; 12:2	Luke 17:26-30; 21:35	2 Thess. 1:7-10; 2 Pet. 3: 7,10
An eternal kingdom	Matt. 25:34, 46	Rev. 11:15; 19:7-9; 21:1	Dan. 7:18, 22,27	Luke 13:28, 29	2 Pet. 3:13
Beast destroyed		Rev. 19:20	Dan. 7:11		2 Thess. 2:8
Rewards	Matt. 25:34	Rev. 11:18	Dan. 12:3	Luke 14:14	2 Tim. 4:1,8

In summary, the gospel of Matthew, Revelation 4-19, and the end-time prophecies of Daniel are best interpreted as being written primarily to the Church, not to the Jews. Considering these passages separately, and comparing them to other scriptures, both support this interpretation. Therefore, the end-time events expressed in these passages refer primarily to the Church.

7

The Church Gathered—Secretly or Openly?

Jesus said, "I come as a thief" (Rev. 16:15). Does this imply a secret rapture?

Sensational preaching about the secret rapture often depicts the following scenario. Jesus will come quietly as a thief to snatch away His jewels. Autos with Christian drivers, trains with Christian conductors, and aircraft with Christian pilots will crash. Newspaper headlines will announce that multitudes have disappeared. The public will be filled with fear and confusion. Sinners will cry out for their Christian mothers, wives, babies, or other loved ones who are gone. They will be in anguish, knowing that the Lord came secretly as a thief and stole away His Church. They will have to face the Antichrist and the mark of the beast without the Church and the Holy Spirit.

Such preaching may be well-meaning, but it is not scriptural. Jesus isn't coming "to snatch away" His Church secretly and under cover of darkness to hide what He does. When He comes, "every eye shall see him" (Rev. 1:7). But He is coming as a thief in the sense of bringing sudden destruction upon the unprepared. "But know this, that if the goodman of the house had known in what watch the thief would come, he would have watched, and would not have suffered his house to be broken up" (Matt. 24:43). For this reason Jesus warns, "Therefore be ye also ready: for in such an hour as ye think not the Son of man cometh" (Matt. 24:44).

The apostle Paul illustrated the same truth of the thief's coming with "sudden destruction" and overtaking the children of darkness, not the children of light: "For yourselves know perfectly that the day of the Lord so cometh as a *thief* in the night. For when they shall say, Peace and safety; then *sudden destruction* cometh upon them, as travail upon a woman with child; and they shall not escape. But ye, brethren, are not in darkness, that that day should overtake you as a *thief.* Ye are all the children of light, and the children of the day: we are not of the night, nor of darkness" (1 Thess. 5:2-5).

Does every "thief" reference about the Second Coming teach that Jesus is coming after the Tribulation and that He will bring sudden destruction upon the unprepared?

Yes. The verses in the diagram below confirm two things:

1. The Lord is coming as a thief after the Tribulation, on the Day of the Lord.

2. The Lord is described as a thief because He will bring sudden destruction upon the unprepared.

Scripture Text	The Lord coming as a "thief" *after* the Tribulation:	The Lord described as a "thief" because He will bring sudden destruction upon the unprepared:
Matthew 24: 29-51	After the tribulation . . . . The thief—Matt. 24:29,43.	House to be broken up. . . . Cut him asunder, and appoint him his portion with the hypocrites—Matt. 24:43,51.
Luke 12:39-46	The thief—Luke 12:39. Compare with Matt. 24:29,42.	House to be broken through. Cut him in sunder . . . appoint him his portion with the unbelievers—Luke 12:39,46.
First Thessalonians 4:16 to 5:3	The day of the Lord so cometh as a thief—1 Thess. 5:2.	Then sudden destruction cometh upon them . . . and they shall not escape—1 Thess. 5:3.
Second Peter 3:7-11	The day of the Lord will come as a thief—2 Pet. 3:10.	The heavens shall pass away with a noise—2 Pet. 3:10. Day of judgment and perdition of ungodly men—2 Pet. 3:7.
Revelation 3:3	I will come on thee as a thief. Keepeth my works unto the end—Rev. 3:3; 2:26.	Repent. If therefore thou shalt not watch, I will come on thee as a thief, and thou shalt not know what hour I will come upon thee—Rev. 3:3.
Revelation 16: 14-21	That great day of God Almighty. Behold, I come as a thief—Rev. 16:14,15.	Blessed is he that watcheth, and keepeth his garments, lest he walk naked, and they see his shame—Rev. 16:15.

Is a secret rapture described anywhere in the Bible?

There is not a hint of a secret rapture in the Bible. In fact, Jesus cautions us not to believe those who attach secrecy to His coming: "Wherefore if they shall say unto you, Behold, he is in the desert; go not forth: behold, he is in the *secret* chambers; believe it not" (Matt. 24:26).

First, our Lord's coming will not be secret, but will be seen by all.

- "Every eye shall *see* Him" (Rev. 1:7). See also Matt. 26:64; Mark 13:26; 14:62; Luke 21:27; John 1:51; Rev. 11:11,12.
- "The Lord Jesus shall be *revealed* [not concealed] . . . in *flaming fire*" (2 Thess. 1:7,8). "For, behold, the Lord will come with *fire*, and with his chariots like a whirlwind, to render his anger with fury, and his rebuke with *flames of fire*. For by *fire* and by his sword will the Lord plead with all flesh: and the slain of the Lord shall be many" (Isa. 66:15,16). See also Psa. 11:6; 21:9; 97:3,5; Isa. 30:30; 33:14; Jer. 51:58; Joel 1:15,19,20; 2:30; Zeph. 1:18; 3:8; Heb. 10:27; 12:29; Rev. 17:16; 18:8; 20:9.
- The Lord Jesus shall *appear*, instead of being hidden. It will be a day of "thick darkness" when "the sun and the moon shall be dark, and the stars shall withdraw their shining" (Joel 2:2,10; Matt. 24:29). Then, "shall appear the sign of the Son of man in heaven: and then shall all the tribes of the earth . . . see the Son of man coming in the clouds of heaven" (Matt. 24:30). According to Strong, "appear" means "to lighten (shine), to show, to be seen." See also Col. 3:4; 1 Tim. 6:14; 2 Tim. 4:1,8; Titus 2:13; Heb. 9:28; 1 Pet. 1:7; 5:4; 1 John 2:28; 3:2.
- "His *lightnings* enlightened the world: the earth *saw*, and trembled" (Psa. 97:4). "For as the *lightning* cometh out of the east, and shineth even unto the west; so shall also the coming of the Son of man be" (Matt. 24:27). See also Rev. 11:19 and 16:18.
- "All the people [shall] *see his glory*" (Psa. 97:6); it will be an event too glorious to be hidden. Jesus is coming "with power and great glory," in His "own glory," in His "Father's glory," and in the glory of all His "holy angels" to be "glorified in his saints" (Luke 9:26; 21:27; 2 Thess. 1:10). See Psa. 102:16; Matt. 16:27; 24:30; 25:31; Mark 8:38; John 1:51; Eph. 5:27.

Second, our Lord's coming will not be secret, but will be heard by all.

• Jesus will come "with a *great sound* of a trumpet" (Matt. 24:31). "Blow ye the trumpet in Zion, and *sound an alarm* in my holy mountain: let all the inhabitants of the land tremble: for the day of the Lord cometh" (Joel 2:1). See also 1 Cor. 15:52; 1 Thess. 4:16; Isa. 27:13; Zeph. 1:16.

• He "shall descend from heaven with a *shout*, [and] with *the voice* of the arch-angel"; therefore, "all that are in the graves *shall hear his voice*" (1 Thess. 4:16; John 5:28). According to Strong, "shout" means "a cry of incitement." Notice how the prophets describe this same event: "And the Lord shall cause *his glorious voice to be heard*" (Isa. 30:30); "The Lord also shall *roar* out of Zion, and *utter his voice* from Jerusalem; and the heavens and the earth shall shake" (Joel 3:16); "The Lord *thundered* from heaven, and the most High *uttered his voice*" (2 Sam. 22:14). See also Rev. 16:17,18; Isa. 66:6; Joel 2:11; Zeph. 1:14.

• All the tribes of the earth will be *mourning* (Matt. 24:30), *languishing* (Isa. 24:4), *howling* (Isa. 13:6), *wailing and gnashing their teeth* (Matt. 13:42; Luke 13:28), and *crying bitterly* (Zeph. 1:14). They will say to the mountains and rocks, "Fall on us, and hide us from the face of him that sitteth on the throne, and from the wrath of the Lamb" (Rev. 6:15,16).

• "The heavens shall pass away with a *great noise*" (2 Pet. 3:10). See also Matt. 24:35.

Finally, our Lord's coming will not be secret, but will be felt by all.

• In that day, the Lord will arise "*to shake terribly* the earth" (Isa. 2:19). There will be "*a great earthquake*, such as was not since men were upon the earth" (Rev. 16:18); "the powers of the heavens shall be *shaken*" (Matt. 24:29); and "the sea and the waves *roaring*" (Luke 21:25). See also Psa. 18:7; Isa. 13:13; 24:13,18,19; Jer. 10:10; Joel 2:10; 3:16; Hag. 2:6,7,21; Heb. 12:26.

• Every *mountain* and *island* will be moved (Rev. 6:14; 16:20). "All the men that are upon the face of the earth, shall shake at my presence, and the mountains shall be thrown down, and the steep places shall fall, and every wall shall fall to the ground" (Ezek. 38:20). See also Psa. 18:7-16; 46; Micah 1:3,4; Nah. 1:5,6.

• *Great hail stones*, each weighing one-hundred and thirty pounds, will fall from heaven. "And there fell upon men a great hail out of heaven, every stone about the weight of a talent" (Rev. 16:21). See also Rev. 11:19; Ezek. 38:22.

Truly, our Lord's coming will not be secret or silent. "Our God shall come, and *shall not keep silence*" when He shall gather His saints together (Psa. 50:3,5).

Objections Answered

Isn't Christ coming secretly "for his saints" before the Tribulation and openly "with his saints" afterwards?

These exact terms "for his saints" and "with his saints" are not found in the Bible but are often used by those who teach two phases of our Lord's coming, or a split-rapture. The Scripture does not teach a secret rapture before the Tribulation because Christ Himself said that He will come for His saints "immediately after the tribulation" (Matt. 24:29-31). Compare with Acts 2:20. The apostle Paul wrote the same thing—that it will be on the Day of the Lord (1 Thess. 4:16 to 5:2). Therefore, it is clear that Jesus Christ is coming for His saints after the Tribulation on the Day of the Lord, not before.

Moreover, the New Testament shows that He is coming "for his saints" at the same time He comes "with his saints":

1. For His saints. "For the Lord himself shall descend from heaven . . . and the dead in Christ shall rise first: Then we which are alive and remain shall be *caught up together* with them in the clouds to meet the Lord in the air" (1 Thess. 4:16,17).

2. With His saints. "For if we believe that Jesus died and rose again, even so them also which sleep in Jesus will God bring *with him*" (1 Thess. 4:14).

The following scriptures further show that when Christ comes *for* His saints, they will be "caught up," glorified, and appear *with* Him in glory:

"When Christ, who is our life, shall appear, then shall ye also appear *with* him in glory" (Col. 3:4).

"At the coming of our Lord Jesus Christ *with* all his saints" (1 Thess. 3:13).

"For what is our hope, or joy, or crown of rejoicing? Are not even ye *in the presence* of our Lord Jesus Christ at his coming?" (1 Thess. 2:19).

"Behold, the Lord cometh *with* ten thousands of his saints" (Jude 1:14). See also Zech. 14:5; Mal. 4:2,3; Rev. 17:14; 19:14.

This truth of the Church's appearing with Christ in glory is lost to those who are affected by the secret rapture teaching. Christ's coming "for His saints" and "with His saints" are not two comings or one coming in two phases, but one glorious event that occurs on the Day of the Lord, after the Tribulation.

Doesn't Titus 2:13 teach that the Second Coming will be in two phases—the "blessed hope" (a secret coming) and the "glorious appearing" (Christ appearing openly at the end of the world)?

The "blessed hope" and "the glorious appearing" describe the same event. Titus 2:13 tells believers to be "looking for that blessed hope, and the glorious appearing." Elsewhere, they are instructed to be "looking for . . . the day of God, wherein the heavens being on fire shall be dissolved" and "for new heavens and a new earth" (2 Pet. 3:12,13).

Therefore, if the "blessed hope" is supposed to be the secret gathering of believers at the so-called "first phase" of our Lord's return, why would Scripture instruct them *to look* for the "glorious appearing," "the day of God," and the "new heavens and a new earth"?

Scripture confirms that "the blessed hope" is indeed the "glorious appearing." Notice that the believer's "hope" is linked not only with "the appearing," but with "the end": "*Hope* to the *end* for the grace that is to be brought unto you at *the revelation* [appearing] of Jesus Christ" (1 Pet. 1:13).

Moreover, Jesus and the apostles used various terms synonymously to describe the Second Coming: His coming (*parousia*); His revelation (*apokalupsis*); His appearing (*epiphania, phaino*, or *phaneroo*). The following chart shows that these terms, which are associated with the believer's hope and with the Lord's appearing, are all associated with one and only one event—"the day of the Lord" or "that day," which is at the end of the world.

Synonymous Terms that Describe the Second Coming and Show That it Occurs on the Day of the Lord, at the End of the World

Coming **Greek—*Parousia***	**Revealed-Revelation** ***Apokalupsis***	**Appear-Appearing** ***Epiphania*** ***Phaino-Phaneroo***	**Day of the Lord** **"That Day" or The** **End of the World**
Matt. 24:27,37, 39	Luke 17:30	Matt. 24:30	Matt. 24:29; Acts 2:20 The Day of the Lord
	1 Cor. 1:7 ("Coming" in Greek is *apokalupsis*—revelation.)		1 Cor. 1:8 The end The Day of our Lord
1 Cor. 15:23			1 Cor. 15:24 The end
1 Thess. 2:19; 3:13; 4:15; 5:23			1 Thess. 5:2,4 The Day of the Lord
	2 Thess. 1:7		2 Thess. 1:10 That day
2 Thess. 2:1,8		2 Thess. 2:8 ("Brightness" in Greek is *epiphania*—appearing.)	2 Thess. 2:2,3 The Day of Christ That day
		1 Tim. 6:14; 2 Tim. 4:1,8; Titus 2:13	2 Tim. 4:8 That day
	1 Pet. 1:7, ("Appearing" in Greek is *apokalupsis*—revelation.) 1 Pet. 1:13; 4:13; 5:1	1 Pet. 5:4	1 Pet. 1:13 The end
2 Pet. 1:16			2 Pet. 1:19 The day
2 Pet. 3:4			2 Pet. 3:7,10,12 The Day of the Lord
1 John 2:28		1 John 2:28; 3:2	1 John 4:17 The Day of Judgment

Doesn't the Word of God teach that our Lord's return to gather the Church is an event that we should believe can take place at any moment?

The New Testament admonishes us to watch and to wait with reference to our Lord's return:

After the Tribulation—Jesus said, "After that tribulation. . . . then shall they see the Son of man coming in the clouds with great power and glory. And then shall he send his angels, and shall gather together his elect. . . . *watch* and pray: for ye know not when the time is" (Mark 13:24,26,27,33). See also Matt. 24:29-31,42; Luke 21:25-28,36.

On the Day of the Lord—"The day of the Lord so cometh as a thief in the night. . . . Let us *watch* and be sober" (1 Thess. 5:2,6). "If therefore thou shalt not *watch*, I will come on thee as a thief" (Rev. 3:3). "Behold, I come as a thief. Blessed is he that *watcheth*" (Rev. 16:15). Jesus will come as "a thief" on the Day of the Lord. Compare First Thessalonians 4:16,17 with 5:2.

Paul taught the Church to be "*waiting* for the coming of our Lord Jesus Christ: who shall also confirm you to the end, that ye may be blameless in *the day of our Lord Jesus Christ*" (1 Cor.1:7,8). The Day of the Lord cannot take place just at any moment because certain events must first happen, including the apostasy and the revelation of the man of sin. See 2 Thess. 2:1-3.

When He shall appear—"For the earnest expectation of the creature *waiteth* for the manifestation of the sons of God" (Rom. 8:19). The manifestation of the sons of God is "when he [Jesus Christ] shall appear," because it is then that "we shall be like him" (1 John 3:2). He shall "appear" after the Tribulation. See Matt. 24:29 and 30.

On the day of redemption—"For we know that the whole creation groaneth and travaileth in pain together until now. And not only they, but ourselves also, which have the firstfruits of the Spirit, even we ourselves groan within ourselves, *waiting* for the adoption, to wit, the redemption of our body. For we are saved by hope: but hope that is seen is not hope: for what a man seeth, why doth he yet hope for? But if we hope for that we see not, then do we with patience *wait* for it" (Rom. 8:22-25).

Notice two things in this passage:

1. We are to *wait* for "the redemption of our body." According

to Luke 21:25-28, the day of redempetion is after the Tribulation.

2. We are to *wait* with patience and with hope. The word "hope" is used six times in Romans 8:20-25.

What is the Christian's hope? It is the "glorious appearing" (Titus 2:13), a hope to "the end" (1 Pet. 1:13). Scripture exhorts believers to watch and to wait for their Lord's return, which will be after the Tribulation on the Day of the Lord, not an "any moment" rapture before the end.

If the gathering of the Church is immediately after the Tribulation, won't it be possible to calculate "the day and hour" of our Lord's coming (Matt. 24:36)?

Jesus gave this verse with reference to His coming immediately after the Tribulation, not concerning a secret rapture before the Tribulation. (Compare Matthew 24:36 with 24:29-31.) Verse 22 indicates that the days of the Great Tribulation will be shortened for the elect's sake. Only the Father knows how many days it will be shortened; therefore, it will be impossible to calculate the exact day and hour.

Doesn't Hebrews 9:28 teach that before the Great Tribulation, Jesus will appear only to those who look for Him?

No. Hebrews 9:28 states, "So Christ was once offered to bear the sins of many; and unto them that look for him shall he appear the second time without sin unto salvation." The use of "many" in the first half of the verse is a typical use of understatement in the Bible. "Many" actually represents "all," namely, Jesus died for all. Similarly, "them that look for him" is simply synonymous with believers, since unbelievers would be those who definitely don't look for or believe in His Second Coming. Peter exhorted believers to look for Jesus when He returns after the Tribulation, which is the end of the world (2 Pet. 3:12-14). Consider the remaining phrases in this verse:

"Shall he appear"—Jesus Himself tells us that He "shall appear" to gather His Church "after the tribulation" (Matt. 24:29-31).

"The second time"—This verse does not say anything about Christ's coming before the Great Tribulation, but refers to "the second time." Jesus appeared to the world once when He came to die for our sins. Here He promises to appear the second time; He makes no mention of a *third* time. When He comes the second and final time, it will be openly and after the Tribulation.

Doesn't Jesus teach a secret rapture in John 14:2,3?

John 14:2,3 states, "In my Father's house are many mansions: if it were not so, I would have told you. I go to prepare a place for you. And if I go and prepare a place for you, I will come again, and receive you unto myself; that where I am, there ye may be also." There is no indication here of a secret rapture. Clearly, Jesus is in heaven preparing a place for us and is coming again to receive us to be with Him forever in that place. In Matthew 24:29-31, He tells us *when* He will come again—"immediately after the tribulation."

8

One Second Coming— All in Christ Gathered on the Last Day

How did Jesus describe His coming in Matthew 24 and 25?

The Second Coming, as described in Matthew 24 and 25, is the only coming Jesus spoke of in the Bible. Here's how He described it:

- It will be as difficult to hide as lightning (24:27).
- It will take place immediately after the tribulation (24:29).
- The sun shall be darkened, and the moon shall not give her light (24:29).
- The stars shall fall from heaven, and the powers of the heavens shall be shaken (24:29).
- Then shall appear the sign of the Son of Man in heaven (24:30).
- All the tribes of the earth shall mourn (24:30).
- All shall see the Son of Man coming (24:30).
- He is coming in the clouds of heaven (24:30).
- He is coming with power and great glory (24:30).
- He is coming with all His holy angels (24:31; 25:31).
- He is coming with a great sound of a trumpet (24:31).
- The saints shall be gathered by the angels (24:31).
- Heaven and earth shall pass away (24:35).
- Destruction shall come on sinners as in Noah's day (24:39).
- They that are ready shall go in with Him to the marriage supper (25:10).

• The door shall be shut (25:10).

• Christ shall sit on the throne of His glory with all His angels (25:31).

• All nations shall be gathered before Him (25:32).

• The righteous shall inherit the eternal kingdom of God (25:34-40,46).

• The wicked will be condemned to everlasting fire (25:41-46).

How did the apostles describe Christ's Second Coming?

The apostles described the Second Coming the same way Jesus did.

Paul's description of Christ's coming in First Thessalonians 4:16-18 agrees with the description Jesus gave in Matthew 24:29-31, including the Lord's coming from heaven, the clouds, the angels, the trumpet, the gathering of the saints, and the Day of the Lord.

Peter's portrayal of our Lord's return in Second Peter 3:4 to 13 is also in harmony with the post-tribulational description given in Matthew 24 and 25. They both describe the Day of the Lord (compare with Matt. 24:29-31 and Acts 2:20), the destruction of the wicked as in the day Noah entered into the ark (compare with Matt. 24:38), the destruction of heaven and earth (compare with Matt. 24:35), and the new heavens and a new earth where the saints will abide forever (compare with Matt. 25:34,46).

In Revelation 6:12-17, John also described the coming of the Lord Jesus much the same as the description in Matthew 24:29-31: the unmistakable signs in the sun, moon, and stars; the powers of heaven shaken; the Lord's coming from heaven; all the tribes of the earth mourning; and their seeing the Son of Man coming in power and great glory.

The chart below shows that the apostles' description of the Second Coming corresponds with the description given by our Lord Jesus Christ in Matthew 24 and 25. None of these passages mention a secret coming.

Jesus Matt. 24,25	1 Cor. 15	**Paul** 1 Thess.	2 Thess.	**Peter** 1 and 2 Pet.	**John** Revelation
Coming after the Tribulation (24:29)	At the end. The last trump (15:24,52)	Saints from tribulation "remain" (4:15,17)	Antichrist is destroyed (2:8)	At the end (1 Pet. 1:13)	Antichrist is destroyed (19:20)
Signs in sun, moon, and stars—Day of the Lord (24:29)	Last trump (15:52; see Rev. 11:15,19)	The Day of the Lord (5:2)	The Day of Christ (2:2)	The Day of the Lord (2 Pet. 3:10)	The great day of His wrath (6:12,17)
Power Clouds Angels Trumpet (24:30,31)	Trumpet (15:52)	Clouds Angels Trump of God (4:16,17)	Power Glory Angels (1:7,9)	Power (2 Pet. 1:16)	Clouds (1:17)
Visible and audible—He "shall appear" (24:30)	"The trumpet shall sound" (15:52)	Shout, voice of arch-angel, trump of God (4:16)	"The Lord Jesus shall be revealed" (1:7)	"At the appearing of Jesus" (1 Pet. 1:7, 13)	"Every eye shall see him" (1:7; 6:16)
The elect gathered together (24:31)	All made alive—All changed (15:22,51)	"Caught up together" (4:17)	"Glorified in his saints" (1:10)	Salvation (2 Pet. 3:15)	The marriage supper (19:7)
The thief (24:43)		Day of the Lord—thief (5:2)		As a thief (2 Pet. 3:10)	"I come as a thief" (16:15)
Heaven and earth pass—Judgment (24:35,51)	Christ puts down all rule (15:24)	Sudden destruction, no escape (5:3)	Everlasting destruction (1:9)	All is burned up (2 Pet. 3:10)	"Heaven departed as a scroll" (6:14)

How did the prophets describe the Second Coming?

Consider two prophecies:

"Our God shall come, and shall not keep silence: a fire shall devour before him, and it shall be very tempestuous round about him. He shall call to the heavens from above, and to the earth, that he may judge his people. *Gather my saints together unto me*; those that have made a covenant with me by sacrifice" (Psa. 50:3-6).

"The Lord reigneth; let the earth rejoice; let the multitude of isles be glad thereof. Clouds and darkness are round about him: righteousness and judgment are the habitation of his throne. A fire goeth before him, and burneth up his enemies round about. His lightnings enlightened the world: the earth saw, and trembled. The hills melted like wax at the presence of the Lord, at the presence of the Lord of the whole earth. The heavens declare his righteousness, and all the people see his glory" (Psa. 97:1-6).

As in Matthew 24 and 25, the above passages mention the clouds, the throne, the lightning, the visible glory of the Lord, the gathering of His saints, the judgment of the wicked, and the destruction of the world.

Some other inspiring Old Testament prophecies about the Lord's coming are Job 19:25,26; Psa. 17:15; 46; 96:13; 98:9; 99:1; 149:5-9; Isa. 2; 13; 24; 25; 26; 63:1-3; 66; Zeph. 1:14-18; 2:1-3; Dan. 7:9-13; 12:2; Mic. 1:2-4; Mal. 3:17,18 through 4:3. These shed additional light on the New Testament scriptures, making us realize that the Bible is "a more sure word of prophecy" (2 Pet. 1:19), a truly marvelous and inspiring book!

What events of significance did the angels in Acts 1:9-11 foretell would accompany Christ's return?

The angels foretold that Jesus will return from heaven in the same manner as He was taken up to heaven: visibly ("they beheld"), with a cloud, with angels, and only once. Jesus did not ascend to heaven in two phases; therefore, He will not return in two phases, as some incorrectly teach.

"And when he had spoken these things, while they beheld, he was taken up; and a cloud received him out of their sight. And while they looked stedfastly toward heaven as he went up, behold, two men stood by them in white apparel; which also said, Ye men of Galilee, why stand ye gazing up into heaven? This same Jesus, which is taken up from you into heaven, shall so come in like manner as ye have seen him go into heaven" (Acts 1:9-11).

Does this mean, then, that there will be only one resurrection of the just?

Yes. When the Bible speaks of "the coming" of our Lord and of "the resurrection," it's always in the singular. Therefore, there's only one Second Coming of our Lord and only one resurrection of the just—not two or one in two phases. The following scriptures illustrate these truths:

"Waiting for *the coming* of our Lord Jesus Christ" (1 Cor. 1:7).

"Be patient . . . unto *the coming* of the Lord" (James 5:7).

"Be recompensed at *the resurrection* of the just" (Luke 14:14).

"If by any means I might attain unto the resurrection of the dead" (Phil. 3:11).

What biblical terminologies relate to "the resurrection of the just"?

Expressions related to this resurrection are

- the harvest (Matt. 13:30,39)
- the gathering (Matt. 24:31; Mark 13:27; 2 Thess. 2:1)
- be made alive (1 Cor. 15:22)
- raise him up (John 6:54)
- to receive you (John 14:3)
- the redemption of our body (Rom. 8:23)
- be caught up (1 Thess. 4:17)
- be glorified (2 Thess. 1:10)
- we shall all be changed (1 Cor. 15:51; Phil. 3:21)
- we shall be like Him (1 John 3:2)
- we shall see Him as He is (1 John 3:2; Job 19:26,27)
- appear with Him in glory (Col. 3:4)

Since several of these terms are often used interchangeably, we know they are speaking of the same event—the coming of our Lord Jesus Christ.

Will the wicked dead see Christ's coming?

Yes, because "*all* that are in the graves shall hear his voice. And shall come forth . . . " (John 5:28,29). Scripture states that they who pierced Jesus will see Him. "Behold, he cometh with clouds; and every eye shall see him, and they also which pierced him: and all kindreds of the earth shall wail because of him" (Rev. 1:7). Jesus said to the high priest who condemned him to death, "Ye shall see the Son of man sitting on the right hand of power, and coming in the clouds of heaven" (Mark 14:62).

> Every eye shall now behold Him,
> Robed in dreadful majesty.
> Those who "set at nought" and sold Him,
> Pierced and nailed Him to the tree.
> Deeply wailing, deeply wailing—
> Shall the true Messiah see.
>
> Author unknown

What is meant by the expression "the last day"?

"The last day" means no other days will follow. It refers to the end of the world when time shall be no more. In John's gospel, this phrase is used in connection with the resurrection five times and with the Day of Judgment once:

"And this is the Father's will which hath sent me, that of all which he hath given me I should lose nothing, but should raise it up again at *the last day*" (John 6:39).

"And this is the will of him that sent me, that every one which seeth the Son, and believeth on him, may have everlasting life: and I will raise him up at *the last day*" (John 6:40).

"No man can come to me, except the Father which hath sent me draw him: and I will raise him up at *the last day*" (John 6:44).

"Whoso eateth my flesh, and drinketh my blood, hath eternal life; and I will raise him up at *the last day*" (John 6:54).

"Martha saith unto him, I know that he shall rise again in the resurrection at *the last day*" (John 11:24).

"He that rejecteth me, and receiveth not my words, hath one that judgeth him: the word that I have spoken, the same shall judge him in *the last day*" (John 12:48).

The last day is both resurrection day and Judgment Day. Other expressions synonymous with *the last day* are:

- the last trump (1 Cor. 15:52,53)
- the end (Matt. 13:39,40,49)

- immediately after the tribulation (Matt. 24:29)
- the coming of our Lord Jesus Christ (1 Cor. 1:7)
- the day of the Lord (1 Thess. 5:2; 2 Pet. 3:10)
- his appearing (2 Tim. 4:1)
- the revelation of Jesus Christ (1 Pet. 1:13)
- the day of judgment and perdition of ungodly men (2 Pet. 3:7)
- the day of God (2 Pet. 3:12).

Since the Lord is coming on the last day, when will the marriage supper of the Lamb take place?

On that same day. Jesus spoke of the marriage supper with reference to His coming after the Tribulation. (Compare Matt. 25:1-13 in context with 24:29-31.)

Second, Jesus said, "And at midnight there was a cry made, Behold, the bridegroom cometh; go ye out to meet him" (Matt. 25:6). Midnight is the last hour of the day. This signifies that Jesus is coming at the end of the world. No doubt the midnight hour also implies the dark days of persecution that will be on the earth just prior to our Lord's return.

Third, Jesus linked the time of the marriage supper with the Judgment Day. Once the Bridegroom comes, it's too late to prepare. "And while they went to buy, the bridegroom came; and they that were ready went in with him to the marriage: and the door was shut. Afterward came also the other virgins, saying, Lord, Lord, open to us. But he answered and said, Verily I say unto you, I know you not. Watch therefore, for ye know neither the day nor the hour wherein the Son of man cometh" (Matt. 25:10-13). See also Matt. 22:11-14.

Fourth, according to the context of Revelation 19:7-9, the marriage supper is after the destruction of Babylon at the end of the world (compare with Rev. 16:19 through 19:9).

Fifth, because the Bride is the Church (Eph. 5:23-25), the body of Christ (Eph. 5:30-32), the wife of the Lamb (Rev. 19:7), and the saints (Rev. 19:8), the marriage supper cannot possibly occur before the last day since Jesus will not come for His Bride until she is complete (James 5:7,8; 2 Pet. 3:9).

Does the Bible teach that the whole body of Christ will be raised together at one time?

Yes, because "the body is one" (Rom. 12:5; 1 Cor. 12:12,13). Scripture repeatedly emphasizes this truth: "one fold" (John 10:16); "one bread" (1 Cor. 10:17); "one new man" (Eph. 2:15). Furthermore, the Church is Christ's bride (Rev. 19:7); His people (1 Pet. 2:10; 2 Cor. 6:16; Heb. 8:10); a holy nation (1 Pet. 2:9); a royal priesthood (1 Pet. 2:5); a holy temple (Eph. 2:21); the olive tree (Rom. 11:17); and His elect people (Matt. 24:31; Rom. 8:33).

Since "the body is one," *all* who are in Christ Jesus will be raised on the last day. This is seen in the following verses:

"*His elect*" are gathered "after the tribulation" (Matt. 24: 29,31).

"*All* which he hath given me . . . [I] should raise it up again at the last day" (John 6:39).

"*Every one* which seeth the Son . . . I will raise him up at the last day" (John 6:40).

"*Whoso . . . hath eternal life* . . . I will raise him up at the last day" (John 6:54).

"*All* be changed. . . . At the last trump" (1 Cor. 15:51,52).

"*The dead in Christ*" and "*we which are alive* . . . shall be caught up together. . . . The day of the Lord" (1 Thess. 4:16,17; 5:2).

"*All* them that believe" will be glorified "in that day" (2 Thess. 1:10).

"*All* . . . that love his appearing" will be given a crown "at that day" (2 Tim. 4:8).

The truth that the Church is one body and that *all* in Jesus Christ will be raised together on the last day is further evidence that a resurrection of the Church before the Great Tribulation is impossible.

In summary, Jesus, the apostles, the Old Testament prophets, and the angels described the return of our Lord as a one-time event—the consummation of all things at the end of the world, on the last day. Then, and not before, the Church as one body—the Bride of Christ—will be resurrected to be with her Lord forever.

Objections Answered

Isn't it true that there are two types of believers: true believers or the Bride of Christ—those who are raptured before the Tribulation, at the main harvest; and nominal believers—those who missed the rapture, but because they refused the number of the beast (666), were ready for the second phase of the harvest at our Lord's coming afterwards?

According to the parable of the wheat and the tares and the general teaching of the Bible, there are not two types of believers, but one—wheat (the Bride of Christ); there are not two harvests, but one—the harvest at the end of the world (Matt. 13:30,39). Therefore, there is no opportunity for salvation after Jesus comes. At the harvest the wheat will be gathered and the tares will be burned.

Given the premise, however, that there will be a pre-tribulation rapture, nominal Christians who are left behind would not be able to save themselves by merely refusing the number of the beast and giving their own lives, as some claim. Salvation is "by grace . . . through faith; and that *not of yourselves*; it is the gift of God: *Not of works*, lest any man should boast" (Eph. 2:8,9). During the Tribulation, true believers will be able to resist receiving the number because their sins have been cleansed by the blood of Jesus and their names are written in the book of life (Rev. 7:14; 13:8). They'll be willing to suffer because they are saved, but *not* to get saved.

Doesn't the Bible teach that there are three companies of saints to be resurrected separately: the bride, the bridal party, and the guests?

Jesus did not make such a distinction. Those who wear a wedding garment include the Lord's bride, the bridal party, and the guests (Matt. 22:2,10,11).

Doesn't First Corinthians 15:22 and 23 depict different orders of the resurrection?

First Corinthians 15:22 and 23 reads, "For as in Adam all die, even so in Christ shall all be made alive. But every man in his own order: Christ the firstfruits; afterward they that are Christ's at his coming."

These verses show only one resurrection of believers, which will occur at Christ's coming. The order is Christ first, then the Church—Christ the firstfruits, then the harvest ("the precious fruit of the earth," James 5:7). This chapter also teaches that "in Christ shall *all* be made alive" and "we shall all be changed" at "the last trump" (1 Cor. 15:22,51,52). How, then, can there be a resurrection of the Church before the "last trump"?

9

Noah and Lot— Deliverance and Judgment on the Same Day

Why did Jesus give Noah and Lot as examples of His coming?

Jesus gave them as examples because in the day when He is revealed, the Church will be saved and the wicked will be destroyed. Just as in the days of Noah and Lot, deliverance and judgment will come *on the same day.*

"And as it was in the days of Noe [Noah], so shall it be also in the days of the Son of man. They did eat, they drank, they married wives, they were given in marriage, until *the day* that Noe entered into the ark, and the flood came, and *destroyed them all.*

"Likewise also as it was in the days of Lot; they did eat, they drank, they bought, they sold, they planted, they builded; but *the same day* that Lot went out of Sodom it rained fire and brimstone from heaven, and *destroyed them all.* Even thus shall it be in the day when the Son of man is revealed" (Luke 17:26-30).

As Noah entered the ark before the flood, won't the Church be gathered before the Great Tribulation?

According to the words of Jesus, Noah's entering the ark before the flood is a type of the Church's being gathered *when* Jesus comes to destroy the ungodly—after the Tribulation when heaven and earth pass away. (Compare Matt. 24:37-39 with 24:29,35.) Jesus stated that on "the day that Noe entered into the ark . . . the flood came, and destroyed them all" (Luke 17:27). Notice the phrases "the day" and "destroyed them all." Just as the entire population was destroyed on the day Noah entered the ark, so the entire population will be destroyed on the day when the Church is gathered. Jesus confirms this truth in verse 30:

"Even thus shall it be in *the day* when the Son of man is revealed."

Peter also discussed these events and made two relevant observations:

1. The destruction of the world and of the ungodly will be by fire, not by water as in Noah's day.

2. It will occur when Jesus comes on the "day of judgment," which is "the day of the Lord" (2 Pet. 3:5-10).

These biblical passages clearly indicate that Noah's entering the ark before the flood is not a type of the Church's being raptured out before the Great Tribulation.

What are the similarities between the days of Noah and Lot and "the day when the Son of Man is revealed" (Luke 17:30)?

At least six such similarities exist:

1. Judgment will come when iniquity has come to the full.

In Noah's day—"And God saw that the wickedness of man was great in the earth, and that every imagination of the thoughts of his heart was only evil continually. And it repented the Lord that he had made man on the earth, and it grieved him at his heart. And the Lord said, I will destroy man whom I have created from the face of the earth; both man, and beast, and the creeping thing, and the fowls of the air; for it repenteth me that I have made them" (Gen. 6:5-7).

In Lot's day—"And the Lord said, . . . the cry of Sodom and Gomorrah is great, and . . . their sin is very grievous" (Gen. 18:20). See also Gen. 19:13,15.

In the last days—"Iniquity shall abound, the love of many shall wax cold" (Matt. 24:12). "Put ye in the sickle, for the harvest is ripe: come, get you down; for the press is full, the fats overflow; for their wickedness is great" (Joel 3:13). See also Isa. 13:11; 24:5,6,16,20; 26:21; Zeph. 1:17,18; 2 Tim. 3:1-5,13; 2 Pet. 2:5,6; Jude 1:14,15; Rev. 18:5.

2. Believers must be ready.

Noah—"Noah found grace in the eyes of the Lord. . . . Noah was a just man and perfect in his generations, and Noah walked with God. . . . And the Lord said unto Noah, Come thou and all thy house into the ark; for thee have I seen righteous before me in this generation" (Gen. 6:8,9; 7:1).

Lot—"And Lot said unto them [the angels], Oh, not so, my Lord: Behold now, thy servant hath found grace in thy sight, and thou hast magnified thy mercy" (Gen. 19:18,19). "Just Lot. . . . that righteous man" (2 Pet. 2:7,8).

The Church—"For the grace of God that bringeth salvation hath appeared to all men, teaching us that, denying ungodliness and worldly lusts, we should live soberly, righteously, and godly, in this present world; looking for that blessed hope, and the glorious appearing of the great God and our Saviour Jesus Christ" (Titus 2:11-13).

3. *Many will be hindered by the cares of life.*

Noah—"In the days of Noe. . . . They did eat, they drank, they married wives, they were given in marriage, until the day that Noe entered into the ark, and the flood came, and destroyed them all" (Luke 17:26,27).

Lot—"In the days of Lot; they did eat, they drank, they bought, they sold, they planted, they builded; but the same day that Lot went out of Sodom it rained fire and brimstone from heaven, and destroyed them all" (Luke 17:28,29).

The last days—"Even thus [as in the days of Noah and Lot] shall it be in the day when the Son of man is revealed" (Luke 17:30). "And take heed to yourselves, lest at any time your hearts be overcharged with surfeiting, and drunkenness, and *cares of this life*, and so that day come upon you unawares" (Luke 21:34). "Remember Lot's wife" (Luke 17:32).

4. *The righteous will be delivered before judgment.*

Noah—"In the selfsame day entered Noah . . . into the ark. . . . And the Lord shut him in" (Gen. 7:13,16).

Lot—"Lot went out of Sodom" (Luke 17:29). "The Lord being merciful unto him: and they brought him forth, and set him without the city" (Gen. 19:16).

The Church—"The bridegroom [Jesus] came; and they that were ready went in with him to the marriage: and the door was shut" (Matt. 25:10). "Come, my people, enter thou into thy chambers, and shut thy doors about thee: hide thyself as it were for a little moment, until the indignation be overpast. For, behold, the Lord cometh out of his place to punish the inhabitants of the earth for their iniquity: the earth also shall disclose her blood, and shall no more cover her slain" (Isa. 26:20,21). See also 2 Pet. 2:5-9.

5. *God's people will be gathered openly, not secretly.*

Noah—Noah entered the ark not only with his family, but with "every beast after his kind, and all the cattle after their kind, and every creeping thing that creepeth upon the earth after his kind, and every fowl after his kind, every bird of every sort" (Gen. 7:14).

Lot—Lot, his wife, and their two daughters were delivered openly by the angels: "And when the morning arose, then the angels hastened Lot. . . . And while he lingered, the men laid hold upon his hand, and upon the hand of his wife, and upon the hand of his two daughters; the Lord being merciful unto him: and they brought him forth, and set him without the city" (Gen. 19:15,16).

The Church—"And then shall *they see* the Son of man coming in the clouds with great power and glory. And then shall he send his angels, and shall gather together his elect from the four winds, from the uttermost part of the earth to the uttermost part of heaven" (Mark 13:26,27).

6. *On the same day the Church is gathered, destruction will come from the Almighty. All who are left will be destroyed; none will escape.*

In Noah's day—"*The day* that Noe entered into the ark . . . the flood came, and *destroyed them all*" (Luke 17:27). See also Gen. 7:11-13.

In Lot's day—"*The same day* that Lot went out of Sodom it rained fire and brimstone from heaven, and *destroyed them all*" (Luke 17:29).

In the Day of the Lord—"Even thus [as in the days of Noah and Lot] shall it be in *the day* when the Son of man is revealed" (Luke 17:30). "For as a snare shall it come on *all* them that dwell on the face of the whole earth" (Luke 21:35). "For when they shall say, Peace and safety; then *sudden destruction* cometh upon them, as travail upon a woman with child; and they shall not escape" (1 Thess. 5:3).

Do other scriptures support the teaching that deliverance and judgment will occur on the same day?

Yes, there are many. Let's examine some of them. Notice the scriptural details in the chart below:

Deliverance for the Righteous	Judgment for the Wicked—the Same Day
Matthew 13:30,39-43 The wheat will be gathered.	The tares will be burned.
Matthew 13:47-50 The good fish will be gathered into vessels.	The bad fish will be cast away.
Matthew 24:31,50,51 The elect will be gathered.	The unprepared will be cut asunder.
Matthew 25:10-13 The wise virgins will enter the marriage supper.	The foolish virgins will be shut out.
Matthew 25:34,41 The sheep will inherit the kingdom.	The goats will inherit everlasting fire.
Luke 21:34-36 The watchful and prayerful will be accounted worthy to escape judgment.	The worldly-minded will be caught unawares.
2 Peter 3:7,10-13 Salvation will come to the Church.	Judgment will come upon the ungodly.
Revelation 7:9,14; 6:12-17 A great multitude will stand before the throne of the Lamb of God.	A great multitude will cry, "Hide us from the face of him that sitteth on the throne."
Revelation 11:18 The saints will be rewarded.	The nations will face God's wrath.
Revelation 15:2; 14:19 The prepared will "stand on the sea glass, having the harps of God."	The unprepared will face "the great winepress of the wrath of God."
Malachi 3:17; 4:1 The jewels will be spared.	The wicked will be made stubble.
1 Thessalonians 4:16,17; 5:3 The Church will be caught up to meet the Lord.	The ungodly will face sudden destruction; none shall escape.
2 Thessalonians 1:7-10 The saints will be glorified.	Fiery vengeance will come on them that know not God and obey not the gospel.

Will anyone have a chance to be saved after the Church is gathered?

The Bible indicates that the coming of Christ is the Day of Judgment when the door of salvation will be shut forever. None was saved after Noah entered the ark and the door was shut. Sodom and Gomorrah did not have a second chance after the angels delivered Lot out of Sodom. Similarly, Jesus warned that those who are left after the Church is gathered are left for destruction. In the immediate context, He admonished, "Watch therefore: for ye know not what hour your Lord doth come" (Matt. 24:42). In fact, almost every passage of Scripture that speaks of the Second Coming gives an admonition about readiness and holy living. Therefore, the time to prepare is now, because there will be no chance for salvation once Jesus appears. We must be as "men that wait for their lord" (Luke 12:36). "Now is the acceptable time; behold, now is the day of salvation" (2 Cor. 6:2).

Objections Answered

Isn't Enoch an Old Testament type of the Church's being raptured out secretly?

Enoch is mentioned three times in the New Testament, but not once with reference to a secret rapture (Luke 3:37; Heb. 11:5; Jude 1:14). If Enoch were a type of the Church, her being raptured out secretly, Jesus and the apostles apparently would have told us, as they do with Noah and Lot—types of the Church's being gathered when Jesus comes to judge the world after the Great Tribulation (Matt. 24:29,37-39; Luke 17:26-30; 2 Pet. 2:5-9; 3:5-7).

Doesn't "one shall be taken and the other left" mean that the prepared shall be taken up in a secret rapture and the unprepared shall be left to go through the Great Tribulation?

Jesus said, "one shall be taken and the other left" in the context of discussing Noah and Lot, and His coming *after* the Tribulation. (Compare Matt. 24:40,41 with 24:29,37-39 and Luke 17:34-37 with 17:26-30.)

When Jesus said, "Two men shall be in the field; the one shall be taken, and the other left," the disciples asked, "Where, Lord?" (Luke 17:36,37). They knew that the saved would be taken to be with their Lord, but they were wondering what would happen to those who were left. Jesus responded, "Wheresoever the body [or carcass] is, thither will the eagles be gathered together" (Luke 17:37; Matt. 24:28). In other words, those who are left will be slain, and eagles will gather to eat their dead flesh. See also Job 39:27-30.

John foresaw the entire end-time scene and likened it to two suppers: "The marriage supper of the Lamb" for the saints who were *taken*; "the supper of the great God" for the fowls that are called to eat the flesh of the ungodly who were *left*. These fowls will "eat the flesh of kings, and the flesh of captains, and the flesh of mighty men, and the flesh of horses, and of them that sit on them, and the flesh of all men, both free and bond, both small and great" (Rev. 19:9,17,18). See also Psa. 110:6; Ezek. 39:17-20.

Therefore, Jesus did not teach a secret rapture, nor that the unprepared will be left to go through the Tribulation with a second opportunity for salvation. Rather, that when He comes after the Tribulation, the prepared will be *taken* to be with Him, and the unprepared will be *left* for destruction. As in the days of Noah and Lot, deliverance and judgment will come on the same day—"the day when the Son of man is *revealed*" (Luke 17:30).

10

The Day of the Lord

To what day was Jesus referring when He said, "Many will say unto me in that day, Lord, Lord" (Matt. 7:22)?

Jesus was referring to the Day of the Lord when He will come to gather His Church and judge the world. Scripture commands us to look and to prepare for that day. Every New Testament writer and at least nineteen Old Testament prophets specifically mention the Day of the Lord.

The Day of the Lord is referred to as "a day" (Acts 17:31); "the day" (1 Cor. 3:13; Heb. 10:25); "that day" (Luke 21:34; 1 Thess. 5:4; 2 Tim. 4:8); "the day of destruction" (Job 21:30); "the day of the Lord's vengeance" (Isa. 34:8; 61:2); "the day of the Lord's anger" (Zeph. 2:3; Isa. 13:13); "the great and dreadful day of the Lord" (Mal. 4:5); "the day of judgment" (2 Pet. 2:9; 1 John 4:17); "the last day" (John 12:48); "the great and notable day of the Lord" (Acts 2:20); "the day of wrath and revelation of the righteous judgment of God" (Rom. 2:5); "the day of trouble" (Nah. 1:7; Zeph. 1:15); "the day of our Lord Jesus Christ" (1 Cor. 1:8); "the day of the Lord Jesus" (2 Cor. 1:14); "the day of redemption" (Eph. 4:30); "the day of Jesus Christ" (Phil. 1:6); "the day of Christ" (2 Thess. 2:2); "the day of visitation" (1 Pet. 2:12); "the day of judgment and perdition of ungodly men" (2 Pet. 3:7); "the day of God" (2 Pet. 3:12); "the great day" (Jude 1:6); "the great day of his wrath" (Rev. 6:17); and the "great day of God Almighty" (Rev. 16:14).

A proper understanding of the Day of the Lord gives abundant proof that the Church will go through the Great Tribulation and makes the truth of the Second Coming and the end of the world come into focus. It also gives a fresh awareness of the fear of the Lord and an urgency to warn others "to flee from the wrath to come" (Matt. 3:7).

What major events will unfold on the Day of the Lord?

The Scripture clearly tells us about several events that will happen on that momentous day:

1. *Jesus will come as Savior for His Church.* "For the Lord himself shall descend from heaven with a shout, with the voice of the archangel, and with the trump of God: and the dead in Christ shall rise first: then we which are alive and remain shall be caught up together with them in the clouds to meet the Lord in the air: and so shall we ever be with the Lord" (1 Thess. 4:16,17). See also 2 Thess. 1:10; 2:1-3.

2. *Jesus will come as Judge of the world.* "For yourselves know perfectly that the *day of the Lord* so cometh as a thief in the night. For when they shall say, Peace and safety; then sudden destruction cometh upon them, as travail upon a woman with child; and they shall not escape" (1 Thess. 5:2). The apostle Paul discussed Jesus' coming as Savior and as Judge in the same context (1 Thess. 4:16-5:2); therefore, both occur on the Day of the Lord.

3. *Babylon will be utterly burned with fire.* In "that *great day of God Almighty*. . . . the great city was divided into three parts, and the cities of the nations fell: and great Babylon came in remembrance before God, to give unto her the cup of the wine of the fierceness of his wrath" (Rev. 16:14,19). "And she shall be utterly burned with fire: for strong is the Lord God who judgeth her" (Rev. 18:8). See Chapter Fifteen.

4. *The battle of Armageddon will occur.* "For they are the spirits of devils, working miracles, which go forth unto the kings of the earth and of the whole world, to gather them to the battle of that *great day of God Almighty*. . . . And he gathered them together into a place called in the Hebrew tongue Armageddon" (Rev. 16:14,16).

5. *The beast and the false prophet will be destroyed.* In "*the day of Christ*. . . . the Lord shall consume [the man of sin] with the spirit of his mouth, and shall destroy [him] with the brightness of his coming" (2 Thess. 2:2,8).

6. *The fallen angels will be judged.* "And the angels which kept not their first estate, but left their own habitation, he hath reserved in everlasting chains under darkness unto the judgment of *the great day*" (Jude 1:6).

7. Jesus will reward those who love His appearing. "Henceforth there is laid up for me a crown of righteousness, which the Lord, the righteous judge, shall give me at *that day*: and not to me only, but unto all them also that love his appearing" (2 Tim. 4:8).

8. The earth will be destroyed with fire. "But the *day of the Lord* will come as a thief in the night; in the which the heavens shall pass away with a great noise, and the elements shall melt with fervent heat, the earth also and the works that are therein shall be burned up" (2 Pet. 3:10). See also Isa. 13:10-13; 34:1-10.

9. The righteous look for new heavens and a new earth. "What manner of persons ought ye to be . . . looking for and hasting unto the coming of *the day of God*, wherein the heavens being on fire shall be dissolved, and the elements shall melt with fervent heat? Nevertheless we, according to his promise, look for new heavens and a new earth, wherein dwelleth righteousness" (2 Pet. 3:11-13). The new heavens and a new earth will come simultaneously with the destruction of the present heaven and earth. How do we know that? Scripture commands us to look not only for "the coming of *the day of God*, wherein the heavens being on fire shall be dissolved," but also for "new heavens and a new earth, wherein dwelleth righteousness."

What is an unmistakable sign of the Day of the Lord?

Scripture mentions several signs that pinpoint the Day of the Lord. "The sun [shall] be darkened, and the moon shall not give her light, and the stars shall fall from heaven, and the powers of the heavens shall be shaken" (Matt. 24:29). Whenever we see these cosmic signs in the Scripture, we know they concern the Day of the Lord. The Bible lists these signs at least six times in reference to that day.

"Behold, *the day of the Lord*. . . . the stars of heaven and the constellations thereof shall not give their light: the sun shall be darkened in his going forth, and the moon shall not cause her light to shine" (Isa. 13:9,10).

"The earth shall quake before them; the heavens shall tremble: the sun and the moon shall be dark, and the stars shall withdraw their shining. . . . for *the day of the Lord* is great and very terrible" (Joel 2:10,11).

"The sun shall be turned into darkness, and the moon into

blood, before the great and the terrible *day of the Lord come*" (Joel 2:31).

"*The day of the Lord* is near. . . . The sun and the moon shall be darkened, and the stars shall withdraw their shining" (Joel 3:14,15).

"The sun shall be turned into darkness, and the moon into blood, before that great and notable *day of the Lord* come" (Acts 2:20).

"And I beheld when he had opened the sixth seal, and, lo, there was a great earthquake; and the sun became black as sackcloth of hair, and the moon became as blood; and the stars of heaven fell unto the earth. . . . For *the great day of his wrath* is come; and who shall be able to stand?" (Rev. 6:12,13,17).

Does the Day of the Lord include the Great Tribulation?

There is no biblical evidence that the Day of the Lord includes the tribulation period. According to Scripture, the Day of the Lord cannot begin until at least six things occur:

1. Elijah must come (Mal. 4:5). This was fulfilled by John the Baptist's ministry (Matt. 11:13,14; 17:11,12.)
2. The gospel must be preached in all the world (Matt. 24:14; 2 Pet. 3:9,10).
3. There must be a falling away (2 Thess. 2:2,3).
4. The man of sin must be revealed (2 Thess. 2:2,3).
5. The Great Tribulation must have occurred. (Compare Rev. 6:12-17 with 6:9-11; Matt. 24:21 with 24:29-31).
6. The end of the world must come (1 Cor. 1:8).

In Acts 2:20, Peter called the Day of the Lord, "that great and notable day." According to Strong, notable means "manifestation," "conspicuous," "memorable." It is the root word of "appearing" that Paul used when he described "the glorious appearing" in Titus 2:13. This truth suggests that the Day of the Lord is not stretched out over a long series of events, but is one great, conspicuous, memorable event. It will come suddenly as a thief in the night and will be a catastrophic event in which "the heavens shall pass away with a great noise, and the elements shall melt with fervent heat" (2 Pet. 3:10). Paul also linked the Day of the Lord with the end of the world: "Who shall also confirm you unto *the end*, that ye may be blameless in the *day of our Lord Jesus Christ*" (1 Cor. 1:8).

Moreover, the Bible does not say that the Great Tribulation will come as a thief in the night (Matt. 24:21), but that the Day of the Lord will come as a thief in the night (1 Thess. 5:2; 2 Pet. 3:10). In the light of these truths, it is impossible for the Day of the Lord to include the Great Tribulation. They are two distinct events. One follows the other; the Day of the Lord begins immediately *after* the Tribulation.

Can it be proven that Christ's coming as described in Matthew 24 and 25 occurs on the Day of the Lord?

Yes, by numerous proofs. They show once again that the Day of the Lord comes immediately after the Tribulation. The following comparisons show that the events of Matthew 24 and 25 occur on the Day of the Lord.

Matthew 24:29—"The sun [shall] be darkened, and the moon shall not give her light." Isaiah prophesied, "Behold, *the day of the Lord*. . . . The sun shall be darkened in his going forth, and the moon shall not cause her light to shine" (Isa. 13:9,10).

Matthew 24:30—"All the tribes of the earth [shall] mourn." The prophets depict this as occurring on the Day of the Lord: "Howl ye; for *the day of the Lord* is at hand" (Isa. 13:6). "*The great day of the Lord* is near . . . the mighty man shall cry there bitterly" (Zeph. 1:14).

Matthew 24:31—The "great sound of a trumpet." Joel declared, "Blow ye the trumpet in Zion, and sound an alarm in my holy mountain: let all the inhabitants of the land tremble: for *the day of the Lord* cometh" (Joel 2:1).

Matthew 24:31—"And he shall send his angels . . . and they shall gather together his elect." The apostle Paul indicated that the Church will be gathered on the Day of the Lord: "The dead in Christ shall rise first: then we which are alive and remain shall be caught up together. . . . *The day of the Lord*" (1 Thess. 4:16,17; 5:2). See also 2 Thess. 2:1,2.

Matthew 24:35—"Heaven and earth shall pass away." Peter wrote about heaven and earth passing away on the Day of the Lord. "*The day of the Lord* will come . . . the heavens shall pass away . . . the earth also" (2 Pet. 3:10).

Matthew 24:43—Christ's reference to "the thief." The apostles declared, "*The day of the Lord* so cometh as a thief in the night" (1 Thess. 5:2; 2 Pet. 3:10).

Matthew 25:41—"Depart from me, ye cursed, into everlasting fire." Paul described the Day of the Lord as a day of flaming fire and everlasting destruction upon the ungodly: "The Lord Jesus shall be revealed . . . in flaming fire taking vengeance on them that know not God, and that obey not the gospel of our Lord Jesus Christ: Who shall be punished with everlasting destruction . . . *in that day*" (2 Thess. 1:7-10). "*The day of the Lord* cometh. . . . Then sudden destruction cometh" (1 Thess. 5:2,3).

Do other scriptures liken the Day of the Lord to the Day of Judgment?

Yes, the Day of the Lord is seen as the Day of Judgment in each of the following verses:

Paul wrote about the Day of the Lord as "the day of wrath and revelation of the righteous judgment of God" (Rom. 2:5); "the day when God shall judge the secrets of men by Jesus Christ" (Rom. 2:16); and a day appointed by God "in the which he will judge the world in righteousness" (Acts 17:31).

Peter referred to the Day of the Lord as "the day of judgment and perdition of ungodly men." (Compare 2 Pet. 3:10 with 3:7.)

Jude wrote of "the judgment of the great day" and of the coming of "the Lord with ten thousands of his saints, to execute judgment upon all" (Jude 1:6,14,15).

John declared, "The great day of his wrath is come; and who shall be able to stand?" (Rev. 6:17) and "Herein is our love made perfect, that we may have boldness in the day of judgment" (1 John 4:17).

The prophet Isaiah warned, "Behold, the day of the Lord cometh, cruel both with wrath and fierce anger, to lay the land desolate: and he shall destroy the sinners thereof out of it" (Isa. 13:9). See also Joel 1:15; Jer. 46:10; Obad. 1:15.

Jesus Himself said, "But I say unto you, That every idle word that men shall speak, they shall give account thereof in the day of judgment. For by thy words thou shalt be justified, and by thy words thou shalt be condemned" (Matt. 12:36,37). He also warned the unrepentant cities, "Woe unto thee, Chorazin! woe unto thee, Bethsaida! for if the mighty works, which were done in you, had been done in Tyre and Sidon, they would have repented long ago in sackcloth and ashes. But I say unto you, It shall be more tolerable for Tyre and Sidon at the day of judgment, than for you" (Matt. 11:20-22). See also Matt. 10:15; Mark 6:11; John 12:48.

Will the true Church be protected on the Day of the Lord?

Yes. Paul wrote that on the Day of the Lord, Jesus will come to gather His Church *before* sending sudden destruction on the wicked. In the same context, He assured, "For God hath not appointed us to wrath, but to obtain salvation by our Lord Jesus Christ" (1 Thess. 5:9).

The following verses further promise the Lord's protection to His people when He pours out His wrath and indignation upon the wicked on that day:

The saints will experience "glory and honour and immortality" on the "day of wrath and revelation of the righteous judgment of God" (Rom. 2:5,7).

"God is our refuge and strength, a very present help in trouble. Therefore will not we fear, though the earth be removed, and though the mountains be carried into the midst of the sea; though the waters thereof roar and be troubled, though the mountains shake with the swelling thereof. . . . The Lord of hosts is with us; the God of Jacob is our refuge. . . . Be still, and know that I am God: I will be exalted among the heathen, I will be exalted in the earth. The Lord of hosts is with us; the God of Jacob is our refuge. Selah" (Psa. 46:1-3,7,10,11).

"The mountains quake at him, and the hills melt, and the earth is burned at his presence, yea, the world, and all that dwell therein. Who can stand before his indignation? and who can abide in the fierceness of his anger? his fury is poured out like fire, and the rocks are thrown down by him. The Lord is good, a strong hold in *the day of trouble*; and he knoweth them that trust in him" (Nah. 1:5-7). See also Isa. 25:9; 26:20,21; 2 Thess. 1:7-10; 2 Pet. 3:7-13.

What will happen to those who are not prepared for that day?

They will cry bitterly. "The *great day of the Lord* is near, it is near, and hasteth greatly, even the voice of the day of the Lord: the mighty man shall cry there bitterly. That day is a day of wrath, a day of trouble and distress, a day of wasteness and desolation, a day of darkness and gloominess, a day of clouds and thick darkness, a day of the trumpet and alarm against the fenced cities, and against the high towers. And I will bring distress upon men, that they shall walk like blind men, because they have sinned against the Lord: and their blood shall be poured out as dust, and their flesh as the dung" (Zeph. 1:14-17).

They will flee to escape, but there will be no place of refuge. "Woe unto you that desire *the day of the Lord!* to what end is it for you? the day of the Lord is darkness, and not light. As if a man did flee from a lion, and a bear met him; or went into the house, and leaned his hand on the wall, and a serpent bit him. Shall not the day of the Lord be darkness, and not light? even very dark, and no brightness in it?" (Amos 5:18-20).

"Fear, and the pit, and the snare, are upon thee, O inhabitant of the earth. And it shall come to pass, that he who fleeth from the noise of the fear shall fall into the pit; and he that cometh up out of the midst of the pit shall be taken in the snare: for the windows from on high are open, and the foundations of the earth do shake" (Isa. 24:17,18).

"Enter into the rock, and hide thee in the dust, for fear of the Lord, and for the glory of his majesty. The lofty looks of man shall be humbled, and the haughtiness of men shall be bowed down, and the Lord alone shall be exalted *in that day*" (Isa. 2:10,11). See also Isa. 2:19,21; Lam. 2:22; Rev. 6:12-17.

What must I do to prepare for the Day of the Lord?

The following scriptures instruct us how to prepare for that great day:

1. Repent. "God . . . now commandeth all men every where to repent: Because he hath appointed a day, in the which he will judge the world in righteousness by that man whom he hath ordained; whereof he hath given assurance unto all men, in that he hath raised him from the dead" (Acts 17:30,31). See Chapter Twenty-Four.

2. *Believe on the Lord Jesus Christ.* "For I know whom I have believed, and am persuaded that he is able to keep that which I have committed unto him against *that day*" (2 Tim. 1:12).

3. *Seek the Lord, seek righteousness, and seek meekness.* "Seek ye the Lord, all ye meek of the earth, which have wrought his judgment; seek righteousness, seek meekness: it may be ye shall be hid in the *day of the Lord's anger*" (Zeph. 2:3). "*The day of the Lord* will come. . . . What manner of persons ought ye to be in all holy conversation and godliness" (2 Pet. 3:10,11).

4. *Don't be enticed by the things of this life.* "And take heed to yourselves, lest at any time your heart be overcharged with surfeiting, and drunkenness, and cares of this life, and so *that day* come upon you unawares. For as a snare shall it come on all them that dwell on the face of the whole earth" (Luke 21:34,35).

5. *Awake! Be revived!* "Knowing the time . . . that now it is high time to awake out of sleep: for now is our salvation nearer than when we believed. The night is far spent, *the day* is at hand: let us therefore cast off the works of darkness, and let us put on the armour of light" (Rom. 13:11,12). See also 1 Thess. 5:2,6.

6. *Do all things without murmuring and quarreling.* "Do all things without murmuring and disputings: that ye may be blameless and harmless, the sons of God, without rebuke, in the midst of a crooked and perverse nation, among whom ye shine as lights in the world: Holding forth the word of life; that I may rejoice in *the day of Christ*, that I have not run in vain, neither laboured in vain" (Phil. 2:14-16). See also Jude 1:15,16.

7. *Let love abound in knowledge and in all judgment.* "And this I pray, that your love may abound yet more and more in knowledge and in all judgment; that ye may approve things that are excellent; that ye may be sincere and without offence till *the day of Christ*" (Phil. 1:9,10). "Herein is our love made perfect, that we may have boldness in *the day of judgment*: because as he is, so are we in this world" (1 John 4:17).

8. *Beware of the deceitfulness of riches.* "Riches profit not in *the day of wrath*: but righteousness delivereth from death" (Pro. 11:4). "Neither their silver nor their gold shall be able to deliver

them in *the day of the Lord's wrath*" (Zeph. 1:18). See also Job 20:28; Ezek. 7:19; Mark 4:19; Luke 18:24,25; 1 Tim. 6:6-16.

9. Grieve not the Holy Spirit of God by sin or loose talk. "And grieve not the holy Spirit of God, whereby ye are sealed unto *the day of redemption.* Let all bitterness, and wrath, and anger, and clamour, and evil speaking, be put away from you, with all malice" (Eph. 4:30,31).

10. Fast and pray. "Sanctify ye a fast, call a solemn assembly, gather the elders and all the inhabitants of the land into the house of the Lord your God, and cry unto the Lord. Alas for *the day*! for *the day of the Lord* is at hand, and as a destruction from the Almighty shall it come" (Joel 1:14,15; 2:10-17). See also Luke 21:34-36.

11. Be diligent in the work of the Lord. "The Lord give mercy unto the house of Onesiphorus; for he oft refreshed me, and was not ashamed of my chain: but, when he was in Rome, he sought me out very diligently, and found me. The Lord grant unto him that he may find mercy of the Lord *in that day*: and in how many things he ministered unto me at Ephesus, thou knowest very well" (2 Tim. 1:16-18).

12. Abide in the grace of God. "I thank my God always on your behalf, for the grace of God which is given you by Jesus Christ; that in every thing ye are enriched by him, in all utterance, and in all knowledge; even as the testimony of Christ was confirmed in you: So that ye come behind in no gift; waiting for the coming of our Lord Jesus Christ: Who shall also confirm you unto the end, that ye may be blameless in *the day of our Lord Jesus Christ*" (1 Cor. 1:4-8).

Since God gave the above admonitions about the Day of the Lord to the Church, she certainly will be on earth until then.

Objection Answered

Isn't there a difference between the Day of the Lord and the Day of Christ?

In order to prove their point, some who teach a secret rapture claim that there is a difference. The Bible, however, makes no distinction. By comparing the events of the Day of the Lord with those of the Day of Christ, one can see that they are one and the same.

Events of the Day of the Lord (1 Thess. 4:15-18; 5:1-8)	**Events of the Day of Christ (2 Thess. 1:7-12; 2:1-8)**
The coming of the Lord (4:15).	The coming of our Lord (2:1).
The Lord descends from heaven (4:16).	The Lord is revealed from heaven (1:7).
With the voice of the arch-angel (4:16).	With His mighty angels (1:7).
Caught up together to meet the Lord (4:17).	Our gathering together unto Him (2:1).
Sudden destruction (5:3).	Everlasting destruction (1:9).
Exhortation to faith (5:8).	Exhortation to faith (1:11).
"That day" (5:4).	"That day" (1:10; 2:3).

In addition, the apostles speak of the Day of the Lord as follows:

The Day of Christ (Phil. 1:10; 2:16; 2 Thess. 2:2).
The Day of Jesus Christ (Phil. 1:6).
The Day of the Lord (Acts 2:20; 1 Thess. 5:2; 2 Pet. 3:10).
The Day of our Lord Jesus (1 Cor. 5:5; 2 Cor. 1:14).
The Day of our Lord Jesus Christ (1 Cor. 1:8).

Obviously, each of these terms cannot refer to separate events any more than can the terms "the coming of the Son of man," "the coming of the Lord," or "the coming of our Lord Jesus Christ."

Finally, the Scripture uses interchangeably admonitions concerning the Day of Christ, the Day of Jesus Christ, the Day of the Lord Jesus Christ, and the Day of the Lord Jesus.

Consider the following three comparisons:

1. "Rejoice in the day of Christ" (Phil. 2:16).
   "Rejoicing . . . in the day of the Lord Jesus" (2 Cor. 1:14).
2. "Without offence till the day of Christ" (Phil. 1:10).

"Blameless in the day of our Lord Jesus Christ" (1 Cor. 1:8).

3. "Until the day of Jesus Christ" (Phil. 1:6).

"Till the day of Christ" (Phil. 1:10).

Since Scripture teaches that the events of the Day of the Lord and the Day of Christ are the same and that these terms are used interchangeably in Scripture, there can be no difference between the Day of the Lord and the Day of Christ.

11

Who Are the Elect?

Who are the elect in Matthew 24:22, 24, and 31?

Jesus referred to the Church in these verses. He mentioned the elect three times with reference to their going through the Great Tribulation and to being gathered by the angels immediately afterwards. (This same account is given in Mark 13:20,22,27.) While it is obvious that the elect of the New Testament is the Church, some obscure this truth by insisting that the elect refers to Israel.

By comparing each of these verses with parallel verses in the New Testament, we will see clear evidence that the elect is the Church.

First, compare Matthew 24:22 with Luke 18:7,8. Both passages speak of the elect and show that the days of the Great Tribulation will be shortened for their sake. Not even those who teach that the elect of Matthew are the Jews would make the same claim for Luke's gospel.

"And except those days should be shortened, there should no flesh be saved: but for *the elect's* sake those days shall be shortened" (Matt. 24:22).

"And shall not God avenge *his own elect*, which cry day and night unto him, though he bear long with them? I tell you that he will avenge them speedily. Nevertheless when the Son of man cometh, shall he find faith on the earth?" (Luke 18:7,8).

Second, Matthew 24:24 and Second Thessalonians 2:9 both show that false prophets and lying wonders will deceive many during the days before the coming of our Lord. So "the very elect" in Matthew 24:24 are as much the Church as those whom Paul addresses in Second Thessalonians.

Third, a comparison of Matthew 24:30,31 with First Thessalonians 4:16,17 suggests unmistakable similarities between the two passages: the Lord's descending from heaven, the angels, the clouds, the trumpets, and the gathering. Surely, "the elect" of Matthew 24:31 and "the dead in Christ" and "we which are alive and remain" of First Thessalonians 4:16,17 are the same company of people—the Church.

Fourth, the apostle Peter stated, "The *church* that is at Babylon, *elected* together with you, saluteth you" (1 Pet. 5:13), which also supports the truth that the elect refers to the Church.

Lastly, the words "elect," "elect's," and "election" are found twenty-three times in the New Testament, not once referring to the nation of Israel. In addition to the six times they are used in Matthew 24 and Mark 13, fifteen times in other verses they pertain to the Church, once to Christ, and once to the angels. In fact, we can see a clear distinction between Israel and the elect in two particular verses: "What then? *Israel* hath not obtained that which he seeketh for; but the *election* hath obtained it, and the rest were blinded" (Rom. 11:7); "As concerning the gospel, *they* [Israel] are enemies for your sakes: but as touching the election, they are beloved for the fathers' sakes" (Rom. 11:28).

What else does the Bible say about the Church's being the elect?

1. *The elect are "the chosen."* The words "elect" and "chosen" are the same in the Greek. Both of these terms are used in Mark 13:20: "And except that the Lord had shortened those days, no flesh should be saved: but for the *elect's* sake, whom he hath *chosen*, he hath shortened the days." In the New Testament, the word "chosen" often refers to the Church. "According as he hath *chosen* us in him before the foundation of the world, that we should be holy and without blame before him in love" (Eph. 1:4). See also John 15:16,19; 2 Thess. 2:13; Jam. 2:5; Rev. 17:14.

2. *The elect are brothers and sisters in Christ, the Church.* "Paul . . . unto the church of the Thessalonians which is in God the Father and in the Lord Jesus Christ . . . Knowing, *brethren* beloved, your *election* of God" (1 Thess. 1:1,4).

3. *The elect are the saints and the faithful in Christ Jesus.* "To the *saints* . . . and to the *faithful* in Christ Jesus . . . According as he hath chosen [elected] us in him" (Eph. 1:1,4).

4. *The elect are they who are in Christ Jesus.* "There is therefore

now no condemnation to them which are in *Christ Jesus*. . . . Who shall lay any thing to the charge of God's *elect*?" (Rom. 8:1,33).

5. *The elect are all who believe in Jesus, the chosen cornerstone of the Church.* "Wherefore also it is contained in the scripture, Behold, I lay in Zion a chief corner stone, *elect*, precious: and he that *believeth on him* shall not be confounded. . . . But ye are a *chosen* [elected] generation, a royal priesthood, an holy nation, a peculiar people; that ye should shew forth the praises of him who hath called you out of darkness into his marvelous light" (1 Pet. 2:6,9).

6. *The elect are those who are saved by grace, not those who are Israelites by birth.* "Even so then at this present time also there is a remnant according to the election of *grace*. And if by grace, then is it no more of works: otherwise grace is no more grace. But if it be of works, then it is no more grace: otherwise work is no more work. What then? Israel hath not obtained that which he seeketh for; but the *election* hath obtained it, and rest were blinded" (Rom. 11:5-7).

Thus, the Bible uses various terms to describe the elect, who are the Church: the chosen, the brethren, the saints, the faithful, they who are in Christ Jesus, all who believe in Him, and they who are saved by grace.

Are believers, then, spiritual Israel?

Yes, because the seed of Abraham is Christ (Gal. 3:16). Therefore, they who are Christ's are "Abraham's seed and heirs according to the promise" (Gal. 3:29). In other words, if we belong to Christ, by grace through faith, we are Abraham's seed—the spiritual Israel—the elect of God: "Know ye therefore that they which are of *faith*, the same are the children of Abraham" (Gal. 3:7). See also Rom. 3:28-30; 4:1-18; 9:24-26,30-32; Gal. 3:8-14.

Throughout the New Testament, believers are seen as the people of God: "But ye are a chosen generation. . . . Which in time past were not a people, but are now the *people of God*" (1 Pet. 2:9,10). "I will be their God, and they shall be *my people*" (2 Cor. 6:16). "And I heard a great voice out of heaven saying, Behold, the tabernacle of God is with men, and he will dwell with them, and they shall be *his people*, and God himself shall be with them, and be their God" (Rev. 21:3). See also Hos. 2:23; Isa. 65:1-16; Titus 2:14; Rev. 18:4.

Believers are even called the Israel of God: "For in Christ Jesus neither circumcision availeth any thing, nor uncircumcision, but a new creature. And as many as walk according to this rule, peace be on them, and mercy, and upon *the Israel of God*" (Gal. 6:15-16). Consider the following chart:

Natural Israel	**Spiritual Israel, the Church**
Romans 2:28,29 For he is not a Jew, which is one outwardly; neither is that circumcision, which is outward in the flesh.	But he is a Jew, which is one inwardly; and circumcision is that of the heart, in the spirit.
Romans 11:7 What then? Israel hath not obtained that which he seeketh for;	But the election hath obtained it, and the rest were blinded.
Romans 9:7 Neither, because they are the seed of Abraham, are they all children:	But, in Isaac shall thy seed be called. [Isaac represents those who are God's "children of promise" (Gal. 4:28), through "faith" (Rom. 4:16).]
Romans 9:8 They which are the children of the flesh, these are *not* the children of God:	But the children of the promise are counted for the seed.
John 1:11,12 He came unto to his own, and his own received him not.	But as many as received him, to them gave he power *to become the sons of God*, even to them that believe on his name.

Who are the 144,000 redeemed mentioned in Revelation chapters 7 and 14?

By comparing various scriptures, we find that the description of the 144,000 is identical to that of the elect, the Church. First, consider the following chart.

The 144,000	The Church
Hurt not . . . till we have *sealed* the servants of our God—Rev. 7:3.	Ye [the Church] are *sealed* unto the day of redemption—Eph. 4:30.
The *servants* of our God—Rev. 7:3.	A great multitude. . . . are they before the throne of God, and *serve* him—Rev. 7:15; 22:3.
A Lamb stood on the *mount Sion*, and with him an hundred forty and four thousand—Rev. 14:1.	But ye [the Church] are come to *Mount Zion*—Heb. 12:22.
Having his Father's *name* written in their foreheads—Rev. 14:1.	I will write upon him the *name of my God*—Rev. 3:12; 22:4.
And I heard a voice from heaven, as *the voice of many waters*, and as the voice of a great *thunder*—Rev. 14:2.	And I heard as it were the voice of a great multitude, and as the *voice of many waters*, and as the voice of mighty *thunderings*, saying, . . . the marriage of the Lamb is come—Rev. 19:6,7.
And I heard the voice of harpers harping with their *harps*: And they sung as it were *a new song*—Rev. 14:2,3.	Having every one of them *harps*, and golden vials full of odours, which are the prayers of the saints. And they sung *a new song*—Rev. 5:9; 15:2,3.
Were redeemed from the earth—Rev. 14:3.	Christ hath *redeemed* us—Gal. 3:13.
Were not defiled with women; for they are *virgins*—Rev. 14:4.	[The Church is] a *chaste virgin* to Christ—2 Cor. 11:2; Rev. 3:4; 21:27.
These are they which *follow* the Lamb—Rev. 14:4.	My sheep hear my voice, and I know them, and they *follow* me—John 10:27.
Being the *firstfruits* unto God—Rev. 14:4.	Of his own will begat he us with the word of truth, that we should be a kind of *firstfruits* of his creatures—James 1:18; see also Heb. 12:23.
And in their mouth was found *no guile*—Rev. 14:5.	For our exhortation was *not . . . in guile*—1 Thess. 2:3.
For they are *without fault* before the throne of God—Rev. 14:5.	*Faultless* before the presence of his glory—Jude 1:24; Rev. 7:14,15.

Second, as already discussed, the Church is spiritual Israel: "And if ye be Christ's, then are ye Abraham's seed, and heirs according to the promise" (Gal. 3:29).

Third, by comparing Ephesians 2 with Revelation 21, we see that the twelve tribes of the children of Israel (the 144,000) are symbolic of the Church, which is built on the foundation of the twelve apostles:

"And are built upon the foundation of the apostles and prophets, Jesus Christ himself being the chief corner stone" (Eph. 2:20).

"And [the holy Jerusalem] had a wall great and high, and had *twelve gates*, and at the gates twelve angels, and names written thereon, *which are the names of the twelve tribes of the children of Israel*. . . . And the wall of the city had twelve foundations, in them the names of the twelve apostles of the Lamb. . . . And he measured the *wall* thereof, an *hundred and forty and four cubits* [144]" (Rev. 21:9-12,14,17).

Fourth, it is interesting to note how often the number twelve is used with reference to the holy Jerusalem: twelve gates, twelve angels, the names of the twelve tribes of Israel, twelve foundations, the names of twelve apostles, twelve manner of precious stones, twelve pearls, and twelve manner of fruits (Rev. 21:12-21; 22:2).

Finally, since the holy Jerusalem where the Bride of Christ (the Church) dwells is measured in terms of 12 and 144, it is reasonable to believe that the 144,000 redeemed is a figure that represents the complete Church or elect of God, whether they be Jewish or Gentile believers.

Who are the two witnesses in Revelation 11?

We know that the two witnesses must be symbolic of the Church because the Church is alluded to in four specific ways:

1. *The temple of God (Rev. 11:1,2)*—John was told to measure the temple, the altar, and them that worship therein. What does the temple represent, and who are they who worship in the temple and at the altar? The temple of God represents the Church (1 Cor. 3:16; Eph. 2:21) as well as those who worship in the temple and at the altar. The Church has "boldness to enter into the holiest by the blood of Jesus" (Heb. 10:19), and their prayers

are as "incense . . . upon the golden altar" (Rev. 8:3; Psa. 141:2). (According to Exodus 31:7-11, "the holiest" and "the golden altar" represent the holy place in the Old Testament tabernacle or temple.) The temple of God (the Church) in Revelation 11:1 is contrasted in verse two with the court that is outside the temple. This represents the Gentiles, those who know not God.

2. *The holy city (Rev. 11:2)*—The trampling of the holy city relates to the destruction of the mighty and the holy people by the Antichrist. (Compare Dan. 8:13 with 8:23,24 and Rev. 13:4-7.) In Revelation 21:9,10, the holy city is seen as "the bride, the Lamb's wife," which is the Church. In contrast, Jerusalem is symbolically called "Sodom and Egypt" (Rev. 11:8). It is also called "the great city," a term that is used eight times with reference to Babylon in Revelation.

3. *An olive tree (Rev. 11:4)*—Paul refers to the Church as a good olive tree: "For if thou wert cut out of the olive tree which is wild by nature, and wert graffed [grafted] contrary to nature into a *good olive tree*: how much more shall these, which be the natural branches, be graffed into their own olive tree?" (Rom. 11:24). See also Psa. 52:8; Zech. 4:3,11-14.

4. *A candlestick (Rev. 11:4)*—Jesus said to John, "And the seven candlesticks which thou sawest are the seven churches" (Rev. 1:20). He also said to His followers (the Church), "Ye are the light of the world. A city that is set on an hill cannot be hid. Neither do men light a candle, and put it under a bushel, but on a candlestick; and it giveth light unto all that are in the house" (Matt. 5:14,15).

What additional scriptures suggest similarities between the two witnesses and the Church?

As the Church, the two witnesses are:

1. *Witnesses of our Lord Jesus Christ (Rev. 11:3,7)*—Jesus says to His followers, "Ye are witnesses of these things" (Luke 24:48). The Church is depicted as giving witness (or testimony): "And they overcame him by the blood of the Lamb, and by the word of their testimony; and they loved not their lives unto the death" (Rev. 12:11) and "I saw the souls of them that were beheaded for

the witness of Jesus, and for the word of God" (Rev. 20:4). See also Rev. 12:17.

2. *Able to speak with Holy Ghost fire (power) (Rev. 11:5)*—God said to Jeremiah, "Because ye speak this word, behold, I will make my words in thy mouth fire, and this people wood, and it shall devour them" (Jer. 5:14). Jesus gave a similar promise to the Church: "For I will give you a mouth and wisdom, which all your adversaries shall not be able to gainsay nor resist" (Luke 21:15). When "certain of the synagogue" were disputing with Stephen, "they were not able to resist the wisdom and the spirit by which he spake" (Acts 6:9,10).

3. *Avenged by God of their adversaries (Rev. 11:5)*—Jesus promised His Church that "God [shall] avenge his own elect, which cry day and night unto him" (Luke 18:7). Paul wrote that "it is a righteous thing with God to recompense tribulation to them that trouble you" (2 Thess. 1:6).

4. *Promised that their enemies will be killed in the same manner that they are killed (Rev. 11:5)*—This same promise is given to the saints—"He that leadeth into captivity shall go into captivity: he that killeth with the sword must be killed with the sword. Here is the patience and the faith of the saints" (Rev. 13:10). In fact, just as "their dead bodies [the two witnesses, the Church] shall lie in the street" (Rev. 11:8) to be "meat unto the fowls of the heaven" (Psa. 79:2), so the slain bodies of the wicked will be left for the fowls of the air when Jesus comes in judgment (Rev. 19:17,18; Matt. 24:28; Luke 17:37).

5. *Endued with all power so that nothing is impossible (Rev. 11:6)*—When writing to the Church, James indicated that the fervent prayer of a righteous man is able to control the rain as did the prayers of Elijah (James 5:16-18). See also Matt. 17:20,21; Luke 10:19; John 15:7; Acts 1:8.

6. *Persecuted by the beast who "shall make war against them" (Rev. 11:7)*—If the beast were coming against only two men—the two witnesses—why the term "war"? According to Revelation 13:7 and Daniel 7:21, the beast makes "war with the saints."

7. *Killed (Rev. 11:7)*—But at the resurrection, "the Spirit of life from God entered into them, and they stood upon their feet" (Rev. 11:11). Ezekiel's prophecy says almost the exact same thing. "The breath came into them, and they lived, and stood up

upon their feet" and adds, "an exceeding great army" (Ezek. 37:10). In Revelation 19:19, the Church is referred to as an army.

8. Seen by their enemies ascending "up to heaven in a cloud" (Rev. 11:12)—Paul wrote that the Church will be "caught up . . . in the clouds, to meet the Lord in the air" (1 Thess. 4:17). And Jesus declared that "all the tribes of the earth" shall see this event (Matt. 24:30,31).

Is election for one particular nationality or for people of all nationalities?

Jesus and the apostles give us reason to believe that election is for all:

"Of a truth . . . God is no respecter of persons: But in *every nation* he that feareth him, and worketh righteousness, is accepted with him" (Acts 10:34,35).

"Peter, an apostle of Jesus Christ, to the strangers scattered throughout Pontus, Galatia, Cappadocia, Asia, and Bithynia, *elect* according to the foreknowledge of God the Father" (1 Pet. 1:1,2).

"But *as many as received him*, to them gave he power to become the *sons of God*, even to them that believe on his name" (John 1:12).

In Christ, is there any difference between Jew or Gentile? Is one the elect of God more than the other?

It's wonderful to know that in Christ Jesus there is no difference between Jew or Gentile! We are made one through His blood. The apostle Paul states:

"There is neither Jew nor Greek, there is neither bond nor free, there is neither male nor female: for ye are *all one* in Christ Jesus" (Gal. 3:28).

"For as the *body is one*, and hath many members, and all the members of that *one body*, being many, are *one body*: so also is Christ. For by *one Spirit* are we all baptized into *one body*, whether we be *Jews or Gentiles*, whether we be bond or free; and have been all made to drink into *one Spirit*" (1 Cor. 12:12,13).

The chart below confirms that in Christ there's no difference between Jew and Gentile; one isn't more the elect of God than the other.

The Elect Described	Old Testament (Believing Jews)	New Testament (Believers—Jew and Gentile)
A holy people	Lev. 19:2	1 Pet. 1:16
A chosen people	Deut. 7:6,7	1 Pet. 2:9; Eph. 1:4
A peculiar people	Ex. 19:5	1 Pet. 2:9; Titus 2:14
A kingdom of priests	Ex. 19:6	1 Pet. 2:5; Rev. 1:6
A holy nation	Ex. 19:6	1 Pet. 2:9
A covenant people	Ex. 19:5	Heb. 8:10-12; 10:16-19
A separated people	Lev. 20:24	2 Cor. 6:16-18
"My people"	Lev. 26:11,12	2 Cor. 6:16; Rev. 21:3,7

How may I become one of God's elect?

By faith in Jesus—"For ye are all the children of God by faith in Christ Jesus" (Gal. 3:26). True faith includes repentance (Mark 1:15; Acts 20:21). See also 2 Tim. 2:10; Titus 1:1.

By believing the truth—"But we are bound to give thanks alway to God for you, brethren beloved of the Lord, because God hath from the beginning *chosen* you to salvation through sanctification of the Spirit and belief of the truth" (2 Thess. 2:13).

By the grace of God—"Even so then at this present time also there is a remnant according to the *election of grace*" (Rom. 11:5). "For the grace of God that bringeth salvation hath appeared to all men, teaching us that, denying ungodliness and worldly lusts, we should live soberly, righteously, and godly, in this present world" (Titus 2:11,12).

By being justified by God (declared righteous)—"Who shall lay any thing to the charge of God's *elect*? It is God that justifieth" (Rom. 8:33).

By the Spirit, the Word, and the blood of Jesus—"Elect according to the foreknowledge of God the Father, through sanctification of the Spirit, unto obedience [to the Word] and sprinkling of the blood of Jesus Christ" (1 Pet. 1:2).

Each of these is a facet of the same precious gem and an experience of personal salvation that makes us God's elect.

How should the elect live in everyday life?

Since the elect are the Church, the New Testament is full of exhortations concerning godly living. Specific exhortations to the elect include the following:

Be merciful, kind, and humble. "Put on therefore, as the *elect* of

God, holy and beloved, bowels of mercies, kindness, humbleness of mind, meekness, longsuffering; forbearing one another, and forgiving one another, if any man have a quarrel against any: even as Christ forgave you, so also do ye" (Col. 3:12,13).

Be holy and blameless in love. "According as he hath *chosen* us in him, before the foundation of the world, that we should be holy and without blame before him in love . . . To the praise of the glory of his grace, wherein he hath made us accepted in the beloved" (Eph. 1:4,6).

Be adding diligently to your faith. "And beside this, giving all diligence, add to your faith virtue; and to virtue knowledge; and to knowledge temperance; and to temperance patience; and to patience godliness; and to godliness brotherly kindness; and to brotherly kindness charity. . . . Give diligence to make your calling and *election* sure: for if ye do these things, ye shall never fall: For so an entrance shall be ministered unto you abundantly into the everlasting kingdom of our Lord and Saviour Jesus Christ" (2 Pet. 1:5-7,10,11).

Objection Answered

In the context of Revelation 7, the 144,000 are declared to be of the twelve tribes of Israel and are contrasted with an innumerable host of white-robed Gentiles. Therefore, how can they be symbolic of the Church?

Nowhere does the Bible say that the white-robed throng are Gentiles. Rather, they consist of "*all nations*, and kindreds, and people, and tongues" (Rev. 7:9). Also, as discussed earlier in this chapter, the description of the 144,000 is identical to that of the elect, the Church. In fact, several of these descriptions of the 144,000 are the same as the white-robed throng in Revelation 7:

- The 144,000 are "the servants of our God" (7:3); the white-robed throng "serve him [God] day and night in his temple" (7:15; 22:3).
- The 144,000 are "they which follow the Lamb" (14:4); the white-robed throng are they whom "the Lamb shall lead" (7:17).
- The 144,000 are "before the throne of God" (14:5); the white-robed throng are "before the throne of God" (7:15).

12

Will All Israel be Saved?

What is meant by "And so all Israel shall be saved" (Rom. 11:26)?

"And so all Israel shall be saved" (Rom. 11:26) does not mean that the entire nation of Israel will be saved when Jesus returns, as many teach. This verse refers to the salvation of the Church. In other words, "all Israel" speaks of the Church, both Jew and Gentile, and Paul describes *in what manner* she "shall be saved." This teaching is supported by the following scriptural truths:

1. *The context speaks of believing Jews and Gentiles.* Paul described believing Jews as the "remnant according to the election of grace" (11:5,7), and believing Gentiles as the "wild olive tree" that has been grafted into the "good olive tree" (11:17,24). The believing remnant of Israel could be referred to as "the fulness of the Jews," just as believing Gentiles are referred to as "the fulness of the Gentiles" (11:25). Together, believing Jews and Gentiles comprise "all Israel," the Church.

2. *God does not differentiate between Jew and Gentile.* There are not two separate olive trees, but *one*, consisting of *all* believers, whether Jew or Gentile (11:17). God does not show favoritism; therefore, He doesn't have a separate plan of salvation for the nation of Israel: "*For there is no difference between the Jew and the Greek*: for the same Lord over *all* is rich unto *all* that call upon him. For *whosoever* shall call upon the name of the Lord shall be saved" (Rom. 10:12,13). The following scriptures also emphasize this truth: Acts 10:34,35; 20:21; Rom. 1:16; 2:9-11; 3:9,22,23; Eph. 2:13-18.

3. *The Church is the true Israel of God.* The Bible describes the Church as "the olive tree" (Rom. 11:17,24); "fellow citizens" of "the commonwealth of Israel" (Eph. 2:12,19); "one new man" (Eph. 2:15); "one body" (Eph. 2:16); "the bride, the Lamb's wife" (Rev. 21:9); "heirs of God, and joint-heirs with Christ"

(Rom. 8:17); "the children of the living God" (Rom. 9:26); "an holy nation" (1 Pet. 2:9); the "elect" (1 Pet. 1:2); "Abraham's seed" (Gal. 3:29); the "Jerusalem which is above" (Gal. 4:26); "the children of promise" (Gal. 4:28); "the city of the Lord, the Zion of the Holy One of Israel" (Isa. 60:14); and "the Israel of God" (Gal. 6:15,16). These terms show that the Bible does not speak of two Israels being saved (Israel, the nation, and Israel, the Church), but of one Israel, the Church, which Paul refers to as "all Israel."

Moreover, a true Israelite is one whose heart has been changed by God. The term "Israel" means "prince with God." The angel said to Jacob, "Thy name shall be called no more Jacob, but Israel: for as a prince hast thou power with God and with men, and hast prevailed" (Gen. 32:28). Similarly, all who come to Jesus [the Holy One of Israel] in repentance and faith are given "power to become the sons of God" (John 1:12), are washed from their "sins in his own blood," and are made "kings and priests" unto God (Rev. 1:5,6).

The Bible further describes true Israelites: "Truly God is good to Israel, even to *such as are of a clean heart*" (Psa. 73:1). When Jesus met Nathanael, He said, "Behold an Israelite indeed, *in whom is no guile!*" (John 1:47). David prayed, "Do good, O Lord, unto *those that be good, and to them that are upright in their hearts.* As for such as turn aside unto their crooked ways, the Lord shall lead them forth with the workers of iniquity: but peace shall be upon Israel" (Psa. 125:4,5). Paul declared that "*he is a Jew, which is one inwardly*; and circumcision is that of the heart, in the spirit, and not in the letter; whose praise is not of men, but of God" (Rom. 2:29).

4. The context of Romans 11:26 indicates that only a remnant of Israel will be saved.

Romans 11:1-4—All Israelites by birth are not God's people, but those whom He "foreknew." For example, when Elijah thought that all of Israel had killed the prophets and destroyed God's altars and that he alone was left, God said to him, "I have reserved to myself seven thousand men, who have not bowed the knee to the image of Baal" (11:3,4). These seven thousand were the true Israel, the remnant whom God foreknew. See also 1 Kings 19:18.

Romans 11:5—"Even so . . . at this present time . . . there

is a *remnant* [a small, believing minority] according to the election of grace," not according to national identity. This truth is confirmed in Romans 9:27: "Though the number of the children of Israel be as the sand of the sea, *a remnant shall be saved.*" See also Rom. 9:6-8,28,29; Isa. 1:9; 10:20-23; 46:3; Jer. 31:7; Joel 2:32; Micah 4:7; Zeph. 3:13.

Romans 11:7—Paul made a distinction between Israel, the nation (unbelieving Jews), and Israel, the elect of God (believing Jews)—"What then? Israel hath not obtained that which he seeketh for; but the election [the remnant] hath obtained it, and the rest were blinded."

Romans 11:14—Paul hoped for only "some" or a remnant of his fellow Jews to be saved, and that by hearing and believing the gospel. See also Rom. 3:22; 10:12,13. Certainly, he would not have wished himself "accursed from Christ" for his "kinsmen according to the flesh" (Rom. 9:3) if he believed the whole nation of Israel would be saved when Jesus comes.

Romans 11:17-22—Some of the branches (unbelieving Israel) had been broken off. According to the words of Paul, they judged themselves "unworthy of everlasting life" because they rejected Christ and His gospel (Acts 13:46). This truth is especially illustrated in Matthew 21:33-45 and Jeremiah 11:16,17. See also Matt. 22:1-14; 23:37,38; Luke 19:41-44; Acts 18:6; 28:23-28. God, however, will save individual Jews (the remnant) and "graft them in again," not because of their nationality, but on the condition of faith—"if they abide not still in unbelief" (Rom. 11:23). For this reason, Paul testified "both to *the Jews*, and also to the Greeks, repentance toward God, and faith toward our Lord Jesus Christ" (Acts 20:21). See also Acts 26:20; Rom. 9:30-33; 10:1-4,9-13.

Romans 11:25—Natural Israel, except for the remnant, will remain in spiritual blindness until "the fulness of the Gentiles be come in," that is, until the ingathering of believing Gentiles at the Second Coming. On that "day of wrath and revelation of the righteous judgment of God," there will be no opportunity for unbelieving Jews (or Gentiles) to be saved. Paul wrote that "tribulation and anguish" will come "upon every soul of man that doeth evil, of *the Jew first*, and also of the Gentile; . . . for there is no respect of persons with God" (Rom. 2:5,9-11). This truth is in accordance with the words that Moses spoke to Israel. "A prophet shall the Lord your God raise up unto you of your brethren, like unto me; him shall ye hear in all things whatsoever he shall say unto you. And it shall come to pass, that *every soul* [whether Jew or Gentile], which will not hear that prophet, *shall be destroyed* from among the people" (Acts 3:22,23; Deut. 18:15-19).

5. *Romans 11:25 and 26 do not speak about when Israel will be saved, but how.* These verses are often interpreted to mean "*When* the time of the Gentiles is fulfilled, *then* all Israel will be saved." It is important, however, to note that verse 26 does not say, "And *then* all Israel shall be saved" but, "And *so* all Israel shall be saved." (The word "so" is in the original Greek.) Throughout Romans 11 we see *how* "all Israel [the Church] shall be saved":

Verse 11, "I say then, Have they [natural Israel] stumbled that they should fall? God forbid: but rather through their fall *salvation is come unto the Gentiles*, for to provoke them to jealousy."

Verse 12, "the fall of them [natural Israel] *be the riches of the world.*"

Verse 15, "the casting away of them [natural Israel] *be the reconciling of the world.*"

Verse 19, "Thou wilt say then, The branches [natural Israel] were broken off, that *I* [*a Gentile*] *might be graffed in.*"

Verse 20, "because of unbelief they [natural Israel] were broken off, and *thou standest by faith.*"

Verse 25, "blindness in part is happened to [natural] Israel, until *the fulness of the Gentiles be come in.*"

"And *so* all Israel shall be saved" (11:26). Knowing that natural Israel would refuse the gospel, God ordained that it should be preached to the Gentiles in order to save those who would believe (Rom. 11:30-33; Acts 13:46). Therefore, the above six verses in Romans 11 show that the *so* of Romans 11:26 refers to the *how* of Israel's (the Church's) salvation, namely, by believing the Word of God that was spoken to her as a result of natural Israel's unbelief.

In summary, "And so all Israel shall be saved" refers to the salvation of the Church, not to the salvation of the entire nation of Israel. The context speaks of only a remnant of Israel being saved and of the conversion of Gentiles. Also, God makes no difference between Jew and Gentile. Furthermore, the Church is the true Israel of God, which is saved by having the opportunity to hear and believe the gospel that unbelieving Israel rejected.

Do the promises of Romans 11:26 and 27, which speak of the Deliverer that shall come out of Zion and of His covenant, apply to the future salvation of the nation of Israel?

The promise, "There shall come out of Sion [Zion] the Deliverer, and shall turn away ungodliness from Jacob" (11:26), is a quotation from Isaiah 59:20: "And the Redeemer shall come to Zion, and unto them that turn from transgression in Jacob, saith the Lord." It cannot possibly refer to Jesus' coming as a future deliverer to the Jews, as many assume, because He already fulfilled this prophecy in His first coming. "God according to his promise *raised unto Israel a Saviour* [Greek, deliverer], Jesus" (Acts 13:23); "The God of our fathers raised up Jesus, whom ye slew and hanged on a tree. Him hath God exalted with his right hand to be a Prince and a *Saviour*, for to give *repentance to Israel*, and forgiveness of sins" (Acts 5:30,31); "Unto you first [Israel] God, having raised up his Son Jesus, sent him to bless you, in *turning* away every one of you from his iniquities" (Acts 3:26).

Concerning "Sion," God declares to the Church (whether Jew or Gentile), "But ye are come unto *mount Sion*, and unto the city of the living God, the heavenly Jerusalem" (Heb. 12:22). Scripture contrasts natural Israel, who reject Jesus the "chief corner stone" in "Sion," and spiritual Israel (the Church), who receive Him and become a "holy nation: . . . the people of God." "Behold, I lay in *Sion* a chief corner stone, elect, precious: and he that believeth on him shall not be confounded. Unto you therefore which believe he is precious: but unto them which be disobedient, the stone which the builders disallowed, the same is made the head of the corner. And a stone of stumbling, and a rock of offence, even to them which stumble at the word, being disobedient: whereunto also they were appointed. But ye are a chosen generation, a royal priesthood, an holy nation, a peculiar people, that ye should shew forth the praises of him who hath called you out of darkness into his marvellous light: Which in time past were not a people, but are now the people of God: which had not obtained mercy, but now have obtained mercy" (1 Pet. 2:6-10).

The promise, "For this is my *covenant* unto them, when I shall take away their sins" (Rom. 11:27) has also been fulfilled by the first coming of Jesus and is *now* a reality for believing Jews and Gentiles—the Church. "This is the *covenant* that I will make with them after those days, saith the Lord, I will put my laws into their hearts, and in their minds will I write them; and their sins and iniquities will I remember no more. Now where remission of these is, there is no more offering for sin. Having therefore, brethren, boldness to enter into the holiest by the blood of Jesus . . . . Let us draw near with a true heart in full assurance of faith" (Heb. 10:16-18,22). See also Jer. 31:31-34; Matt. 26:27,28; 1 Cor. 11:25; 2 Cor. 3:6. The Gentiles who were "strangers from *the covenants* of promise" are now "made nigh by the blood of Christ" (Eph. 2:12,13).

Since Christ has already come as Deliverer and has given the Church His new covenant, the promises of Romans 11:26 and 27 apply to the present salvation of Jews and Gentiles, not to the future salvation of the nation of Israel.

Are there other Old Testament prophecies to Israel that have been fulfilled in the Church?

Yes. They include the following ten prophecies:

1. The "seed" in which all nations shall be blessed (Gen. 22:18) is fulfilled in Christ (Gal. 3:16,29) and in the Gentiles receiving the gospel by faith (Gal. 3:7-9).

2. The "Prince of Peace" of Isaiah 9:6 and Micah 5:5 is fulfilled in Jesus Christ because "he is our *peace*, who hath made both one [believing Jews and Gentiles], and hath broken down the middle wall of partition between us; . . . for to make in himself of twain [two] one new man, so making *peace*; and that he might reconcile both unto God in one body by the cross, having slain the enmity thereby" (Eph. 2:14-18).

3. The enlargement of Zion's tent (Isa. 12:6; 54:1-3; Zeph. 3:14) is fulfilled in the conversion of the Gentiles (Gal. 4:27,28).

4. Zion's "corner stone" (Isa. 28:16) is fulfilled in Jesus Christ Himself "in whom all the building fitly framed together groweth unto an holy temple in the Lord: In whom ye also are builded together for an habitation of God through the Spirit" (Eph. 2:20,21). Thus, the earthly temple in Jerusalem is replaced

by the spiritual temple of believing Jews and Gentiles. See also 1 Cor. 3:16,17; 6:19,20; 1 Pet. 2:5 and Chapter Twenty-three.

5. The water that God promised to pour upon Jacob's offspring (Isa. 44:3; 12:3) is fulfilled by the outpouring of the Holy Spirit upon believers (John 7:37-39), both Jew (Acts 2:36-38) and Gentile (Acts 10:44,45).

6. The raising up of the tribes of Jacob (Isa. 49:6) is fulfilled when the gospel is preached to the Gentiles (Acts 13:47).

7. The giving of "peace to him that is far off, and to him that is near" (Isa. 57:19) is also fulfilled in Jesus Christ who "came and preached *peace* to you which were afar off, and to them that were nigh. For through him we both [believing Jews and Gentiles] have access by one Spirit unto the Father" (Eph. 2:17,18).

8. "My people" (Hos. 1:9,10; 2:23) is fulfilled in whom the Lord calls "not of the Jews only [the remnant], but also of the Gentiles." Together these comprise "the children of the living God"—the Church (Rom. 9:24-27; 1 Pet. 2:10).

9. The restoration of "the tabernacle of David" (Amos 9:11,12) is fulfilled in God's visiting the Gentiles "to take out of them a people for his name" (Acts 15:13-17).

10. The offering up of "incense" and "a pure offering" (Mal. 1:11) by the "sons of Levi" (Mal. 3:3) is fulfilled in the "holy priesthood" of believers whose prayers are as incense and who "offer up spiritual sacrifices, acceptable to God by Jesus Christ" (1 Pet. 2:5; Rev. 8:3; Rom. 15:16). See also Chapter Twenty-three.

Since these Old Testament prophecies have been fulfilled in the Church, they confirm that the Church is spiritual Israel. Therefore, they should not be taken to imply the future salvation of Israel.

Is Romans 11:29, "For the gifts and calling of God are without repentance," a promise that all Israel will be saved?

This verse cannot mean that all Israel will be saved because the context clearly refers to:

- Only a remnant being saved "according to the election of grace" (11:5,7).
- The salvation of "some of them" (11:14).

- Jews who will be saved on the condition—"if they abide not still in unbelief" (11:23).

Romans 11:29 does mean, however, that although some do not believe, God has not changed His mind about His gifts and calling that have come as a result of the redeeming work of Jesus Christ. With longsuffering He waits for souls, even unbelieving Jews, to come to Him. Notice the part that believers have in leading unconverted Jews to Christ: "For as ye in times past have not believed God, yet have now obtained mercy through their unbelief: Even so, *have these also now not believed, that through your mercy they also may obtain mercy*" (Rom. 11:30,31). God's door of love and mercy is yet open for all who will come to Him. "O the depth of the riches both of the wisdom and knowledge of God! How unsearchable are his judgments, and his ways past finding out!" (Rom. 11:33).

What is "the hope of Israel" (Acts 28:20)?

According to Paul's teaching, the hope of Israel that God promised is Jesus and the resurrection of the dead. (Compare Acts 28:20 with 23:6; 24:15,21; 26:6-8.) It can be attained by repenting and turning to Him. (Compare Acts 26:6-8 with 26:20-23; 28:20 with 28:23.)

Notice that Paul connects this hope with the Church and God's grace: "There is one body [the Church], and one Spirit, even as ye are called in *one hope* of your calling. . . . But unto every one of us is given *grace* according to the measure of *the gift of Christ*" (Eph. 4:4,7).

Since there is only one body and one hope, the hope of Israel is the same as the hope of the Church—"Christ in you, the hope of glory" (Col. 1:27), which is the blessed hope of His glorious appearing on resurrection day (Titus 1:13). See also 1 Pet. 1:2-4.

When will the remnant of Israel be saved?

God is saving the remnant of Israel now. Paul wrote, "Even so then *at this present time* also there is a remnant according to the election of grace" (Rom. 11:5). When addressing Jews at Antioch, Paul expected them to repent rather than to judge themselves "unworthy of everlasting life" (Acts 13:46).

The Bible teaches men to repent now, not to put it off until later: "*Now* [God] commandeth all men every where to repent" (Acts 17:30). "Behold, *now* is the accepted time; behold, *now* is the day of salvation" (2 Cor. 6:2).

What should be our attitude towards the Jews?

We should have the same Christ-like attitude toward them as we would have for any unsaved person. With tender compassion, we should pray and do all we can to win them to the Lord because His gospel "is the power of God unto salvation to every one that believeth; *to the Jew first*, and also to the Greek" (Rom. 1:16). God is "not willing that any should perish, but that all should come to repentance" (2 Pet. 3:9). Above all, we should not give the Jewish people the false hope that, as a nation, they will automatically be saved in the future.

Objections Answered

Doesn't the parable of the fig tree teach the restoration of the nation of Israel as a sign of the Second Coming of Christ and of her eventual salvation as a nation?

Not one Scripture verse shows that the fig tree represents Israel, as some suppose. God refers to Israel as His vineyard, which shall be trodden down because it brought forth wild grapes: "*O inhabitants of Jerusalem*, and *men of Judah*, judge, I pray you, betwixt me and my vineyard. What could have been done more to my vineyard, that I have not done in it? Wherefore, when I looked that it should bring forth grapes, brought it forth wild grapes? And now go to; I will tell you what I will do to *my vineyard*: I will take away the hedge thereof, and it shall be eaten up; and break down the wall thereof, and it shall be trodden down" (Isa. 5:3-5). See also Ezek. 19:10; Psa. 80:15,16; Matt. 21:33-44; Mark 12:1-12; Luke 20:9-18. Moreover, believing that the fig tree in Luke 21 represents Israel is inconsistent with Matthew 21:18-20 and Mark 11:12-14, passages in which Jesus cursed the fig tree.

An examination of the following scriptural truths will show

that the parable of the fig tree represents the signs of the last days and does not refer to Israel.

"And he spake to them a parable: Behold *the fig tree, and all the trees*; When they now shoot forth, ye see and know of your own selves that summer is now nigh at hand. So likewise ye, when ye see *these things* come to pass, know ye that the kingdom of God is nigh at hand. Verily I say unto you, This generation shall not pass away, till all be fulfilled" (Luke 21:29-32).

1. Jesus referred to trees in general, not just the fig tree. Notice that He said, "the fig tree, and all the trees."

2. Jesus mentioned several signs, not just one sign. He said, "When ye see *these things* come to pass" (the signs mentioned in the context), not "When you see this thing come to pass" (the single sign of the restoration of Israel). Jesus referred to the signs He had already given in the context, such as the appearance of false prophets and the occurrence of wars, earthquakes, famines, etc. See Matt. 24:3-29 and Luke 21:5-25.

3. Jesus said, "This generation shall not pass away, till all be fulfilled" (Luke 21:32; Matt. 24:34). We believe this means the generation that sees all the signs of His coming fulfilled is the generation that will see His return. Since more than a generation (forty years) has passed since Israel was declared a nation on May, 14, 1948, and since Christ has not yet returned, we know He was not referring to Israel's restoration. (Many are now awakening to this fact and are feeling disillusioned with a loss of confidence in their Bible teachers. How much sadder it would be to awaken to the truth about the Second Coming after receiving the mark of the beast!)

4. As a sign of His coming, Jesus foretold not the restoration of Israel but that "Jerusalem shall be trodden down of the Gentiles, until the times of the Gentiles be fulfilled" (Luke 21:24). The times of the Gentiles will be fulfilled when Jesus comes.

5. Jesus had already rejected the nation of Israel and had predicted the destruction of Jerusalem without making any mention of its restoration (Luke 19:41-44).

In summary, the parable of the fig tree is simply teaching this: just as the budding of trees in the springtime signifies that summer is near, so the fulfillment of the signs of the end-time indicates that the coming of our Lord Jesus is near.

Doesn't First Corinthians 10:32 teach that God has a separate plan of salvation for the Jews than for the Church?

This verse simply teaches believers not to offend the unsaved (whether Jews or Gentiles) and the saved (the church of God, which consists of Jewish and Gentile converts). "Give none offence, neither to the Jews, nor to the Gentiles, nor to the church of God" (1 Cor. 10:32).

God does not have a separate plan of salvation for the Jews. Paul wrote, "*For there is no difference between the Jew and the Greek*: for the same Lord over all is rich unto all that call upon him. For whosoever shall call upon the name of the Lord shall be saved" (Rom. 10:12,13).

Doesn't Zechariah 12:10, "They shall look upon me whom they have pierced, and they shall mourn for him," teach that all of Israel will be saved?

Some teach that when Jesus comes, the nation of Israel will look upon Him and mourn in repentance and thereby be saved. Here are seven reasons why that teaching is unscriptural:

1. Zechariah 12:10 was fulfilled at the crucifixion of Jesus: "For these things were done, that the scripture should be *fulfilled*, a bone of him shall not be broken. And again another scripture saith, *They shall look on him whom they pierced*" (John 19:36,37).

2. If Israel rejected Jesus when He came as Savior (Luke 19:14,27), they are not likely to receive Him when He comes as Judge.

3. Before Jesus comes, "All that dwell upon the earth shall worship him [the beast], whose names are not written in the book of life of the Lamb" (Rev. 13:8), and, consequently, "shall drink of the wine of the wrath of God" (Rev. 14:9,10) and "be damned" (2 Thess. 2:9-12). Jesus warned unbelieving Jews, "I am come in my Father's name, and ye receive me not: if another shall come in his own name, him ye will receive" (John 5:43). Therefore, what hope would Israel or any unbeliever have of being saved at Christ's return after the Tribulation?

4. According to the words of Jesus, when all the nations of the earth face the wrath of the Lamb, the mourning that will be heard will be that of anquish and fear, not of repentance. They will say to the mountains and rocks, "Fall on us, and hide us from the

face of him that sitteth on the throne, and from the wrath of the Lamb" (Rev. 6:16), and "all the tribes of the earth [shall] *mourn*, and they shall see the Son of man coming in the clouds of heaven with power and great glory" (Matt. 24:30). See also Zeph. 1:14-18.

5. As has been stated, not all Israel shall be saved, only a remnant (Rom. 9:27).

6. When Jesus comes, all Jews (and Gentiles) who rejected Him will be judged, not saved. "But after thy hardness and impenitent heart treasurest up unto thyself wrath against the day of wrath. . . . Tribulation and anguish, upon every soul of man that doeth evil, *of the Jew first*, and also of the Gentile. For there is no respect of persons with God" (Rom. 2:5,9-11). Examine the words of Jesus and the apostles: Matt. 8:11,12; 10:6,12-15; 12:41,42; 15:13,14; 21:31,32,44; 23:13-15,33; Luke 19:27; 20:18; Acts 3:22,23; 13:40,41,46,50,51; 18:6; 1 Thess. 2:14-16. Study the words of the Old Testament prophets: Isa. 2:6-12; 34:8; 65:1-15; Ezek. 13:5-8; Amos 5:17,18; Zeph. 1:12-18. See also Matt. 7:21,24-27. (The words "whosoever" and "everyone" include the Jews). Compare John 1:11 with 12:48; Rom. 10:19 with Deut. 32:20-29.

7. When Paul said, "If *any man* love not the Lord Jesus Christ, let him be Anathema Maranatha" (1 Cor. 16:22), he made no distinction between Jew and Gentile. Anathema means "accursed, condemned, devoted to destruction." Maranatha means "our Lord cometh or will come." Together they mean "let him be accursed—the Lord cometh." When Jesus comes, all who do not love Him will be accursed and will face the eternal wrath of God without measure.

The unprepared will have no second opportunity for salvation. "He that is unjust, let him be unjust still: and he which is filthy, let him be filthy still: and he that is righteous, let him be righteous still: and he that is holy, let him be holy still. And, behold I come quickly; and my reward is with me, to give *every man* according as his work shall be" (Rev. 22:11,12).

God clearly demonstrates His unfailing love and concern to save unconverted Jews because He sends forth His witnesses to preach to "the Jew first" (Rom. 1:16). The time to repent and get ready is *now*. When Jesus comes, it will be too late.

13

The Man of Sin

Who is the man of sin?

Scripture shows him to be one who will rule the world through deception, false miracles, and through the power of his image and of the number of his name (666) until he is destroyed by the brightness of the Second Coming of the Lord Jesus Christ. The apostle Paul called him "the son of perdition" and "that Wicked" (2 Thess. 2:3,8). In the Book of Revelation, he is called "the beast." It's evident that the terms "man of sin" and "the beast" are speaking of the same person because the Bible describes both as follows:

- receiving power from Satan (2 Thess. 2:9; Rev. 13:2,4)
- being lawless and wicked (2 Thess. 2:3,7,9; Rev. 16:13,14)
- deceiving with all power, signs, and lying wonders—witchcraft (2 Thess. 2:9; Rev. 13:14; 16:14; 19:20)
- being self-exalted to think he is God and is worthy to receive worship (2 Thess. 2:4; Rev. 13:4)
- being against the Lord Jesus Christ and His true followers (2 Thess. 2:4; Rev. 13:6,7-10,15; 17:14)
- speaking great things and blasphemies (2 Thess. 2:4; Rev. 13:5,6)
- being destroyed at the coming of Jesus (2 Thess. 2:8; Rev. 19:19,20)

How does the Bible contrast Christ and Antichrist?

Christ came from heaven (John 6:38); Antichrist will ascend out of the bottomless pit (Rev. 11:7).

Christ humbled Himself (Phil. 2:8); Antichrist will exalt himself (2 Thess. 2:4).

Christ was despised and rejected of men (Isa. 53:3); Antichrist will be worshiped by all (Rev. 13:3,4).

Christ is the truth (John 14:6); Antichrist will be a deceiver (2 Thess. 2:8-10).

Christ is sinless (2 Cor. 5:21); Antichrist is referred to as the man of sin (2 Thess. 2:3).

Christ is obedient to God, the Father (John 15:10); Antichrist will blaspheme God, the Father (Rev. 13:6).

Christ loves the Church (Eph. 5:25); Antichrist will war against the Church (Rev. 13:7).

Christ was God incarnate (John 1:1); Antichrist will be Satan incarnate (2 Thess. 2:9; Rev. 13:2-4).

Christ was received up into heaven (Mark 16:19); Antichrist will go down into perdition; he will be "cast alive into a lake of fire burning with brimstone" (Rev. 17:11; 19:20).

Will the Church be present during the reign of the man of sin?

Yes. The Bible plainly declares that:

1. The coming of the Lord, our gathering together unto him, and the Day of Christ are one event that cannot take place "except . . . that man of sin be revealed" (2 Thess. 2:1-3). Here, we see that the man of sin must be revealed before the Church is gathered.

2. The man of sin will not be revealed to the world, but to the Church. The world will be deceived by his lying wonders and will worship him to their own destruction (Rev. 13:3,4,7,8,15-18). See also Matt. 24:24 and 2 Thess. 2:9-12.

On the other hand, by the power of the Holy Spirit, those who love and obey the truth will recognize the man of sin as a deceiver and an Antichrist. They will resist him, his image, and his mark even to the point of losing their own lives. See also John 16:13; 2 Thess. 2:10-14; 1 John 2:20,27; 4:1-4; Rev. 15:2; 20:4.

3. The man of sin will "make war with the saints" (Rev. 13:7). See also Dan. 7:21,22.

4. When Jesus comes to gather His Church, the man of sin will be destroyed "with the brightness of his coming" (2 Thess. 2:8). See also Dan. 7:8-11. This leaves no doubt that the Church will be present during the reign of the man of sin.

Do the phrases in Second Thessalonians 2:6 and 7, "ye know what withholdeth" and "he be taken out of the way," inform us that the Church or the Holy Spirit must be removed before the man of sin can be revealed?

No, they do not. The Church is the Bride of Christ; therefore, in the Scripture, she is not referred to as "he" ("he be taken out of the way") but as "she," "her," or "herself." Consider, for example, Revelation 19:7 and 8: "The marriage of the Lamb is come, and his wife hath made *herself* ready. And to *her* was granted that *she* should be arrayed in fine linen, clean and white." See also Rom. 9:25.

Also, the Holy Spirit will be working through the Church until the end of the world in order to give wisdom in times of persecution (Mark 13:11,19), to seal the Church "unto the day of redemption" (Eph. 4:30), and to empower the Church to witness the gospel (Matt. 24:14; 28:19,20).

Moreover, these phrases ("ye know what withholdeth" and "until he be taken out of the way") do not refer to the Church or to the Holy Spirit because that would contradict other truths of the passage, particularly what we have already seen in Second Thessalonians 2:1-3: that the Church cannot be gathered until *after* the man of sin is revealed. Also, such an interpretation would contradict the teaching of verse eight, which shows that the man of sin will be *destroyed* with the brightness of Christ's coming to gather the Church. Therefore, the phrases "ye know what withholdeth" and "he be taken out of the way," do not refer to the Church or to the Holy Spirit.

What, then, is hindering the man of sin from being revealed?

The following scriptures speak of the Lord Jesus as being a restraining force against the powers of Satan, implying that He is presently hindering the man of sin from being revealed:

Jesus said, "But if I cast out devils by the Spirit of God, then the kingdom of God is come unto you. Or else how can one enter into a strong man's house, and spoil his goods, except he first bind the strong man? and then he will spoil his house" (Matt. 12:28,29). "When a strong man armed keepeth his palace, his goods are in peace: but when a stronger than he shall come upon him, and overcome him, he taketh from him all his armour wherein he trusted, and divideth his spoils" (Luke 11:21,22). See also Matt. 28:18; Luke 10:18,19.

Why will many be deceived by the man of sin?

Many will be deceived because they have not genuinely received Jesus: "I am come in my Father's name, and ye receive me not: if another shall come in his own name, him ye will receive" (John 5:43).

Deception also comes for many reasons:

When we do not love the truth—"Even him, whose coming is after the working of Satan with all power and signs and lying wonders, and with all deceivableness of unrighteousness in them that perish; because they received not the love of the truth, that they might be saved. And for this cause God shall send them strong delusion, that they should believe a lie: That they all might be damned who believed not the truth, but had pleasure in unrighteousness" (2 Thess. 2:9-12).

When we do not walk in the light of God's Word—"Walk while ye have the light, lest darkness come upon you: for he that walketh in darkness knoweth not whither he goeth" (John 12:35). "Be ye doers of the word, and not hearers only, deceiving your own selves" (James 1:22).

When we are unthankful—"Because that, when they knew God, they glorified him not as God, neither were thankful; but became vain in their imaginations, and their foolish heart was darkened. Professing themselves to be wise, they became fools" (Rom. 1:21,22).

"For man shall be lovers of their own selves . . . unthankful. . . . For of this sort are they which creep into houses, and lead captive silly women laden with sins, led away with divers lusts, ever learning, and never able to come to the knowledge of the truth. Now as Jannes and Jambres withstood Moses, so do these also resist the truth: men of corrupt minds, reprobate concerning the faith" (2 Tim. 3:2,6-8).

When we allow pride to fill our hearts—"The pride of thine heart hath deceived thee" (Obad. 3). "For if a man think himself to be something, when he is nothing, he deceiveth himself" (Gal. 6:3).

When we are materialistic—"Because thou sayest, I am rich, and increased with goods, and have need of nothing; and knowest not that thou art wretched, and miserable, and poor, and blind, and naked" (Rev. 3:17). See also Psa. 49:6; 52:7; 62:10; Pro. 11:28; Matt. 13:22; Luke 21:34; 1 Tim. 6:9,10.

When we allow ourselves to be guided by influences other than the Word of God—Paul wrote, "That ye be not soon shaken in mind, or be troubled, neither *by spirit*, nor *by word*, nor *by letter* as from us, as that the day of Christ is at hand. Let no man deceive you by any means. . . ." (2 Thess. 2:2,3). Misconceptions about the Second Coming will come through spirit (false spiritual impressions), word (what we've heard), or letter (what we've read). When we are influenced by feelings, revelations, visions, dreams, prophecies, or similar personal experiences that do *not* agree with the Word of God, then we know it's not from the Spirit of God, but from another spirit. The Spirit of God is "the Spirit of truth" (John 16:13); therefore, He will always agree with the Word of God (1 John 5:7). He guides us into all the truth of God's Word (John 16:13), not into revelations that contradict the Word.

Paul further cautioned us about seducing spirits. "Now the Spirit speaketh expressly, that in the latter times some shall depart from the faith, giving heed to seducing spirits, and doctrines of devils" (1 Tim. 4:1). He linked seducing spirits with doctrines of devils as a reason why men depart from the faith. That's why we should check out all subjective impressions and teachings with the objective truth of the Bible to keep from being deceived.

When we follow miracles and sensationalism instead of truth—The masses will be deceived into making and worshiping an image in honor of the beast because of "those miracles which he [the false prophet] had power to do" (Rev. 13:14). Scripture labels such miracles "lying wonders" (2 Thess. 2:9). Therefore, it is important to seek the truth, not miracles. Jesus said, "And ye shall know the truth, and the truth shall make you free" (John 8:32).

When we hold to the traditions of men instead of God's Word—Multitudes are being deceived by this seemingly innocent practice of following the traditions of men that are upheld by their church or denomination. *Before* his conversion, the apostle Paul was deceived to think he was doing right by "being more exceedingly zealous of the traditions of [his] fathers" (Gal. 1:14). After his conversion, however, he realized his ignorance and unbelief (1 Tim. 1:13), denounced the traditions of men (Col. 2:8), and declared that the gospel he preached was "not after man" nor received "of man," but by the revelation of Jesus Christ (Gal. 1:11,12).

Moreover, Paul never taught believers to keep the unscriptural traditions of men but to "keep the ordinances [Greek, traditions]" that he "received of the Lord." (Compare 1 Cor. 11:2 with 11:23.) These traditions were in accordance with the gospel of the grace of God; therefore, he gave them "in the name of our Lord Jesus Christ" (2 Thess. 2:14-16; 3:6). See Chapter Fourteen.

When we fail to heed our Lord's warnings to "beware of false prophets" (Matt. 7:15)—"Take heed that no man *deceive* you. For many shall come in my name, saying, I am Christ: and shall *deceive* many. . . . And many false prophets shall rise, and shall *deceive* many. . . . For there shall arise false Christs, and false prophets, and shall show great signs and wonders; insomuch that, if it were possible, they shall *deceive* the very elect" (Matt. 24:4,5,11,24). "Beloved, believe not every spirit, but try the spirits whether they are of God: because many false prophets are gone out into the world" (1 John 4:1).

Doesn't Acts 2:17 teach that before Jesus returns there will be a great worldwide revival with God pouring out His Spirit on "all flesh"?

Acts 2:17 reads, "And it shall come to pass in the last days, saith God, I will pour out of my Spirit upon *all flesh*: and your sons and your daughters shall prophesy, and your young men shall see visions, and your old men shall dream dreams." On the basis of this one verse, many claim that a great, worldwide revival will occur before Jesus comes. They stress that God will pour out His Spirit on "all flesh" regardless of one's spiritual condition. We will see, however, that the term "all flesh" means all who are genuinely saved and obeying God's Word. We will also see that the New Testament describes worldwide apostasy and deception in the last days rather than worldwide turning to God.

To begin with, the next verse (Acts 2:18) specifically tells us that God will pour out His Spirit upon His servants and handmaidens, that is, upon His sons and daughters. Scripturally, who are God's sons and daughters? We become the children of God by placing our faith in Christ Jesus (Gal. 3:26); by receiving Him (John 1:12); by mortifying the deeds of the body through the Spirit and being led by the Spirit of God (Rom. 8:13,14); by doing the will of the Father (Matt. 12:50); and by coming out from among unbelievers and idolaters (2 Cor. 6:17,18).

Moreover, Jesus taught that the unregenerate in heart cannot receive the Holy Spirit. He said to His disciples, "If ye love me, keep my commandments. And I will pray the Father, and he shall give you another Comforter, that he may abide with you for ever; even the Spirit of truth; *whom the world cannot receive*, because it seeth him not, neither knoweth him: but ye know him; for he dwelleth with you, and shall be in you" (John 14:15-17). Here Jesus made a distinction: "the world cannot receive" the Spirit of truth, only those who have seen Him and known Him. In other words, to receive the Holy Spirit one must first experience His convicting and regenerating power with the evidence of loving Jesus and keeping His commandments.

Jesus further emphasized this truth, "He that hath my commandments, and keepeth them, he it is that loveth me: and he that loveth me shall be loved of my Father, and I will love him, and will manifest myself to him. Judas saith unto him, not Iscariot, Lord, how is it that thou wilt manifest thyself unto us, and *not unto the world*? Jesus answered and said unto him, If a man love me, he will keep my words: and my Father will love him, and we will come unto him, and make our abode with him" (John 14:21-23).

Peter said that God gives His Spirit to those who obey Him (Acts 5:32). Cornelius and his household are examples of those who received the Holy Spirit *after* they heard the true gospel, repented of their sins, and believed on the Lord Jesus (Acts 11:14-18). Thus, God's promise to pour out His Spirit on all flesh refers to all who repent and obey His Word, whether Jew or Gentile, male or female. He has not promised to indiscriminately pour out His Spirit on all.

In addition, the New Testament describes worldwide apostasy and deception in the last days, not worldwide revival. In the light of increasing wickedness that is flooding the world through godless educational systems, humanism, witchcraft, rock and roll music, pornography, television, video, and religious apostasy—revival is desperately needed! More than ever, we should be on our faces crying out to God for His truth and mercy to prevail. To see souls genuinely converted to the Lord, we should follow the example of the early church. They continued "steadfastly in the apostles' doctrine and fellowship, and in breaking of bread, and in prayers. . . . And the Lord added to the church daily such as should be saved" (Acts 2:42,47). When writing to Timothy, Paul associated the salvation of souls with holy living and continuing in pure doctrine: "Take heed unto thyself, and unto the doctrine; continue in them: for in doing this thou shalt both save thyself, and them that hear thee" (1 Tim. 4:16).

When God's conditions for revival are met, He will surely send revival in local situations, but one fails to find scripture to support the claim of worldwide revival in the last days. When foretelling the signs of His coming and of the end of the world, Jesus declared that many shall be offended, that many shall be deceived by false prophets, and that many shall "wax cold" in their love toward Him. The generation that sees His return will experience great tribulation such as the world has never known (Matt. 24:10-12,22,24). Jesus asked, "When the Son of man cometh, shall he find faith on the earth?" (Luke 18:8). His question implies that there will not be worldwide revival.

Similarly, Paul tells us that in the last days:

- There will come "a falling away" (2 Thess. 2:3).
- "Some shall depart from the faith, giving heed to seducing spirits, and doctrines of devils" (1 Tim. 4:1).
- "Men shall be lovers of their own selves. . . . having a form of godliness, but denying the power thereof" (2 Tim. 3:1-5).
- Men "will not endure sound doctrine" (2 Tim. 4:3).
- "They shall turn away their ears from the truth" (2 Tim. 4:4).
- They "shall be turned unto fables" (2 Tim. 4:4).
- They will be deceived by the man of sin and his "lying wonders," because "they received not the love of the truth, that they might be saved" (2 Thess. 2:3,9,10).

In fact, the deception will be so worldwide that all who "dwell upon the earth shall worship him [the man of sin], whose names are not written in the book of life" (Rev. 13:8). It is obvious, then, that the New Testament describes worldwide apostasy and deception in the last days rather than worldwide turning to God.

Since, as never before, many are claiming to be filled with the Holy Spirit, isn't there a worldwide revival already in progress?

Not necessarily. Scripture shows that not all who cry "Lord, Lord" are genuinely Spirit-filled believers (Matt. 7:21,22). We have already seen that in the last days, many will have only "a form of godliness" (2 Tim. 3:5). They will profess that they know God, but their conduct will show that they deny Him (Titus 1:16). Moreover they will give attention to seducing, unclean spirits, which are the spirits of devils (1 Tim. 4:1; Rev. 16:13,14).

Just as there is "the spirit of truth, and the spirit of error" (1 John 4:6), so there are true believers and false believers; true revival movements and false revival movements. Therefore, we are admonished to "believe not every spirit, but try the spirits whether they are of God: because many false prophets are gone out into the world" (1 John 4:1). How are we to try the spirits? Since the Holy Spirit agrees with and will never violate Scripture, we must try the spirits by the Word of God.

When the following unscriptural conditions exist among those who claim to be Spirit-filled, we know that seducing spirits are working, not the Holy Spirit.

1. When church leaders stress that God will pour out His Spirit on "all flesh," but fail to preach true repentance and salvation through faith in Jesus Christ—Jesus specifically told us to whom He will give His Spirit:

- to those who know the Holy Spirit (John 14:17), which speaks of first experiencing the convicting power of the Spirit and regeneration of heart (John 3:3,5; 16:8; Titus 3:5)
- to those who love Him and keep His commandments (John 14:15,16)
- to those who repent (Acts 2:38)
- to those who believe on Him (John 7:38,39)
- to those who are His sons and daughters (Acts 2:18)
- to those who obey God (Acts 5:32)

2. *When anyone else but Jesus is exalted or glorified*—The Holy Spirit will never glorify Mary, the saints, or any man or woman, only the Lord Jesus Christ. He Himself said that "the Spirit of truth . . . shall testify of me" (John 15:26) and "shall glorify me" (John 16:14).

3. *When there is compromise with sin, the traditions of men, idolatry, false doctrines, and lying wonders*—The Bible associates sin with the devil (1 John 3:8); the traditions of men with worshiping God in vain and making His Word void (Mark 7:7,13); idolatry with devils (1 Cor. 10:19-21); false doctrines with seducing spirits (1 Tim. 4:1); and lying wonders with the spirits of devils (Rev. 16:14; 2 Thess. 2:9).

4. *When "fun ways" are used to present the gospel such as clowns, drama, comedians, and puppets*—The Bible warns believers that foolish talking and jesting should not be once named among us and that they who do such things shall not inherit the kingdom of God (Eph. 5:3-5). Jesus and the apostles did not once use drama to present the gospel even though the theater was popular throughout the ancient world. Moreover, the apostle Paul preached "not with enticing words of man's wisdom, but in demonstration of the Spirit and of power" (1 Cor. 2:4).

When the gospel is preached, God sends His Spirit to save souls and sanctify the Church. With regard to this truth, He specifically commands believers to lay aside all deceit and play-acting. "But the word of the Lord endureth forever. And this is the word which by the gospel is preached unto you. Wherefore laying aside all malice, and all guile [deceit], and hypocrisies [Greek, acting under a feigned part], . . . as newborn babes, desire the sincere milk of the word, that ye may grow thereby" (1 Pet. 1:25; 2:1,2).

In addition, deceit and hypocrisy are characteristic of Satan. He is able to transform (Greek, disguise or masquerade) himself into an angel of light (2 Cor. 11:14). Therefore, play-acting should have no part in presenting the gospel. It gives place for seducing spirits to work deceit in the churches and prepares the way for the man of sin who will pretend that he is God and deceive the nations.

5. *When "love and unity through signs and wonders" or "love and unity through the Spirit" are emphasized rather than "unity*

through the truth and the Spirit"—Scripture shows that the Holy Spirit and the Word of God are inseparable and always agree:

- The Holy Spirit is the Spirit of truth who guides us into all truth (John 16:13; 1 John 2:27).
- The sword of the Spirit is the Word of God (Eph. 6:17).
- Souls are born again by obeying the truth through the Spirit (1 Pet. 1:22,23).
- They who worship God "must worship him in spirit and in truth" (John 4:24).
- God sends His Spirit when His truth is preached and obeyed (Acts 2:38; 5:32; 11:14-18).
- Those who are filled with the Spirit are zealous for the truth. They love the truth, are led into all truth, obey the truth, and speak the truth (Acts 1:8; 6:10).

Therefore, to emphasize unity through the Spirit and the miraculous without the emphasis on truth is unscriptural and deceitful.

6. *When emotionalism, personal prophecies, visions, dreams, personal experiences, and signs and wonders are maximized, but true salvation is minimized*—Jesus warned that many who did wonderful works will be rejected at His coming because they did not obey His Word. "Many will say to me in that day, Lord, Lord, have we not prophesied in thy name? and in thy name have cast out devils? and in thy name done many wonderful works? And then will I profess unto them, I never knew you: depart from me, ye that work iniquity. Therefore, whosoever *heareth* these sayings of mine, and *doeth* them, I will liken him unto a wise man, which built his house upon a rock" (Matt. 7:22-24).

He also taught that the test of genuine salvation is twofold: a practical test of conduct and a doctrinal test.

- A practical test of conduct (John 8:30,42,44)—In His response to Jews who "believed on him" (v. 30) but showed by their conduct that they were *not* true believers, Jesus said, "If God were your Father, ye would love me: . . . Ye are of your father the devil, and the lusts of your father ye will do. He was a murderer from the beginning, and abode not in the truth, because there is no truth in him. When he speaketh a lie, he speaketh of his own: for he is a liar, and the father of it."
- A doctrinal test (John 8:43,46,47)—These Jews also showed

they were *not* true believers by their resistance to God's Word. Jesus said to them, "Why do ye not understand my speech? even because ye cannot hear my word. . . . And if I say the truth, why do ye not believe me? He that is of God heareth God's words: ye therefore hear them not, because ye are not of God." (Practical and doctrinal tests of conversion are further seen in 1 John 1:6; 2:3-6; 3:6-8; 2 John 1:9.) These Jews claimed to be believers, but showed by their conduct and their resistance to God's Word that they did not have genuine salvation. Likewise, many may claim to be saved and Spirit-filled, but if their conduct is unchristian and they have no desire for God's Word, they show that their experience is not genuine.

How is the great falling away affecting churches today?

Sadly, many churches lack the spirit of prayer, the fear of the Lord, true revival, and the strong preaching of the Word to lift up a standard of holiness before the people. Having forsaken the Lord, "the fountain of living waters," they have "hewed them out cisterns, broken cisterns, that can hold no water" (Jer. 2:13). Churches are exchanging:

Separation from the world for conformity to the world
Self-denial for self-indulgence
The joy of the Lord for entertainment
Repentance for "easy believism"
An experience of salvation for mere water baptism
The Word of God for the tradition of men
Their names written in heaven for their names on a church roll
Glorying in the Lord for glorying in men
Holy Spirit revival for fleshly excitement
Glorifying God with praise for glorifying men with applause
The preaching of the Word for films and drama
The wisdom of God for modern psychology
The fear of God for the fear of men
The moral absolutes of God's Word for secular humanism
The upper room for the supper room
Sound doctrine for love and unity
Quality for quantity (crowds)
Spiritual songs for music with Satan's beat
The reproach of Christ for acceptance by the world

Standing alone on truth for ecumenical compromise
The power of God for a form of godliness
A spirit of prayer for a spirit of covetousness
A heavenly vision for television

When will the man of sin be destroyed?

The man of sin will be destroyed:

When Jesus returns to gather His Church—"That Wicked . . . whom the Lord shall consume with the spirit of his mouth, and shall destroy with the brightness of his coming" (2 Thess. 2:8).

At the battle of Armageddon—"And the beast was taken, and with him the false prophet. . . . These both were cast alive into a lake of fire burning with brimstone" (Rev. 19:20).

At the throne judgment when "the books [are] opened"—"A fiery stream issued and came forth from before him: thousand thousands ministered unto him, and ten thousand times ten thousand stood before him: the judgment was set, and the books were opened. I beheld then because of the voice of the great words which the horn spake: I beheld even till the beast was slain, and his body destroyed, and given to the burning flame" (Dan. 7:10,11).

At the end of the world—"The Son of man shall send forth his angels, and they shall gather out of his kingdom all things that offend, and them which do iniquity [this would include the beast and the false prophet]; and shall cast them into a furnace of fire: there shall be wailing and gnashing of teeth" (Matt. 13:41,42).

Not only will the man of sin be cast into a lake of fire, but those who worship him and his image and receive the mark of his name on their forehead or hand will share a similar fate (Rev. 14:9-11). Because our eternal destinies are at stake, we must receive the love of the truth. Our only hope is to obey the gospel (2 Thess. 2:13), which involves repentance and submission to the will of God. We must also put away all sin and worldliness from our lives (1 John 2:15-17).

14

The False Prophet

Who is the second beast in Revelation 13:11?

He is called the false prophet and is described as having "two horns like a lamb" and speaking "as a dragon" (Rev. 13:11; 19:20). Throughout the Book of Revelation, Christ is portrayed as the Lamb. No doubt the false prophet will come as a lamb in the name of Christ to deceive the masses, but when he speaks, we will know by his words that he is sent by Satan, the dragon.

He exercises "all the power of the first beast" and causes "the earth and them which dwell therein to worship the first beast" (Rev. 13:12). More than likely, he will be a leader in the apostate world church, Babylon, since he has much influence on the masses and works hand in hand with the beast.

Moreover, by the power of unclean demonic spirits, he will do "great wonders, so that he maketh fire come down from heaven on the earth in the sight of men" (Rev. 13:13; 16:13,14). He will deceive "them that dwell on the earth by the means of those miracles which he had power to do in the sight of the beast; saying to them . . . that they should make an image to the beast" (Rev. 13:14).

The false prophet will also have "power to give life unto the image of the beast, that the image of the beast should both speak" and he will "cause that as many as would not worship the image of the beast should be killed" (Rev. 13:15). Together with the beast, his aim will be the destruction of those who "keep the commandments of God and the faith of Jesus" (Rev. 14:12).

In addition, he will cause "all, both small and great, rich and poor, free and bond, to receive a mark in their right hand, or in their foreheads: And that, no man might buy or sell, save he that had the mark, or the name of the beast, or the number of his name" (Rev. 13:16; 19:20). Christians will resist this pressure even though it will cost many of them their lives (Rev. 15:2).

Finally, he will be instrumental in deceiving and gathering the kings of the earth to the battle of Armageddon in which he will be defeated by our Lord Jesus Christ and be cast alive into the lake of fire (Rev. 16:13,14; 19:19,20).

What are the marks of false prophets?

Since the rise of false prophets is a clear sign of the end-time, the Church should know what marks them. False prophets, however, are not easily detected because they're deceitful workers sent by Satan who have transformed themselves into "apostles of Christ" and "ministers of righteousness" (2 Cor. 11:13-15). Usually, they preach just enough gospel to convince most of their hearers that they love the truth. They are influenced by evil spirits and often practice divination and sorcery in the guise of Christianity and spiritual gifts (1 Kings 22:21,22; Jer. 14:14; Ezek. 22:28; Acts 13:6; Rev. 16:13,14; 18:23). Jesus said, "Beware of false prophets, which come to you in sheep's clothing, but inwardly they are ravening wolves" (Matt. 7:15). If false prophets are cleverly disguised, how can we know them? Jesus continued, "Ye shall know them by their fruits. Do men gather grapes of thorns, or figs of thistles? Even so every good tree bringeth forth good fruit; but a corrupt tree bringeth forth evil fruit" (Matt. 7:16,17).

We can detect false prophets by the following traits:

They exalt themselves. They love the praise of men more than the praise of God. Jesus said, "All their works they do for to be seen of men" (Matt. 23:5). They love the seats of honor and being called by flattering titles (Matt. 23:6,7). The man of sin will exalt "himself above all that is called God, or that is worshipped" (2 Thess. 2:4). On the other hand, Jesus, our example, is meek and lowly of heart (Matt. 11:29). John wrote, "He that saith he abideth in him ought himself also so to walk, even as he walked" (1 John 2:6). See also Luke 16:15; John 5:44; 2 Cor.11:20; 1 Tim. 6:3,4; Pro. 25:27; Jer. 45:5.

They love money. Jesus rebuked religious leaders who "devour widow's houses" and "are full of extortion and excess" (Matt. 23:14,25). In addition, Peter warned of false prophets and false teachers who "through covetousness . . . with feigned words make merchandise of you" (2 Pet. 2:3). See also Isa. 56:11; Jer.

5:26-31; 8:10; Ezek. 13:19; 22:25; 33:31; Micah 3:11; Acts 20:29-35; Titus 1:11; Jude 1:11.

They work lying signs and miracles. True miracles from God confirm His Word and draw people to Christ, but false miracles from Satan exalt man and deceive the masses. A true servant will give God all the glory for His works and keep himself free from the love of money and the praise of men. He will also emphasize the Word of God and holy living, not miracles. But a false prophet will capitalize on miracles to deceive, to glorify self, and to get rich. See Matt. 24:24; 2 Thess. 2:9-12; Rev. 13:14; 18:23.

They pretend to be sent by God but speak lies. God says, "Behold, I am against the prophets, saith the Lord, that use their tongues, and say, He saith. Behold, I am against them that prophesy false dreams, saith the Lord, and do tell them, and cause my people to err by their lies, and by their lightness; yet I sent them not, nor commanded them: therefore they shall not profit this people at all, saith the Lord" (Jer. 23:31,32).

The New Testament warns about false prophets and false teachers who "bring in damnable heresies" (2 Pet. 2:1) and who speak "lies in hypocrisy; having their conscience seared with a hot iron" (1 Tim. 4:2). Only as we know the truth are we able to detect and to confound the lies of false prophets. See also Titus 1:10-14; Jude 1:3,4.

They cry, "Peace, peace; when there is no peace" (Jer. 8:11). "They say still unto them that despise me, The Lord hath said, Ye shall have peace; and they say unto every one that walketh after the imagination of his own heart, no evil shall come upon you" (Jer. 23:17). They'll deceive many by saying, "The world is not going to be destroyed in a sudden onslaught of bloodletting and catastrophe as today's doom-criers predict. Glorious days lie ahead—a golden age of prosperity and peace." Beware! "For when they shall say, Peace and safety; then sudden destruction cometh. . . ." (1 Thess. 5:3). See also Jer. 6:14; Ezek. 13:10.

They prophesy in the name of the Lord prophecies that do not come to pass. "And if thou say in thine heart, How shall we know the word which the Lord hath not spoken? When a prophet speaketh in the name of the Lord, if the thing follow not, nor come to pass, that is the thing which the Lord hath not spoken, but the prophet hath spoken it presumptuously: thou shalt not be afraid of him"

(Deut. 18:21,22). Deuteronomy 13:1,2 further warns that if whatever a prophet says comes to pass, but his life influences us away from God, then we are not to follow him. See also Jer. 23:16,26; Ezek. 13:1-16.

They do not follow the example of our Lord Jesus Christ and the apostles. "There shall be false teachers among you. . . . that walk after the flesh in the lust of uncleanness" (2 Pet. 2:1,10).

Paul cautioned, "Brethren, be followers together of me, and mark them which walk so as ye have us for an ensample. (For many walk, of whom I have told you often, and now tell you even weeping, that they are the enemies of the cross of Christ: Whose end is destruction, whose God is their belly, and whose glory is in their shame, who mind earthly things)" (Phil. 3:17-19).

They practice phariseeism. Pharisaical leaders are spiritually blind (Matt. 15:14). The Bible describes them as being unrepentant (Matt. 21:31,32); self-righteous (Luke 18:9-12); covetous, proud, and hateful (Luke 16:14); easily offended by the truth (Matt. 15:12); outwardly moral and inwardly wicked (Matt. 23:27); unconcerned for the salvation of sinners (Luke 7:39); oppressive (Matt. 23:4); envious (Acts 17:5); inconsistent (Matt. 23:24); cruel in persecuting (Matt. 23:34); unforgiving toward others (John 8:3-11); crafty (Luke 20:20-26); critical of others (Luke 15:2); and lacking in love and mercy (Matt. 23:23; Luke 11:42).

They also love the praise of men (Matt. 23:6,7; John 12:42,43); do not enter the kingdom and hinder those who would go in (Matt. 23:13); lay heavy burdens that are too grievous to be borne on men's shoulders (Matt. 23:4); and pray and fast to be seen of others (Matt. 6:5,16).

Jesus warned that Pharisees "compass sea and land to make one proselyte, and when he is made, [they] make him *twofold more the child of hell* than [themselves]" (Matt. 23:15).

They hold to the traditions of men. Following those who hold to the traditions of men will spoil our faith, trouble us, remove us from Christ, pervert the gospel of Christ, and lead us into the ditch—hell. "Beware lest any man *spoil* you through philosophy and vain deceit, after *the tradition of men*, after the rudiments of the world, and not after Christ" (Col. 2:8). Paul wrote to the saints at Galatia, "I marvel that ye are so soon *removed from him* [the Lord Jesus] that called you into the grace of Christ unto another gospel: which is not another; but there be some that *trouble you*, and would *pervert the gospel of Christ.* But though we, or an angel from heaven, preach any other gospel unto you than that which we have preached unto you, let him be accursed. . . . For do I now persuade *men*, or God? or do I seek to please *men*? for if I yet pleased *men*, I should not be the servant of Christ. But I certify you, brethren, that the gospel which was preached of me *is not after man.* For I neither received it of *men*, neither was I taught it, but by the revelation of Jesus Christ" (Gal. 1:6-8,10-12). With reference to those who were steeped in traditionalism, Jesus said, "Every plant, which my heavenly Father hath not planted, shall be rooted up. Let them alone: they be blind leaders of the blind. And if the blind lead the blind, both shall *fall into the ditch*" (Matt. 15:13,14).

In summary, false prophets:

1. Exalt themselves
2. Love money
3. Work lying signs and wonders
4. Pretend to be sent by God but speak lies
5. Cry, "Peace, peace; when there is no peace" (Jer. 8:11)
6. Prophesy in the name of the Lord prophecies that do not come to pass
7. Do not follow the example of our Lord Jesus Christ and the apostles
8. Practice phariseeism
9. Hold to the traditions of men

What else does the Bible say about the harmful effects of holding to the traditions of men?

By traditions of men, we mean those doctrines or teachings that are not consistent with the overall teaching of the Word of God. Instead of stressing the importance of God's Word, many today emphasize that we should hold to the traditions of the historic church. This emphasis, instead of giving priority to God's written Word, is leaven that gradually works to deceive many into accepting false religion, which prepares the way for the Antichrist and the false prophet.

By holding to the traditions of men, we also "transgress [go con-

trary to, violate] the commandment of God" (Matt. 15:3). The Pharisees asked Jesus, "Why do thy disciples transgress the tradition of the elders? For they wash not their hands when they eat bread." Jesus answered, "Why do ye also *transgress* the commandment of God by your tradition?" (Matt. 15:2,3). Although it seemed innocent enough, and practical, Jesus and His disciples refused to succumb to this tradition. Since it was not a command of God, they knew it should *not have been imposed on others.*

Moreover, they saw in the lives of the Pharisees the evil effects of keeping this tradition, such as spiritual pride, self-righteousness, and a critical spirit. These effects, in turn, resulted in the Pharisees' transgressing some definite commands of God. By their spiritual pride, they transgressed the command, "*Humble* yourselves in the sight of the Lord" (James 4:10). By their self-righteousness, they transgressed the command, "Purify your *hearts*" (James 4:8). Jesus plainly declared, "Not that which goeth into the mouth [the germs from unwashed hands] defileth a man; but that which cometh out of the mouth [that which is in *the heart*: evil thoughts, murders, adulteries, fornications, thefts, false witness and blasphemies] this defileth a man" (Matt. 15: 11,18,19). "Cleanse first that which is *within* the cup and platter, that the outside of them may be clean also" (Matt. 23:26). In addition, by criticizing the disciples for not complying with their tradition of the washing of hands, the Pharisees transgressed God's Word, which tells us "What God hath cleansed, that call not thou common [or unclean]" (Acts 10:28; 11:9).

By holding to the traditions of men, not only do we transgress the commandment of God, but we lay it aside, make it void, reject it, turn from it, and add to it. As long as the Pharisees were walking "according to the tradition of the elders" and imposing their tradition on others, they were "teaching for doctrines the commandments of men," not the commandments of God (Mark 7:5,7). Jesus strongly rebuked them. Notice what He said they were doing to His precious Word: "For *laying aside* the commandment of God, ye hold the tradition of men" (7:8); "Making the word of God of *none effect* through your tradition" (7:13); and "*Full well ye reject* the commandment of God, that ye may keep your own tradition" (7:9).

Paul warned that the commandments of men turn us from the

truth: "Not giving heed to Jewish fables, and commandments of men, that *turn from the truth*" (Titus 1:14).

Moreover, we add to God's Word when we keep our traditions. We minimize the importance of the Bible because we infer that it is incomplete and therefore insufficient to guide us in the right way—thus, we must add our traditions. Serious consequences await those who add or take away from God's Word: "For I testify unto every man that heareth the words of the prophecy of this book, If any man shall *add* unto these things, God shall *add unto him the plagues* that are written in this book" (Rev. 22:18). "And if any man shall *take away* from the words of the book of this prophecy, God shall *take away his part out the book of life*, and out of the holy city, and from the things which are written in this book" (Rev. 22:19). "Every word of God is pure. . . . *Add* thou not unto his words, lest he reprove thee, and thou shalt be found a liar" (Pro. 30:5,6).

By holding to the traditions of men, we become hypocritical and our worship to God is in vain. Jesus reproved the Pharisees, saying, "Ye hypocrites, well did Esaias prophesy of you, saying, This people draweth nigh unto me with their mouth, and honoureth me with their lips; but their heart is far from me. But in vain they do worship me, teaching for doctrines the commandments of men" (Matt. 15:7-9).

If we also teach as doctrines the commands of men, all our worship and service to God will be in vain. On the Day of the Lord, we will find ourselves shut out of the kingdom of God and frantically crying, "Lord, Lord, have we not prophesied in thy name? . . . and in thy name done many wonderful works?"—only to hear Him answer, "I never knew you: depart from me, ye that work iniquity" (Matt. 7:22,23).

By holding to the traditions of men, we seek to please men, not the Lord Jesus. Paul denounced the tradition of his fathers and testified, "For do I now persuade men, or God? or do I seek to please men? for if I yet pleased men, I should not be the servant of Christ" (Gal. 1:10). See also Gal. 1:14; Col. 2:8.

By holding to the traditions of men, we miss God's true blessings. The Pharisees had no idea of the blessings they missed by holding to their traditions—experiencing salvation and deliverance from sin (Luke 7:30-32; John 9:41); knowing the wisdom and greatness of Christ (Matt. 12:38-42); being filled with the Holy Spirit (Mark 2:22); having spiritual, material, and physical needs met (Luke 4:18-30); rejoicing and praising God (Luke 19:37-40); experiencing heart purity (Luke 11:39); and entering into the kingdom of heaven (Matt. 5:20; 21:43). These blessings and many more can be ours when we hold to the pure Word of God.

By holding to the traditions of men, we experience spiritual death, not spiritual life. No matter how rigidly we keep the traditions of men, they cannot give us spiritual life or true holiness. Tradition produces "vain conversation," an empty, self-deceiving manner of life that often is accompanied by a critical spirit (1 Pet. 1:18; Mark 7:2,3). Such deception spawns a cold, legalistic form of following man-made rules without the love and grace of God flowing from the heart. The result is spiritual death.

When we obey truth, however, the precious blood of Christ, the Spirit, and the incorruptible seed of "the word of God, which *liveth* and abideth for ever," work together to produce a born-again experience that purifies the heart and fills it with God's unfeigned love (1 Pet. 1:18-23). The result is spiritual life.

Why is it harmful to hold to the traditions of men? Let's summarize the damage we may incur.

1. We spoil our faith.
2. We are removed from Christ.
3. We pervert His gospel and hold to "another gospel."
4. We are led into deception and false religion.
5. We become self-righteous and "transgress the commandment of God."
6. We lay aside God's Word, make it void, reject it, turn from it, and add to it.
7. We become hypocritical and worship God in vain.
8. We become men pleasers.
9. We miss God's true blessings.
10. We experience spiritual death, not life.

Clearly, then, we cannot keep the traditions of men and the Word of God—we must choose one or the other. Therefore, we must determine by prayer and diligent Bible study if we are holding to the traditions of men, and, if so, be willing to change and obey God's Word anew.

To what does the Bible liken false prophets?

To "foxes" (Ezek. 13:4); to "ravening wolves" (Matt. 7:15); to "serpents" and "vipers" (Matt. 23:33); to "liars" (Rev. 2:2); to "a fool" (Hosea 9:7); to "a snare" (Hosea 9:8); to "dumb dogs" that "cannot bark" (Isa. 56:10); to "greedy dogs which can never have enough" (Isa. 56:11); to "shepherds that cannot understand" and who "look to their own way, every one for his gain" (Isa. 56:11); to a "child of the devil" and an "enemy of all righteousness" (Acts 13:10); to "natural brute beasts" (2 Pet. 2:12); to "spots" and "blemishes" (2 Pet. 2:13); to "cursed children" (2 Pet. 2:14); to "wells without water [and] clouds that are carried with a tempest" (2 Pet. 2:17); to "trees whose fruit withereth, without fruit, twice dead, plucked up by the roots"; to "raging waves of the sea, foaming out their own shame"; and to "wandering stars, to whom is reserved the blackness of darkness for ever" (Jude 1:12,13).

What influence do false prophets have on the Church and the nation?

False prophets deceive by "good words and fair speeches" (Rom. 16:18)—"Evil men and seducers shall wax worse and worse, deceiving, and being deceived" (2 Tim. 3:13).

False prophets turn people away from the truth. "And they [false teachers] shall *turn away their ears from the truth*, and shall be turned unto fables" (2 Tim. 4:4). "And when they had gone through the isle unto Paphos, they found a certain sorcerer, *a false prophet*, a Jew, whose name was Barjesus: Which was with the deputy of the country, Sergus Paulus, a prudent man; who called for Barnabas and Saul, and desired to hear the word of God. But Elymas the sorcerer (for so is his name by interpretation) withstood them, seeking to *turn away the deputy from the faith.* Then Saul, (who also is called Paul,) filled with the Holy Ghost, set his eyes on him, and said, O full of all subtilty and all mischief, thou child of the devil, thou enemy of all righteousness, wilt thou not cease to pervert the right ways of the Lord?" (Acts 13:6-10). See also Titus 1:14.

False prophets subvert the faith of many. "And their word will eat as doth a canker [gangrene]. . . . and overthrow the faith of some" (2 Tim. 2:17,18). "For there are many unruly and vain talkers and deceivers. . . . who subvert whole houses, teaching things which they ought not, for filthy lucre's sake" (Titus 1:10,11).

False prophets bring believers into bondage. "And that because of false brethren unawares brought in, who came in privily to spy out our liberty which we have in Christ Jesus, that they might bring us into bondage" (Gal. 2:4). "For when they speak great swelling words of vanity, they allure through the lusts of the flesh, through much wantonness, those that were clean escaped from them who live in error. While they promise them liberty, they themselves are the servants of corruption: for of whom a man is overcome, of the same is he brought in bondage" (2 Pet. 2:18,19).

False prophets influence believers toward sin and hypocrisy. "And many shall follow their pernicious [lascivious or unclean] ways" (2 Pet. 2:2). According to this chapter, these lascivious ways include acting in "covetousness" (v. 3,14); walking "after the flesh in the lust of uncleanness" (v. 10); despising "government" (v. 10); being "presumptuous" and "selfwilled" (v.10); "not afraid to speak evil of dignities" (v. 10); speaking "evil of the things that they understand not" (v. 12); counting "it pleasure to riot in the day time" (v. 13); "sporting themselves with their own deceivings" (v. 13); "having eyes full of adultery . . . that cannot cease from sin" (v. 14); "beguiling unstable souls" (v. 14); forsaking "the right way" and going "astray" (v. 15); "following the way of Balaam [covetousness]" (v. 15); speaking "great swelling words of vanity" (v. 18); alluring "through the lusts of the flesh, through much wantonness [immorality]" (v. 18); and being "servants of corruption" (v. 19). See also 2 Pet. 2:20-22; Luke 12:1; Matt. 16:12; 23:13,15; 1 Cor. 15:33.

False prophets resist those whom God sends. "Woe unto you, scribes and Pharisees, hypocrites! . . . Ye serpents, ye generation of vipers, how can ye escape the damnation of hell? Wherefore, behold, I send unto you prophets, and wise men, and scribes: and some of them ye shall kill and crucify; and some of them shall ye scourge in your synagogues, and persecute them from city to city" (Matt. 23:29,33,34). See also 2 Tim. 4:14,15; 2 John 1:9,10.

False prophets hinder true spiritual prayer and worship. "And when the chief priests and scribes saw the wonderful things that he did, and the children crying in the temple, and saying, Hosanna to the son of David; they were sore displeased, and said unto him, Hearest thou what these say? And Jesus saith unto them, Yea; have ye never read, Out of the mouth of babes and sucklings thou hast perfected praise?" (Matt. 21:15,16).

False prophets persecute the saints. "But as then he that was born after the flesh persecuted him that was born after the Spirit, even so it is now" (Gal. 4:29).

False prophets cause the way of truth to be spoken of as evil. "But there were false prophets also among the people, even as there shall be false teachers among you. . . . And many shall follow their pernicious ways; by reason of whom the way of truth shall be evil spoken of" (2 Pet. 2:1,2).

The influence of false prophets causes wickedness to fill the land. "I have seen also in the prophets of Jerusalem an horrible thing: they commit adultery, and walk in lies: they strengthen also the hands of evildoers, that none doth return from his wickedness: they are all of them unto me as Sodom, and the inhabitants thereof as Gomorrah. . . . from the prophets of Jerusalem is profaneness gone forth into all the land. . . . For who hath stood in the counsel of the Lord, and hath perceived and heard his word? . . . But if they had stood in my counsel, and had caused my people to hear my words, then they should have turned them from their evil way, and from the evil of their doings" (Jer. 23:14,15,18,22).

When there is "no truth, nor mercy, nor knowledge of God in the land. By swearing, and lying, and killing, and stealing, and committing adultery, they break out, and blood toucheth blood. Therefore shall the land mourn, and every one that dwelleth therein shall languish" (Hos. 4:1-3).

False prophets will destroy the flock. "For I know this, that after my departing shall grievous wolves enter in among you, not sparing the flock" (Acts 20:29). "For the leaders of this people cause them to err; and they that are led of them are destroyed" (Isa. 9:16).

Their influence of sin will cause many to partake of their plagues. "And he spake unto the congregation, saying, Depart, I pray you, from the tents of these wicked men, and touch nothing of theirs, lest ye be consumed in all their sins" (Num. 16:26). See also Ezra 9:14; Jer. 5:26-31; Rev. 18:4,5.

False prophets hinder souls from entering the kingdom of heaven. Jesus warned, "But woe unto you, scribes and Pharisees, hypocrites! for ye shut up the kingdom of heaven against men: for ye neither go in yourselves, neither suffer ye them that are entering to go in" (Matt. 23:13).

Jesus also observed, "Strait [difficult with many obstacles] is the gate, and narrow is the way, which leadeth unto life, and few there be that find it" (Matt. 7:14). He then named one great obstacle in verse 15—false prophets! And He faithfully warns all who will hear, "Beware of false prophets, which come to you in sheep's clothing, but inwardly they are ravening wolves."

What can we do about false prophets and the apostate church?

To be specific, the Bible tells believers not to fellowship with:

Those who transgress and abide not in the doctrine of Christ—"Whosoever transgresseth, and abideth not in the doctrine of Christ, hath not God. He that abideth in the doctrine of Christ, he hath both the Father and the Son. If there come any unto you, and bring not this doctrine, receive him not into your house, neither bid him God speed: For he that biddeth him God speed is partaker of his evil deeds" (2 John 1:9-11). "If any man teach otherwise, and consent not to wholesome words, even the words of our Lord Jesus Christ, and to the doctrine which is according to godliness. . . . from such withdraw thyself" (1 Tim. 6:3,5).

Those who cause divisions and offenses contrary to the doctrine—The apostle Paul warned the Church at Rome to "avoid them" (Rom. 16:17).

The foolish—"Go from the presence of a foolish man, when thou perceivest not in him the lips of knowledge" (Pro. 14:7). See also Pro. 9:6.

Those who work the unfruitful works of darkness—"And have no fellowship with the unfruitful works of darkness, but rather reprove them" (Eph. 5:11).

Brothers who walk disorderly—"Now we command you, brethren, in the name of our Lord Jesus Christ, that ye withdraw yourselves from every brother that walketh disorderly. . . . For we hear that there are some which walk among you disorderly, working not at all, but are busybodies. . . . And if any man obey not our word by this epistle, note that man, and have no company with him, that he may be ashamed" (2 Thess. 3:6,11,14).

Those who profess that they know God but work abominations—"They profess that they know God; but in works they deny him, being *abominable*, and disobedient, and unto every good work reprobate" (Titus 1:16). "Should we again break thy commandments, and join in affinity with the people of these *abominations*? Wouldest not thou be angry with us till thou hadst consumed us, so that there should be no remnant nor escaping?" (Ezra 9:14).

Abominations include stealing, murder, committing adultery, swearing falsely, burning incense unto Baal, walking after other gods (Jer. 7:9); practicing sodomy (Lev. 18:22,23), idolatry (Deut. 7:25; 1 Pet. 4:3), or witchcraft (Deut. 18:9-12); a woman wearing that which pertains unto a man, and visa-versa (Deut. 22:5); using false weights (Deut. 25:13,16); sowing discord (Pro. 6:19); lying (Pro. 12:22); offering wicked sacrifices (Pro. 15:8); justifying the wicked and condemning the just (Pro. 17:15). Those who work abominations are destined for the lake of fire (Rev. 21:8).

Those who name the name of Christ but do not depart from sin—"Let every one that nameth the name of Christ depart from iniquity. . . . If a man therefore purge himself from these, he shall be a vessel unto honour, sanctified, and meet for the master's use, and prepared unto every good work" (2 Tim. 2:19,21).

Those who are scornful—"Blessed is the man that walketh not in the counsel of the the ungodly, nor standeth in the way of sinners, nor sitteth in the seat of the scornful" (Psa. 1:1). See also Pro. 22:10.

Those who have a form of godliness, but deny the power thereof—They are "lovers of their own selves, covetous, boasters, proud, blasphemers, disobedient to parents, unthankful, unholy, without natural affection, trucebreakers, false accusers, incontinent, fierce, despisers of those that are good, traitors, heady, highminded, lovers of pleasures more than lovers of God" (2 Tim. 3:2-5).

Those who are called brothers but are fornicators, covetous, idolaters, etc.—"But now I have written unto you not to keep company, if any man that is called a brother be a fornicator, or covetous, or an idolater, or a railer, or a drunkard, or an extortioner; with such an one no not to eat" (1 Cor. 5:11). Since the Bible warns that "a little leaven leavened the whole lump" (1 Cor. 5:6), we should avoid all false prophets, false religions, and false doctrines. Just a little bad influence can spread. This would also mean avoiding their meetings, their programs, and their literature.

On the other hand, we should seek fellowship with God-fearing believers (Mal. 3:16-18). David said, "I am a companion of all them that fear thee, and of them that keep thy precepts" (Psa. 119:63). Scripture urges, "And let us consider one another to provoke unto love and to good works: Not forsaking the assembling of ourselves together, as the manner of some is; but exhorting one another: and so much the more, as ye see the day approaching" (Heb. 10:24,25).

Obedience to the above scriptures will help us to be strong in the Lord and to stand in the evil days ahead when all the world is being deceived by the Antichrist and the false prophet.

Objection Answered

Isn't it a noble thing to keep the time-honored traditions of our church or denomination?

Someone has said, "Antiquity is no certain rule of verity. It matters not how old an idea may be, how widely it may be believed, how earnestly propagated, how fervently held—if it is not true, it is false."

God's Word is eternal and true—"Thy word is truth" (John 17:17); "For ever, O Lord, thy word is settled in heaven" (Psa. 119:89); "The word of the Lord endureth for ever. And this is the word which by the gospel is preached unto you" (1 Pet. 1:25). Therefore, why should we hold to the traditions of men?

The Lord commanded, "Walk ye *not* in the statutes of your fathers, neither observe their judgments, nor defile yourselves with their idols: *I am the Lord your God*; walk in *my* statutes, and keep *my* judgments, and do them" (Ezek. 20:18,19) and "Beware lest any man *spoil you* through philosophy and vain deceit, after *the tradition of men*, after the rudiments of the world, and not after Christ" (Col. 2:8). See also Jer. 9:12-16.

Make no mistake about it, there can be no salvation as long as we knowingly resist the truth and hold to the traditions of men. Our Lord could not save the Pharisees as long as they held to their traditions; the same holds true for us. When Paul was converted, he denounced the traditions of men. Likewise, to be saved, we must be redeemed *from* "the tradition of [our] fathers" and be "born again" by obeying "the *truth* through the Spirit" (1 Pet. 1:18,22,23).

To save souls, God uses the instrument of His Word, not the traditions of men: "Being born again, not of corruptible seed, but of incorruptible, by the word of God, which liveth and abideth for ever" (1 Pet. 1:23). "Of his own will begat he us with the word of truth" (James 1:18). "Receive with meekness the engrafted word, which is able to save your souls" (James 1:21). "So then faith cometh by hearing, and hearing by the word of God" (Rom. 10:17). "Take heed unto thyself, and unto the doctrine; continue in them: for in doing this thou shalt both save thyself, and them that hear thee" (1 Tim. 4:16).

15

Babylon

Who is Babylon?

Babylon is the false religious system that mixes biblical truth with heathen customs and practices of ancient Babylon. According to Revelation 17 and 18, Babylon fits the description of a false religious system that:

Has worldwide political power—She "reigneth over the kings of the earth" (Rev. 17:18). See also Rev. 17:1,2,15; 18:3.

Has an alliance with "the beast"—"I saw a woman sit upon a scarlet coloured beast" (Rev. 17:3). See also Rev. 17:7,8.

Has great economic power—"And the merchants of the earth are waxed rich through the abundance [power] of her delicacies" (Rev. 18:3). "The merchandise of gold, and silver, and precious stones, and of pearls, and fine linen, and purple, and silk, and scarlet, and all thyine wood, and all manner vessels of ivory, and all manner vessels of most precious wood, and of brass, and iron, and marble. And cinnamon, and odours, and ointments, and frankincense, and wine, and oil, and fine flour, and wheat, and beasts, and sheep, and horses, and chariots, and slaves, and souls of men" (Rev. 18:12,13). "Thy merchants were the great men of the earth" (Rev. 18:23).

Glorifies herself and lives luxuriously—"How much she hath glorified herself and lived deliciously" (Rev. 18:7); "And the woman was arrayed in purple and scarlet colour, and decked with gold and precious stones and pearls" (Rev. 17:4). See also Rev. 18:3,9,14.

Is "full of abominations and filthiness" (Rev. 17:4)—"And upon her forehead was a name written, Mystery, Babylon the Great, the mother of harlots and abominations of the earth" (Rev. 17:5).

Is the persecutor of true believers—"And I saw the woman drunken with the blood of the saints, and with the blood of the martyrs of Jesus" (Rev. 17:6).

Is located on seven mountains—"The seven heads are seven mountains, on which the woman sitteth" (Rev. 17:9).

Makes "merchandise" of the "souls of men" (Rev. 18:12,13)—See also 2 Pet. 2:3,15; Jude 1:11.

Will eventually be hated and destroyed by ten kings—"These shall hate the whore, and shall make her desolate" (Rev. 17:16).

Will be judged by God "double according to her works" (Rev. 18:6).

How do we know Babylon is a religious system?

The following four reasons indicate that Babylon is a religious system:

1. The mixing of true worship with idolatry and heathen religion is called whoredoms in the Bible. Babylon is referred to as "the mother of harlots" and "the great whore" because of her sin of spiritual fornication (Rev. 17:1,2,4,15,16; 18:3,9; 19:2). This was also the sin of Israel. She professed to serve God, but also followed heathen religion by doing "after the manner of the *Babylonians of Chaldea*" (Ezek. 23:15). God rebuked her by saying, "Thou hast gone a *whoring* after the heathen, and . . . thou art polluted with their *idols*" (Ezek. 23:30). See also Deut. 32:15-17; 2 Kings 9:22; Jer. 3:6-9; Hos. 4:12-19; 2 Tim. 3:1-6; 4:3,4; Rev. 2:14,20.

The name, "Mystery, Babylon the Great, mother of harlots and abominations of the earth" (Rev. 17:5), also suggests that Babylon is a religious system that gives birth to all the abominations that go with pagan religion, such as idolatry, witchcraft, astrology, and human sacrifices. "When thou art come into the land which the Lord thy God giveth thee, thou shalt not learn to do after the abominations of those nations. There shall not be found among you any one that maketh his son or his daughter to pass through the fire, or that useth divination, or an observer of times, or an enchanter, or a witch, or a charmer, or a consulter with familiar spirits, or a wizard, or a necromancer. For all that do these things are an abomination unto the Lord: and because of these abominations the Lord thy God doth drive them out from before thee" (Deut. 18:9-12). See also Deut. 29:17,18; 1 Kings 14:24; 2 Kings 16:3,4; 21:2-11; 2 Chr. 28:2-4; Isa. 47:12,13; Ezek. 16:22-58; 18:12.

The apostles warned against "abominable idolatries" (1 Pet. 4:3) and showed that they are connected with devil worship: "What say I then? that the idol is any thing, or that which is offered in sacrifice to idols is any thing? but I say, that the things which the Gentiles sacrifice, they sacrifice to devils, and not to God: and I would not that ye should have fellowship with devils" (1 Cor. 10:19,20). See also Lev. 17:7; Deut. 32:16,17; 2 Chr. 11:15; Psa. 106:36,37; Rev. 9:20.

2. In Babylon is "found the blood of prophets, and of saints, and of all that were slain upon the earth" (Rev. 18:24). Religious sources often initiated persecution of believers in the New Testament (John 18:3; Acts 4:1,2; 5:17,18; 6:9-13; 9:13,14; 13:50).

3. The description of Babylon in the Book of Revelation corresponds in detail with the description of ancient Babylon in the Old Testament. The comparison in the following chart shows that Babylon, the amassing world church of the end-time, has her roots in the religion of ancient Babylon.

The Religion of Ancient Babylon Old Testament	Babylon, the Amassing World Church Revelation 17 and 18
Dwellest upon many waters—Jer. 51:13.	Sitteth upon many waters. . . . the peoples, and multitudes, and nations, and tongues—Rev. 17:1,15.
Shall commit fornication with all the kingdoms of the world—Isa. 23:17.	The kings of the earth have commited fornication with her—Rev. 18:3.
Babylon hath been a golden cup—Jer. 51:7.	Having a golden cup—Rev. 17:4.
The whoredoms of the well-favoured harlot, the mistress of witchcrafts, that selleth nations through her whoredoms, and families through her witchcrafts—Nah. 3:4.	Mystery, Babylon the Great, the mother of harlots and abominations of the earth—Rev. 17:5. Full of abominations and filthiness—Rev. 17:4.
I shall be a lady forever. . . . I shall not sit as a widow—Isa. 47:7,8.	I sit as a queen, and am no widow—Rev. 18:7.
Babylon is fallen . . . and all the graven images of her gods—Isa. 21:9. Babylon . . . the nations have drunken of her wine—Jer. 51:7.	Babylon is fallen . . . because she made all nations drink of the wine of the wrath of her fornication—Rev. 14:8; 18:2.

The Religion of Ancient Babylon Old Testament	Babylon, the Amassing World Church Revelation 17 and 18
For the multitude of thy sorceries, and for the great abundance of thine enchantments—Isa. 47:9.	By thy sorceries were all nations deceived—Rev. 18:23.
Babylon hath caused the slain of Israel to fall—Jer. 51:49.	In her was found the blood of prophets, and of saints, and of all that were slain upon the earth—Rev. 18:24.
My people, go ye out of the midst of her, and deliver ye every man his soul. . . . I will do jugment upon the graven images of Babylon—Jer. 51:45,47.	Come out of her, my people, that ye be not partakers of her sins—Rev. 18:4. What agreement hath the temple of God with idols?—2 Cor. 6:16.

4. The biblical description of Babylon, the false church, is the opposite of the biblical description of the true Church of Jesus Christ.

- The false church is called a harlot (Rev. 17:5); the true Church is called faithful (Rev. 17:14).
- The false church has a name written on her forehead, "Mystery, Babylon the great, the mother of harlots and abominations of the earth" (Rev. 17:5); the true Church has the name of God on her forehead (Rev. 3:12; 22:4).
- The false church is referred to as Babylon (Rev. 18:21); the true Church is referred to as the new Jerusalem (Rev. 21:2).
- The false church drinks "a golden cup . . . full of abominations and filthiness" (Rev. 17:4), which is "the cup of devils" (1 Cor. 10:21); the Church of Jesus Christ drinks the cup of suffering for His name's sake (Matt. 20:22), which is "the cup of the Lord" (1 Cor. 10:21).
- The false church glorifies herself (Rev. 18:7); the true Church glorifies the Lord (Rev. 15:4).
- The false church lives luxuriously (Rev. 18:7); the true Church lives as "strangers and pilgrims," looking for a heavenly city (Heb. 11:13-16).
- The false church (the harlot) is arrayed in scarlet, which can represent pomp, power, and royalty as well as sin, bloodguiltness, and satanism (Rev. 17:4; 18:24; 12:3; Isa. 1:18); the true

Church (a chaste virgin) is arrayed in "fine linen, clean and white," which speaks of purity and righteousness (2 Cor. 11:2; Rev. 19:8).

• The false church will be judged by God and drink the "wine of the fierceness of his wrath" (Rev. 16:19); the true Church will be blessed and drink the "fruit of the vine" with Christ in His kingdom (Matt. 26:29).

Do the gospels and epistles allude to Babylon?

Yes, very definitely! Consider how the following verses about false religionists relate to that which is written of Babylon in the Book of Revelation:

Persecuting and killing the righteous.

The gospels—Jesus told false religionists, "Ye are the children of them which killed the prophets. . . . I send unto you prophets, and wise men, and scribes: and some of them ye shall kill and crucify; and some of them shall ye scourge in your synagogues, and persecute them from city to city: that upon you may come *all the righteous blood shed upon the earth*, from the blood of righteous Abel unto the blood of Zacharias son of Barachias, whom ye slew between the temple and the altar" (Matt. 23:31,34,35).

The Revelation—"And in her was found the blood of prophets, and of saints, and of *all that were slain upon the earth*" (Rev. 18:24).

Deceiving all nations.

The gospels and epistles—"And many false prophets shall rise, and shall deceive many" (Matt. 24:11). "Now the Spirit speaketh expressly, that in the latter times some shall depart from the faith, giving heed to *seducing spirits*, and *doctrines of devils*; speaking lies in hypocrisy; having their conscience seared with a hot iron; forbidding to marry, and commanding to abstain from meats" (1 Tim. 4:1-3). See also Matt. 24:24; 1 John 4:1.

The Revelation—"For by thy *sorceries* were all nations *deceived*" (Rev. 18:23).

Full of sin and abominations.

The gospels and epistles—The man of sin and false religionists are associated with sin and abominations. "The mystery of iniquity doth already work. . . . that Wicked be revealed" (2 Thess. 2:7,8). "They profess that they know God; but in works they deny him, being abominable, and disobedient, and unto every good work reprobate" (Titus 1:16). "False prophets. . . . shall utterly perish in their own corruption. . . . count it pleasure to riot in the day time. . . . having eyes full of adultery, and that cannot cease from sin" (2 Pet. 2:1,12-14). Many of the scribes and Pharisees appeared righteous to men but were "full of extortion and excess. . . . full of dead men's bones, and of all uncleanness. . . . [and] full of hypocrisy and iniquity" (Matt. 23:25,27,28).

The Revelation—"Mystery, Babylon the Great, the mother of harlots and abominations of the earth" (Rev. 17:5). "Having a golden cup in her hand full of abominations and filthiness of her fornications" (Rev. 17:4).

What great part will Babylon have in the end-time?

The New Testament foretells that there will be great apostasy and the revelation of the man of sin before the coming of the Lord (2 Thess. 2:1-3). As already stated, the false church of "Mystery, Babylon the Great, the mother of harlots and abominations of the earth" (Rev. 17:5) links with "the mystery of iniquity" (2 Thess. 2:7) and, thus, with "the man of sin" (2 Thess. 2:3). The world is seeing an unprecedented resurgence of sorcery (drugs), idolatry, enchantments, human sacrifices, humanism, astrology, and witchcraft, which stem from the religious system of Babylon. Through her, the nations will be deceived, will commit spiritual fornication, and will "drink of the wine of the wrath of her fornication" (Rev. 18:23; 17:2; 14:8). As prophesied, this wickedness will increase as we come closer to the end (Matt. 24:12; Rev. 9:20,21; 16:13-16,19).

The association between Babylon and the beast (the man of sin) is also seen in Revelation 17:3: "I saw a woman sit upon a scarlet coloured beast, full of names of blasphemy, having seven heads and ten horns." See also verses 7 to 11. This description of the beast fits that given in Revelation 13:1.

Through lying wonders, the false religion of Babylon will have a big part in deceiving the peoples of the earth into making and worshiping an image of the beast and into receiving his mark (Rev. 13:12-16). In fact, Scripture reveals a definite parallel between "the beast" and "Babylon":

- Both are wicked (one is "the man of sin" and the other "the mother of harlots").
- Both martyr the saints (Rev. 13:7,15; 17:6; 18:24).
- Both are blasphemous (Rev. 13:5; 17:3).
- Both have power over all the nations (Rev. 13:7; 17:2; 18:3,9).
- Both deceive by spirits of devils (Rev. 16:13,14; 18:23).
- Both are self-exalted (2 Thess. 2:4; Rev. 18:7; Jer. 51:53).
- Both perform lying wonders (2 Thess. 2:9; Rev. 13:13,14).
- Both are idolatrous (Rev. 13:15; Isa. 21:9; Jer. 51:47,52).
- Both cause the nations to drink the wine of the wrath of God (Rev. 14:8-10).
- Both will be destroyed when Jesus comes (2 Thess. 2:8; Rev. 16:19).

What is the relevance of the ecumenical movement to Babylon?

There is an interesting parallel between Babylon, which represents a corrupt, worldwide religious system, and the ecumenical movement—namely that ecumenism, at its heart, attempts to create a worldwide or universal church out of the various denominations. Many sincere people mistakenly believe that Jesus prayed for all churches to be one.

What did Jesus mean when He prayed "that they all may be one" (John 17:21)?

Jesus prayed for His followers to be one with those who would yet believe on Him, but not for all churches to be one. In John 17, Jesus prayed for His followers, then for those who would believe on Him as a result of their preaching. "I pray for them: I pray not for the world, but for them which thou hast given me. . . . Neither pray I for these alone, but for them also which shall believe on me through their word; that they all may be one" (vs. 9,20,21). Clearly, Jesus prayed for two groups to be one: His followers and their future converts.

Consider five additional reasons why we know that Jesus never prayed for all churches to be one:

1. The Lord Jesus commanded separation between His Church,

the spotless Bride (Eph. 5:27), and the false church, "Babylon the Great, the mother of harlots" (Rev. 17:5). He clearly commanded believers not to be one with her, but to "come out of her" (Rev. 18:4).

2. Uniting with false churches will cause greater apostasy and deception in the world: "Know ye not that a little leaven [of sin or false doctrine] leaveneth the whole lump?" (1 Cor. 5:6; Gal. 5:9).

3. Paul warned believers not to unite with those who preach "another gospel" (Gal. 1:7-9). True Christian fellowship and unity must be based on the Word of God, not the traditions of men that make "the word of God of none effect" (Mark 7:13). "Can two walk together, except they be agreed?" (Amos 3:3). John wrote, "Whosoever transgresseth, and abideth not in the doctrine of Christ, *hath not God.* He that abideth in the doctrine of Christ, he hath both the Father and the Son. If there come any unto you, and bring not this doctrine, receive him not into your house, neither bid him God speed" (2 John 1:9,10).

4. Jesus Himself predicted division: "Suppose ye that I am come to give peace on earth? I tell you, Nay; but rather *division*: for from henceforth there shall be five in one house *divided*, three against two and two against three" (Luke 12:51,52). "Think not that I am come to send peace on earth: I came not to send peace, but a *sword*" (Matt. 10:34). The Word of God is described as a sword that divides: "For the Word of God is quick, and powerful, and sharper than any *twoedged sword*, piercing even to the *dividing* asunder of soul and spirit, and of the joints and marrow, and is a discerner of the thoughts and intents of the heart" (Heb. 4:12). Therefore, whenever truth is preached, there will be division between those who love the truth and those who hold to the traditions of men and false doctrines (John 6:66-68; 7:43; 9:16; 10:19; Acts 14:4; 23:6,7).

5. Jesus condemned religious hypocrites and warned His followers to "beware" of them (Luke 12:1) and to "let them alone" (Matt. 15:14). Never once did He pray for His own to be one with worldly church members who resist the truth, nor did He try to unite the two together. But He prayed for His followers to be one with those who would believe on Him through their preaching.

What is the scriptural basis of Christian unity?

True Christian unity can occur only among:

1. Members of "the *same* body," which is the body of Christ—the true Church (Eph. 3:6) See also Rom. 12:5. Not all church members are part of the body of Christ; some are the children of Satan because they will not come to Christ in repentance and faith. (Compare Matt. 21:31,32 and John 5:40-43 with 8:44-47.) See also John 1:12,13; Rom. 8:16; Titus 1:16.

2. Believers who realize that Jesus Christ is the only "head of the body, the church" and that "in all things" He must have "the preeminence" (Col. 1:18). He is "the blessed and only Potentate, the King of kings, and Lord of lords; who only hath immortality" (1 Tim. 6:15,16). Ephesians 4:5 states, "*One Lord*, one faith, one baptism." The Bible teaches that "*one* is your Master, even Christ; and all ye are brethren. And call no man your father upon the earth: for *one* is your Father, which is in heaven. Neither be ye called masters: for *one* is your Master, even Christ" (Matt. 23:8-10). The Bible also says, "holy and reverend is *his name*" (Psa. 111:9). See also Luke 22:24-27; John 3:30.

Jesus is the only Savior (Acts 4:12), the only mediator between God and man (1 Tim. 2:4,5), and the only door by which we may enter and be saved (John 10:9). Jesus alone is sinless (Heb. 7:25,26). He alone died to bring us to God (1 Pet. 3:18) and has the power to redeem us with His precious blood (1 Pet. 1:18,19; Heb. 4:14-16; 9:12-14). Jesus alone is exalted by God to give repentance and forgiveness of sins (Acts 5:30,31; Matt. 9:6). "By him all that believe are justified from all things" (Acts 13:39). Jesus alone is the Author (Heb. 5:9) and the Captain (Heb. 2:10) of our salvation. He declares, "I am the way, the truth, and the life: no man cometh unto the Father, but *by me*" (John 14:6) and invites us to come directly to Him with our burden of sin. "*Come unto me*, all ye that labour and are heavy laden, and I will give you rest" (Matt. 11:28). "If we confess our sins [to Jesus], he is faithful and just to forgive us our sins, and to cleanse us from all unrighteousness" (1 John 1:9). "The blood of Jesus Christ his Son cleanseth us from all sin" (1 John 1:7). Only Jesus can give repentance, cleansing, healing, deliverance from the power of sin, and peace (Luke 4:18; 7:48,50; 18:13,14).

3. Believers who "all speak the *same* thing" (1 Cor. 1:10),

namely scriptural doctrine, not "fables" (2 Tim. 4:2-4), or "the traditions of men" (Mark 7:8-13; Col. 2:8). Paul, with reference to "the unity of the faith," speaks of coming into "the knowledge of the Son of God," which implies a correct doctrinal understanding of who Christ is and what He has done (Eph. 4:13). See also Acts 2:42; Gal. 1:8,9; Col. 1:23,25-28; 2 Tim. 1:13; 3:16; Titus chapter 2.

4. Believers who are willing to be led into all truth by "the *same* anointing"—the Holy Spirit. "These things have I written unto you concerning them that seduce you. But the anointing which ye have received of him abideth in you, and ye need not that any man teach you: but as *the same anointing* teacheth you of all things, and *is truth, and is no lie*, and even as it hath taught you, ye shall abide in him" (1 John 2:26,27). Some people want unity of the Spirit without unity of doctrine, but Jesus tells us that "when he, the Spirit of truth, is come, *he will guide you into all truth*" (John 16:13).

5. Believers who "walk by the *same* rule" and who "mind the *same* thing" (Phil. 3:16)—the pattern set by Jesus Christ and the apostles. Paul exhorts believers to "be perfectly joined together in the *same* mind" (the mind of Christ) and in "the *same* judgment" (1 Cor. 1:10; Phil. 2:3-8). Scripture urges us to walk "in the *same* spirit" and "in the *same* steps" (2 Cor. 12:18). All these verses imply that there will be fellowship among believers who walk in the light (1 John 1:3,7), who are pure in heart (2 Tim. 2:22; Psa. 111:1), who fear God (Psa. 61:5; 89:7), and who keep His commandments (1 John 5:2,3).

6. Believers who have "the *same* spirit of faith" (2 Cor. 4:13).

7. Believers who are willing to suffer "the *same* afflictions" for Christ's sake (1 Pet. 5:9).

8. Believers who have "the *same* care one for another" (1 Cor. 12:25). They have "the *same* purpose" of knowing about and of comforting the saints (Eph. 6:22; Col. 4:8).

9. Believers who have the same "hope" (Eph. 4:4) and are heirs of the same "promise" or "inheritance" (Heb. 11:9; Col. 1:12). Our hope is "the glorious appearing" of Jesus Christ (Titus 2:13) and our inheritance is reserved in heaven (1 Pet. 1:4).

In summary, true Christian unity must be based on biblical

repentance, exalting only the Lord Jesus Christ, being taught by the Spirit of Truth, receiving and abiding in pure doctrine, having living faith in the Lord Jesus Christ, suffering affliction for His name's sake, caring for one another, and having the same hope of the Second Coming when true believers will receive their eternal inheritance.

Why will Babylon be destroyed?

She will be destroyed because "her sins have reached unto heaven, and God hath remembered her iniquities" (Rev. 18:5). Babylon has "a golden cup in her hand full of abominations and filthiness of her fornication" (Rev. 17:4), which include the following:

- hypocrisy (Rev. 17:4)
- spiritual fornication (Rev. 14:8; 17:1,2,3,15; 18:3,9; 19:2)
- idolatry (Isa. 21:9; Jer. 50:2,38; 51:17,47,52)
- magic, witchcraft, and sorceries (Isa. 47:9,12,13; Dan. 2:1,2; Rev. 18:23)
- covetousness (Jer. 51:13; Rev. 18:11-13)
- enslaving and making merchandise of the souls of men (2 Pet. 2:3; Rev. 18:13)
- oppression (Isa. 14:4)
- cruelty and destruction (Isa. 47:5,6; Jer. 51:24,25)
- pride and arrogance (Isa. 14:13,14; 47:8,10; Jer. 50:29-32; Rev. 18:7)
- the martyrdom of the saints (Rev. 17:6; 18:24)
- causing "all nations" to "drink of the wine of the wrath of her fornication" (Rev. 14:8; 17:2; 18:3)

When will Babylon be destroyed?

Babylon will be destroyed on the Day of the Lord (Isa. 13:6,19), when the seventh and last vial is poured forth at the coming of our Lord Jesus Christ (Rev. 16:17-19).

How will Babylon be destroyed?

The false system of Babylon with "a golden cup in her hand full of abominations and filthiness" (Rev. 17:4) will receive from the Lord "the cup of the wine of the fierceness of his wrath"

(Rev. 16:19). The Lord God who is strong will judge her and avenge "the blood of his servants at her hand" (Rev. 18:8; 19:2).

Suddenly, in one hour (Jer. 51:8; Rev. 18:10,17), she will fall in "a great earthquake" (Rev. 16:18,19), be "utterly burned by fire" (Rev. 18:8,18) even as Sodom and Gomorrah (Isa. 13:19; Jer. 50:40), and be violently "thrown down" to "be found no more at all" (Rev. 18:21).

In that day, the "holy apostles and prophets" and "much people in heaven" will rejoice saying, "Alleluia; Salvation, and glory, and honour, and power, unto the Lord our God: For true and righteous are his judgments: for he hath judged the great whore, which did corrupt the earth with her fornication, and hath avenged the blood of his servants at her hand. And again they said, Alleluia. And her smoke rose up for ever and ever" (Rev. 18:20; 19:1-3).

In conclusion, just as God warned Lot and his family to escape for their lives before He destroyed Sodom and Gomorrah with fire and brimstone, so He repeatedly warns His people to come out of the false religious system of Babylon:

"Go ye forth of Babylon, flee ye from the Chaldeans" (Isa. 48:20).

"Depart ye, depart ye, go ye out from thence, touch no unclean thing; go ye out of the midst of her; be ye clean, that bear the vessels of the Lord" (Isa. 52:11).

"Remove out of the midst of Babylon" (Jer. 50:8).

"Flee out of the midst of Babylon, and deliver every man his soul: be not cut off in her iniquity; for this is the time of the Lord's vengeance; he will render unto her a recompence" (Jer. 51:6).

"Deliver thyself, O Zion, that dwellest with the daughter of Babylon" (Zech. 2:7).

"Be ye not unequally yoked together with unbelievers: for what fellowship hath righteousness with unrighteousness? And what communion hath light with darkness? And what concord hath Christ with Belial? Or what part hath he that believeth with an infidel? And what agreement hath the temple of God with idols? For ye are the temple of the living God; as God hath said, I will dwell in them, and walk in them; and I will be their God, and they shall be my people. Wherefore come out from among them, and be ye separate, saith the Lord, and touch not the unclean thing; and I will receive you, and will be a Father unto you, and ye shall be my sons and daughters, saith the Lord Almighty" (2 Cor. 6:14-18).

"Come out of her [Babylon], my people, that ye be not partakers of her sins, and that ye receive not of her plagues" (Rev. 18:4).

16

The Judgment Seat of Christ

When will "the judgment seat of Christ" (2 Cor. 5:10) take place?

At the judgment seat of Christ everyone will "receive the things done in his body, according to that he hath done, whether it be good or bad" (2 Cor. 5:10). Paul spoke of this day of reckoning in the context of the resurrection of the saints (5:4), thus, we know it occurs when Jesus comes after the Tribulation (Matt. 24:29-31), on the Day of the Lord (1 Thess. 4:16-18; 5:2). He also said the Lord "will render to every man" (Rom. 2:6) on "the day of wrath and revelation of the righteous judgment of God" (Rom. 2:5) which, according to Second Peter 3:7 and 10, is "the day of the Lord."

Is "the judgment seat of Christ" (2 Cor. 5:10) exclusively for believers?

This teaching is common among some groups; however, nothing in Second Corinthians 5:10 indicates that this judgment is exclusively for believers—"We must *all* appear before the judgment seat of Christ." "All" includes Jew and Gentile, the living and the dead, the great and the small, believers and unbelievers. Verse eleven also implies that unbelievers will be present: "Knowing therefore the terror of the Lord, we persuade men." Because of this awful judgment, Paul felt compelled to persuade men to repent.

Also, by comparing this verse with Romans 14:10-14, there can be no doubt that the judgment seat of Christ is for all. "But why dost thou judge *thy brother*? or why dost thou set at nought *thy brother*? for we shall *all* stand before the judgment seat of Christ. For it is written, As I live, saith the Lord, every *knee* shall bow to me, and *every tongue* shall confess to God. So then *every one of us* shall give account of himself to God." The words "all," "every knee," "every tongue" and "every one of us" surely speak of believers and unbelievers.

This truth is confirmed in Isaiah 45:23 and 24. Part of the above passage (Romans 14:11) is a quotation from verse 23: "I have sworn by myself, the word is gone out of my mouth in righteousness, and shall not return, That unto me *every knee* shall bow, *every tongue* shall swear." Notice that verse 24 specifically shows that "every knee" and "every tongue" includes both the righteous and the unrighteous: "Surely, shall one [the righteous] say, In the Lord have I righteousness and strength: even to him shall men come; and all that are incensed against him [the unrighteous] shall be ashamed." Therefore, the teaching that the judgment seat of Christ is for believers only is not supported by Scripture.

Is there a difference between the judgment seat of Christ (Rom. 14:10-12; 2 Cor. 5:9-11), the judgment at Christ's throne of glory (Matt. 25:31-46), and the great white throne judgment (Rev. 20:11-15)?

No, there is no difference. Since the resurrection of the just and the unjust occurs on the last day, there can only be one judgment, not three distinct ones. Moreover, the following four similarities between the three accounts give clear evidence that they refer to the same event:

1. They each depict a throne.

Romans 14:10; 2 Cor. 5:10—"The judgment seat of Christ."

Matthew 25:31—"The throne of his glory."

Revelation 20:11—"And I saw a great white throne."

2. They each show that all mankind will stand before God, both believers and unbelievers.

Romans 14:10; 2 Corinthians 5:10—"For we shall all stand before the judgment seat of Christ."

Matthew 25:32—"And before him shall be gathered all nations: . . . his sheep . . . the goats."

Revelation 20:12; 21:7,8 (the context is 20:11-15)—"And I saw the dead, small and great, stand before God. . . . He that overcometh. . . . and the abominable. . . ."

3. *They each show that every man will be judged according to his works.*

Romans 14:12—"So then every one of us shall give account of himself to God."

Matthew 25:40,45—To the righteous, Jesus will say, "Verily I say unto you, Inasmuch as ye have done it unto one of the least of these my brethren, ye have done it unto me." To the ungodly, He will say, "Verily I say unto you, Inasmuch as ye did it not to one of the least of these, ye did it not to me."

Revelation 20:13—"And they were judged every man according to their works."

4. *They each show the righteous rewarded and the ungodly condemned.*

2 Corinthians 5:10—"For we must all appear . . . that everyone may receive the things done in his body, according that he hath done, whether it be *good* or *bad*."

Matthew 25:34,41—"Then shall the King say unto them on his right hand, Come, *ye blessed* of my Father, inherit the kingdom prepared for you from the foundation of the world: . . . Then shall he say also unto them on the left hand, Depart from me, *ye cursed*, into everlasting fire, prepared for the devil and his angels."

Revelation 21:7,8 (the context is 20:11-15)—"*He that overcometh* shall inherit all things; and I will be his God, and he shall be my son. But *the fearful, and unbelieving*, and the abominable, and murderers, and whoremongers, and sorcerers, and idolaters, and all liars, shall have their part in the lake which burneth with fire and brimstone: which is the second death."

Therefore, the judgment seat of Christ, the judgment at Christ's throne of glory, and the great white throne judgment refer to the same event because each shows a throne; all nations present, both believers and unbelievers; every man judged according to his works; and the righteous justified and the ungodly condemned.

How does the great white throne judgment show that Jesus is coming to receive His Church after the Tribulation?

Revelation 20:11-15 depicts two great events of the Second Coming: heaven and earth passing away and the final judgment.

The gospels and epistles show that these events occur when Jesus comes to receive His Church *after* the Tribulation (Matt. 24:29-35; 25:31; 1 Thess. 4:16-5:2; 2 Pet. 3:7,10).

Does the Bible, then, teach one judgment for both the just and the unjust?

Yes. The Bible always speaks of the Day of Judgment as a single event—*the Day* of Judgment, not *the days* (see Matt. 12:36; Rom. 2:5; 2 Pet. 2:9; 3:7; 1 John 4:17). In the same way that there will be only one resurrection of the just and the unjust (Acts 24:15), so there will be only one judgment. "Marvel not at this: for the hour is coming, in the which all that are in the graves shall hear his voice, and shall come forth; they that have done good, unto the resurrection of life; and they that have done evil, unto the resurrection of damnation" (John 5:28,29).

The Bible further says that God has appointed *a day* in which He will judge *the world* in righteousness (Acts 17:31). "A day" speaks of one judgment day; "the world" encompasses the just and the unjust.

On that day Jesus shall "sit upon the throne of his glory: and before him shall be gathered all nations: and he shall separate them one from another, as a shepherd divideth his *sheep* [the just] from the *goats* [the unjust]" (Matt. 25:31,32). Both they who will be justified and they who will be condemned will give account in that day. Jesus warned, "But I say unto you, that every idle word that men shall speak, they shall give account thereof in *the day of judgment.* For by thy words thou shalt be justified, and by thy words thou shalt be condemned" (Matt. 12:36,37).

The parable of the net also shows one judgment for the just and the unjust. "Again, the kingdom of heaven is like unto a net, that was cast into the sea, and gathered of every kind: which, when it was full, they drew to shore, and sat down, and gathered the *good* into vessels, but cast the *bad* away. So shall it be at the end of the world: the angels shall come forth, and sever *the wicked* from among *the just,* and shall cast them into the furnace of fire: there shall be wailing and gnashing of teeth" (Matt. 13:47-50). See also Matt. 25:14-30; Luke 19:12-27; Rev. 21:7,8.

The only possible conclusion one can draw from these passages is that both believers and unbelievers will appear at one judgment to receive their just due.

Who will escape the second death?

The second death is "the lake which burneth with fire and brimstone" (Rev. 21:8). Jesus specifically told us who will escape it: "he that hath part in the first resurrection" (Rev. 20:6) and "he that overcometh" (Rev. 2:11). Together, they speak of possessing true salvation.

The first resurrection is a spiritual resurrection—rising from death to life through faith in Christ (John 5:24,25; 8:51). To overcome is to live victoriously over sin, the flesh, and the devil. The following passages show that they who have part in the first resurrection and live an overcoming life will escape the second death:

"If ye then be risen with Christ [the first resurrection], seek those things which are above, where Christ sitteth on the right hand of God. Set your affection on things above, not on things on the earth [overcoming the world]. . . . When Christ, who is our life, shall appear, then shall ye also appear with him in glory [escape the second death]" (Col. 3:1,2,4). See also Eph. 2:1-6.

"Verily, verily, I say unto you, He that heareth [is hearing] my word, and believeth [is believing] on him that sent me, hath everlasting life, and shall not come into *condemnation*; but is passed from *death* unto life" (John 5:24). This verse shows that by an initial experience of salvation (the first resurrection) and continuous obedience and faith in God (living an overcoming life), we have eternal life and will escape condemnation and the second death. See also 1 John 5:3,4.

"I am the resurrection, and the life: he that believeth in me, though he were dead, yet shall he live [the first resurrection]: and whosoever liveth and believeth [overcoming] in me shall never die [escape the second death]" (John 11:25,26).

Similarly, with reference to salvation, New Testament believers are exhorted to *continue* in fruit-bearing and Christ's love (John 15:7-9); in the grace of God (Acts 13:43); in well doing (Rom. 2:7); in God's goodness (Rom. 11:22); in prayer (Col. 4:2); and in the doctrine of Christ (1 Tim. 4:16). The absolute necessity of continuing in obedience and faith is also seen in the following verses: Luke 18:8; John 3:18,36; 2 Cor. 1:24; Gal. 2:20; Eph. 6:16; Col. 1:22,23; 1 Thess. 3:5; Heb. 3:12-14; 10:38,39; 11:6; 1 John 5:10-13.

Since "the second death hath no power" on those who have "part in the first resurrection" (Rev. 20:6), why will believers be present at the great white throne judgment?

Contrary to what many are teaching, the following scriptures, which are all *addressed to believers*, make it unmistakably clear that Christians have not been given an "exempt status" from being present at the judgment. Consider these four reasons:

First, our accountability to God is inescapable. Jesus declared, "Behold, I come quickly; and my reward is with me, to give every man according as his work shall be" (Rev. 22:12). At that time, He will require us to give an account of our stewardship. "Therefore is the kingdom of heaven likened unto a certain king, which would *take account* of his servants" (Matt. 18:23); "The lord of those servants cometh, and *reckoneth* with them" (Matt. 25:19). See also Matt. 20:1-16; 25:31-46; Luke 12:35-48; 19:12-27.

Second, the apostles warned believers that God will judge our works "for there is no respect of persons with God" (Rom. 2:11):

"Be ye holy in all manner of conversation; because it is written, Be ye holy; for I am holy. And if ye call on the Father, who *without respect of persons* judgeth according to *every* man's work, pass the time of your sojourning here in fear" (1 Pet. 1:15-17).

"And whatsoever ye do, do it heartily, as to the Lord, and not unto men; knowing that of the Lord ye shall receive the reward of the inheritance: for ye serve the Lord Christ. But he that doeth wrong shall receive for the wrong which he hath done: and *there is no respect of persons*" (Col. 3:23-25).

God "will render to every man according to his deeds: To them who by patient continuance in well doing seek for glory and honour and immortality [believers], eternal life: But unto them that are contentious, and do not obey the truth, but obey unrighteousness [unbelievers], indignation and wrath. . . . For *there is no respect of persons with God*" (Rom. 2:6-8,11).

Third, Scripture gives many exhortations to believers in light of the judgment. Each of these would be meaningless if we will not be required to give an account of ourselves to God. As believers, we are exhorted:

- To not judge a brother. "But why dost thou judge thy brother? or why dost thou set at nought thy brother? for we shall all stand before the judgment seat of Christ" (Rom. 14:10).
- To not hold a grudge. "Grudge not one against another, brethren, lest ye be condemned: behold, the judge standeth before the door" (James 5:9).
- To abide in Christ. "And now, little children, abide in him; that, when he shall appear, we may have confidence, and not be ashamed before him at his coming" (1 John 2:28).
- To have our love made perfect. "Herein is our love made perfect, that we may have boldness in the day of judgment: because as he is, so are we in this world" (1 John 4:17).
- To labor to be accepted of Christ. "Wherefore we labour, that, whether present or absent, we may be accepted of him. For we must all appear before the judgment seat of Christ; that every one may receive the things done in his body, according to that he hath done, whether it be good or bad" (2 Cor. 5:9,10).

Fourth, the second death is not the judgment. In other words, the Lord Jesus promised, "He that hath part in the first resurrection: *on such the second death hath no power*" (Rev. 20:6), but nowhere does He promise, "He that hath part in the first resurrection will not stand in the judgment." Overcomers will stand before the *judgment* (the Divine tribunal) to be rewarded according to their works, but they will not be condemned to the second death. At the great white throne judgment, *overcomers* will be justified and "inherit all things"; sinners will be condemned and have their part in the lake of fire, which is the second death (Rev. 21:7,8).

It is plain, then, that he who has part in the first resurrection and overcomes the world must give an account of himself before the great white throne judgment. But he will not be condemned with the world because Jesus promised that on him "the second death hath no power" (Rev. 20:6; 2:11).

Objections Answered

Doesn't the Bible teach that "the Bride of Christ" will not be present at the judgment?

Some groups teach that the real "holy ones" in the church, or the "true" Bride, will *not* have to give an account of themselves to God on the Day of Judgment. This teaching, however, is erroneous because the Church is one body—the Bride of Christ. They are the overcomers whom John foresaw at the great white throne judgment (Rev. 21:7) and the sheep who Jesus said would appear before His throne (Matt. 25:31,32). Nowhere does the Bible make a distinction between the Bride of Christ and other members of His body. According to the words of Jesus concerning His marriage supper, only those who are ready, that is, His Bride or Wife, will enter the marriage. All others will be eternally condemned. Compare Matthew 25:1-13 with Revelation 19:7-21.

In addition, when the Bible says, "Every one of us shall give account of himself to God," it does *not* add, "except the Bride of Christ." Nowhere does the Bible speak of anyone being exempt from giving an account of himself to God. Paul himself expected to be judged of the Lord when He comes. He said, "He that judgeth me is the Lord. Therefore judge nothing before the time, until the Lord come, who both will bring to light the hidden things of darkness, and will make manifest the counsels of the hearts" (1 Cor. 4:4,5). How can humble servants of Christ think of themselves as being greater or holier than the apostle Paul?

Doesn't Romans 8:1 teach that there is "no condemnation to them which are in Christ Jesus"?

Yes, but not without qualification. Let's read the rest of the verse: "*who walk not after the flesh, but after the Spirit.*" The Bible teaches that condemnation comes upon those who walk after the flesh. In that same chapter Paul contrasted walking after the flesh and walking after the Spirit. "For they that are after the flesh do mind the things of the flesh; but they that are after the Spirit the things of the Spirit. For to be carnally minded is death; but to be spiritually minded is life and peace. Because the carnal mind is enmity against God: for it is not subject to the law of God, neither indeed can be. So then they that are in the flesh cannot please God" (Rom. 8:5-8). Those who walk after the flesh pursue those practices that gratify the flesh and cater to the appetites of the carnal nature. They are hostile toward God, disobedient to His law, and cannot please God—consequently, they reap condemnation.

The apostles amplified the meaning of walking after the flesh by listing the works of the flesh in Galatians 5:19-21: "adultery, fornication, uncleanness, lasciviousness, idolatry, witchcraft, hatred, variance, emulations, wrath, strife, seditions, heresies, envyings, murders, drunkenness, revellings, and such like." He also emphatically reminds believers that "*they which do such things shall not inherit the kingdom of God.*" In other words, they shall receive condemnation. In the following four passages Paul listed works of the flesh (sins) and reminded believers of the fatal consequences of committing them. He also admonished them not to be deceived into believing that they can continue to do these things and still be justified at the judgment.

"Being filled with all unrighteousness, fornication, wickedness, covetousness, maliciousness; full of envy, murder, debate, deceit, malignity; whisperers, backbiters, haters of God, despiteful, proud, boasters, inventors of evil things, disobedient to parents, without understanding, covenant breakers, without natural affection, implacable, unmerciful: . . . they which commit such things are worthy of death" (Rom. 1:29-32).

"Know ye not that the unrighteous shall not inherit the kingdom of God? Be not deceived: neither fornicators, nor idolaters, nor adulterers, nor effeminate, nor abusers of themselves with mankind, nor thieves, nor covetous, nor drunkards, nor revilers, nor extortioners, shall inherit the kingdom of God" (1 Cor. 6:9,10).

"But fornication, and all uncleanness, or covetousness, let it not be once named among you, as becometh saints; neither filthiness, nor foolish talking, nor jesting, which are not convenient: but rather giving of thanks. For this ye know, that no whoremonger, nor unclean person, nor covetous man, who is an idolater, hath any inheritance in the kingdom of Christ and of God.

Let no man deceive you with vain words: for because of these things cometh the wrath of God upon the children of disobedience. Be not ye therefore partakers with them" (Eph. 5:3-7).

"Mortify therefore your members which are upon the earth; fornication, uncleanness, inordinate affection, evil concupiscence, and covetousness, which is idolatry: For which things' sake the wrath of God cometh on the children of disobedience" (Col. 3:5,6).

Moreover, Paul admonished believers to examine themselves before partaking of the Lord's table and added, "For if we would judge ourselves, we should not be judged. But when we are judged, we are chastened of the Lord, that we should not be *condemned* with the world" (1 Cor. 11:31,32). These verses imply that if we do not examine ourselves, we could incur condemnation with the world.

He also cautioned believers, "Be not deceived; God is not mocked: for whatsoever a man soweth, that shall he also reap. For he that soweth to his flesh shall of the flesh reap corruption; but he that soweth to the Spirit shall of the Spirit reap life everlasting" (Gal. 6:7,8).

The Bible also warns that condemnation (damnation) comes upon any professing believer who is lifted up with pride (1 Tim. 3:6); who speaks idle words (Matt. 12:37; Titus 2:8); who condemns others (Luke 6:37; Rom. 2:1); who holds a grudge (James 5:9); and who condemns himself in the things which he allows, "for whatsoever is not of faith is sin" (Rom. 14:22,23).

Jesus said to the woman who was taken in the act of adultery, "Neither do I *condemn* thee: go, and sin no more" (John 8:11). Jesus implied that she will be condemned if she continues to sin.

Some of the parables also warn that faithful servants of Christ who have become unfaithful will lose their reward as well as their salvation. They will be condemned with unbelievers at the judgment. Jesus spoke of the servant who will be made ruler over all his lord's possessions because he is found faithful when his lord returns. "But and if *that servant* say in his heart, My lord delayeth his coming; and shall begin to beat the menservants and maidens, and to eat and drink, and to be drunken; the lord of that servant will come in a day when he looketh not for him, and at an hour when he is not aware, *and will cut him in sunder, and will appoint him his portion with the unbelievers*" (Luke 12:45-47).

Similarly, in the parable of the talents, Jesus told of "a man traveling into a far country, who called *his own servants*, and delivered unto them his goods." Upon his return, the servants who gained other talents were promised to be made rulers "over many things" and entered into the joy of their lord. But think of it! One of Christ's own servants, the one who hid his talent in the earth, was condemned and cast "into outer darkness" where "there shall be weeping and gnashing of teeth [the second death]" (Matt. 25:14). See also Luke 19:12-27.

Jesus further warned those who walk after the flesh: "Not every one that saith unto me, Lord, Lord, shall enter into the kingdom of heaven; but he that doeth the will of my Father which is in heaven. Many will say to me in that day, Lord, Lord, have we not prophesied in thy name? And in thy name have cast out devils? And in thy name done many wonderful works? And then will I profess unto them, I never knew you: depart from me, *ye that work iniquity*" (Matt. 7:21-23). Luke's account adds, "there shall be weeping and gnashing of teeth," which again speaks of condemnation and the second death (13:28). These people thought they were saved, but woke to the startling reality that they were eternally damned because of their compromise with iniquity.

These passages drive home the importance of knowing that we "are in Christ Jesus" and that we are walking "not after the flesh, but after the Spirit" (Rom. 8:1). Only then are we free from the shackles of condemnation.

In summary, the judgment seat of Christ will occur at the resurrection, on the last day. All will be there, both the just and the unjust. Overcomers will be justified and inherit everlasting life, but the wicked will be condemned and inherit everlasting punishment, which is the lake of fire—the second death.

17

Overcoming Triumphantly Until Jesus Comes

What does it mean to overcome?

Overcoming is contrary to passivity, to giving up, or to being defeated. It speaks of prevailing or conquering triumphantly over obstacles and difficulties. Therefore, it involves conflict and a fight of faith. Paul compared the Christian with a good soldier who endures hardness (2 Tim. 2:3,4) and an athlete who strives to win in competitive games (2 Tim. 2:5; Heb. 12:1).

As Christians, we are in a spiritual struggle against "the wiles [the strategies and the deceits] of the devil. For we wrestle not against flesh and blood, but against principalities, against powers, against the rulers of the darkness of this world, against spiritual wickedness in high places" (Eph. 6:11,12). Therefore, we are instructed to "put on the whole armour of God," to "hold fast," and to overcome and keep the works of Jesus until the end (Eph. 6:11; Rev. 2:25,26).

Is it possible to live an overcoming life?

Yes, it is. God has made every provision for us to reign in life through Jesus Christ. Consider these scriptures:

"There hath no temptation taken you but such as is common to man: but God is faithful, who will not suffer you to be tempted above that ye are able; but will with the temptation also make a way to escape, that ye may be able to bear it" (1 Cor. 10:13).

"His divine power hath given unto us *all things that pertain unto life and godliness*, through the knowledge of him that hath called us to glory and virtue" (2 Pet. 1:3).

"Nay, in all these things [tribulation, distress, persecution, famine, etc.] we are *more than conquerors* through him that loved us" (Rom. 8:37).

"And God is able to make *all* grace abound toward you; that ye, *always* having *all* sufficiency in *all* things, may abound to *every* good work" (2 Cor. 9:8).

"Now thanks be unto God, which *always* causeth us to *triumph* in Christ, and maketh manifest the savour of his knowledge by us in every place" (2 Cor. 2:14).

How can I be an overcomer?

The Bible tells us not only *how* to overcome, but *what* to overcome:

We overcome the world by being born of God, by keeping His commandments, by exercising faith in Him, and by believing that Jesus is the Son of God. "For this is the love of God, that we *keep his commandments*: and his commandments are not grievous. For whatsoever is *born* of God overcometh the *world*: and this is the victory that overcometh the world, even *our faith.* Who is he that overcometh the world, but he that *believeth* that Jesus is the Son of God?" (1 John 5:3-5). To overcome the world is to overcome sin or all that is opposed to keeping the commandments of God. According to 1 John 2:16, the "world" is defined as "the lust of the flesh, and the lust of the eyes, and the pride of life"—pleasures, possessions, and position.

Notice the importance of *our faith*—"this is the victory that overcometh the world, even *our faith.*" Unbelief, the opposite of faith, is the reason why many are not overcoming the world. The symptoms of unbelief are fearfulness (Mark 4:40; Rev. 21:8); murmuring (Psa. 106:24,25); disobedience (Psa. 106:24,25); resistance to the truth (John 8:45,46; Heb. 4:2); hypocrisy (Matt. 21:23-27); speaking evil against the truth (Acts 14:2; 19:9); an evil heart and backsliding (Heb. 3:12); discouragement (compare Ex. 14:11-13 with Psa. 106:6-12); hardness of heart (Mark 16:14; Luke 24:25); a defiled conscience (Titus 1:15); and unrest and condemnation (John 3:36; Rom. 11:20; Heb. 3:18,19; 4:6,11).

On the other hand, as long as a believer exercises faith in God, he is teachable (Luke 8:13-15; 1 Thess. 2:13); keeps the commandments of God (Rev. 14:12); serves God without hypocrisy

(1 Tim. 1:5; Heb. 10:22); overcomes the world and insurmountable obstacles (1 John 5:4,5; Matt. 17:20); inherits the promises of God (Gal. 3:22; Heb. 6:12); resists the devil (1 Pet. 5:8,9); is valiant in fighting the "good fight" (1 Tim. 6:12; 2 Tim. 4:7; Heb. 11:33,34); does not "draw back" when persecuted (Heb. 10:32-39); is "able to quench all the fiery darts of the wicked" (Eph. 6:16); pleases God (Heb. 11:6); and enters into His rest (Heb. 4:5-11).

We overcome false prophets through having Jesus, the Greater One, abiding in us. "Many false prophets are gone out into the world. . . . Ye are of God, little children, and have overcome them: because greater is he that is in you, than he that is in the world" (1 John 4:1,4). Jesus declared, "My sheep hear my voice, and I know them, and they follow me" (John 10:27) and "a stranger will they not follow, but will flee from him: for they know not the voice of strangers" (John 10:5). Paul testified, "*Christ liveth in me*: and the life which I now live in the flesh I live by the faith of the Son of God, who loved me, and gave himself for me" (Gal. 2:20); "I can do all things through Christ which strengtheneth me" (Phil. 4:13).

We overcome the man of sin by having our names written in the Lamb's book of life. "And all that dwell upon the earth shall worship him [the man of sin, the beast], whose names are not written in the book of life of the Lamb" (Rev. 13:8). This verse implies that all whose names are written in the Lamb's book of life do not worship him. With reference to overcoming the beast, Revelation 14:12 states, "Here is the patience of the saints: here are they that keep the commandments of God, and the faith of Jesus."

We overcome the evil that others do to us by our patience, forbearance, and kindness. "Therefore, if thine enemy hunger, feed him; if he thirst, give him drink: for in so doing thou shalt heap coals of fire on his head. Be not overcome of evil, but overcome evil with good" (Rom. 12:20,21).

We overcome Satan and his temptations by the blood of Jesus, by the Word of God, and by self-denial. "And they overcame him [Satan] by the blood of the Lamb, and by the word of their testimony [speaking the Word of God]; and they loved not their lives unto the death [they were ready to die for the Word of

God]" (Rev. 12:11). "I have written unto you, young men, because ye are strong, and the word of God abideth in you, and ye have overcome the wicked one" (1 John 2:14).

Victory over Satan will never result from a casual attitude toward God's Word. Speaking the powerful Word of God enabled Christ to overcome the temptations of Satan. The Scripture tells us all we need to know for victorious Christian warfare. We must experience God's Word, know it, study it, live it, speak it, and be willing to die for it.

As a believer, what should I do when I am tempted to sin?

God's Word tells you how to overcome temptation:

1. Recognize your enemy, the devil. Satan's seducing spirits tempt you to sin. "And Satan stood up against Israel, and provoked [enticed] David to number Israel" (1 Chr. 21:1). See also Matt. 4:1; John 13:2; 1 Thess. 3:5.

2. Remember that Jesus defeated the devil. Because of Christ's victory, you do not have to commit sin; it has no power over you. "He that committeth sin is of the devil; for the devil sinneth from the beginning. For this purpose the Son of God was manifested, that he might destroy the works of the devil. Whosoever is born of God doth not commit sin; for his seed [the Word of God] remaineth in him: and he cannot sin, because he is born of God" (1 John 3:8,9). See also 1 John 2:29; 5:18.

One who is born again by the incorruptible seed of the Word of God does not practice sin because his heart has been changed by the power of God from sinning to practicing righteousness. "God be thanked, that ye were the servants of sin, but ye have obeyed from the heart that form of doctrine which was delivered you. Being then made free from sin, ye became the servants of righteousness" (Rom. 6:17,18). Jesus has set you free from the power of sin. "If the Son therefore shall make you free, ye shall be free indeed" (John 8:36). "Sin shall not have dominion over you" (Rom. 6:14).

3. Give no place to the devil (Eph. 4:27). In other words, avoid the things that tempt you. Here are some scriptural guidelines:

• Flee wickedness. "Enter not into the path of the wicked and go not in the way of evil men. Avoid it, pass not by it, turn from it, and pass away. For they sleep not, except they have done mischief; and their sleep is taken away, unless they *cause some to fall*" (Pro. 4:14-16). God's Word further tells us to flee fornication (1 Cor. 6:18), idolatry (1 Cor. 10:14), the love of money (1 Tim. 6:11), and youthful lusts (2 Tim. 2:22). See also Psa. 1:1; Pro. 1:10; 7:5; 16:29.

• Set no wicked thing before your eyes. David said, "I will walk within my house with a perfect heart. I will set no wicked thing before mine eyes" (Psa. 101:2,3).

• Guard your speech (Psa. 39:1). "Let no corrupt communication proceed out of your mouth" (Eph. 4:29); "Neither filthiness, nor foolish talking, nor jesting, which are not convenient: but rather giving of thanks" (Eph. 5:4).

• Don't be curious about evil things (1 Cor. 10:6). Going near a hornets' nest is dangerous. "Be separate, saith the Lord, and touch not the unclean thing" (2 Cor. 6:17).

• Keep a good conscience. With reference to warring "a good warfare," Paul admonished Timothy to hold "faith, and a good conscience; which some having put away concerning faith have made shipwreck" (1 Tim. 1:19). To do doubtful things is to be damned because "whatsoever is not of faith is sin" (Rom. 14:23). See also Acts 24:16.

• Fill your heart and mind with the Word of God and think on pure things. "Thy word have I hid in mine heart, that I might not sin against thee" (Psa. 119:11). "Ye are strong, and the word of God abideth in you, and ye have overcome the wicked one" (1 John 2:14). "Whatsoever things are true, whatsoever things are honest, whatsoever things are just, whatsoever things are pure, whatsoever things are lovely, whatsoever things are of good report; if there be any virtue, and if there be any praise, *think on these things*" (Phil. 4:8). Avoid whatever does not measure up to this standard. See also 1 Cor. 15:33; 2 Cor. 10:4,5.

• Do not be idle. An idle person falls into many temptations: "And withal they learn to be idle, wandering about from house to house; and *not only idle*, but tattlers also and busybodies, speaking things which they ought not" (1 Tim. 5:13). David fell into temptation and sin when he was idle (2 Sam. 11:1-3).

• "Abstain from all appearance of evil" (1 Thess. 5:22). To avoid the appearance of evil is to avoid the evil itself.

4. *"Resist the devil, and he will flee from you" (James 4:7).* The context of this verse tells you how to resist the devil:

• Humble yourself and God will give you more grace to overcome.

• Submit to the will of God, not to your temptation. Yielding to temptation leads to sin and its miseries, spiritual death, and the lake of fire (1 Tim. 6:9,10; James 1:14,15; Rev. 21:8). Yielding to God and overcoming temptation brings eternal blessing (James 1:12; Rom. 6:13-22).

• Resist the devil. In the name of Jesus, command him to flee. See Matt. 16:23.

5. *Trust Jesus to help you; He is greater than the devil.* "Greater is he that is in you, than he that is in the world" (1 John 4:4). Without Jesus you can do nothing; depend on Him.

• Jesus is sympathetic. He "was in all points tempted like as we are, yet without sin. Let us therefore come boldly unto the throne of grace, that we may obtain mercy, and find grace to help in time of need" (Heb. 4:15,16). See also Heb. 2:18.

• Jesus is at the right hand of the Father making intercession for you (Rom. 8:34). When Simon Peter was in the midst of temptation, our Lord said to him, "Simon, Simon, behold, Satan hath desired to have you, that he may sift you as wheat: But I have prayed for thee, that thy *faith* fail not: and when thou art converted, strengthen thy brethren" (Luke 22:31,32). See also John 17:15.

What does the Bible say about our living an overcoming life in the midst of tribulation?

God's grace is sufficient even in the midst of tribulation. Although the church at Smyrna suffered tribulation, poverty, the reproach and blasphemy of counterfeit believers, and the threat of imprisonment and death, they overcame triumphantly (Rev. 2:8-11). Also, John foresaw those who "came out of great tribulation" (Rev. 7:14) and "had gotten the victory over the beast, and over his image, and over his mark, and over the number of his name" (Rev. 15:2).

God will enable the following people to endure to the end and emerge victorious through tribulation:

Those who maintain their faith by praying without fainting—In the parable of the unjust judge (Luke 18:1-8), Jesus implied that when He comes again, He will find faith on the earth if men will pray always and not faint. He told of the widow who was avenged by the judge because she came continually saying, "Avenge me of mine adversary." This prayer of submission puts our case in God's hands, the hands of a just and faithful judge, instead of trying to fight our own battles. In times of persecution, we must cry for justice, not vengeance. Take courage in our Lord's words, "And shall not God avenge his own elect, which cry day and night unto him, though he bear long with them? I tell you that he will avenge them speedily." The Lord will come suddenly to "recompense tribulation" to those who persecute His Church (Rev. 6:9-17; 1 Thess. 5:3; 2 Thess. 1:4-8). Prayer, supplication in particular, is the key to sustaining our faith and overcoming our enemies in the dark days ahead.

Those who hear the Word of God and do it—The end-time will be marked by *rains* of lawlessness (2 Tim. 3:1-5), *floods* of persecution (Isa. 59:19; Rev. 12:15,16), and *winds* of false doctrine and deceitfulness (Eph. 4:14; 2 Thess. 2:9-13). Those who hear and obey the Word will not be defeated. "Whosoever heareth these sayings of mine, and doeth them, I will liken him unto a wise man, which built his house upon a rock: And the *rain* descended, and the *floods* came, and the *winds* blew, and beat upon that house; and it fell not: for it was founded upon a rock" (Matt. 7:24,25).

Those who are filled with the Holy Spirit—In times of persecution, the Holy Spirit will give wisdom "which all your adversaries shall not be able to gainsay nor resist" (Luke 21:15; Acts 6:10). He will also impart boldness (Acts 4:31), faith (Acts 6:5), comfort (Acts 9:31), joy (Acts 13:50-52; 1 Thess. 1:6), power (Acts 1:8; 2 Tim. 1:7), and love (Rom. 5:3-5). The Holy Spirit will also intercede through us in prayer according to the will of God (Rom. 8:26,27). What a comfort in times of trouble!

Those who fear the Lord—In the midst of tribulation, God's Word assures us that "the fear of the Lord is strong confidence:

and his children shall have a place of refuge" (Pro. 14:26). The fear of the Lord is also the beginning of knowledge and wisdom (Pro. 1:7; 9:10); a hatred of evil (Pro. 8:13); a treasure to the saints (Pro. 15:16, Isa. 33:6); a fountain of life, to depart from the snares of death (Pro. 14:27); and a reverence for Almighty God that we need to serve Him acceptably (Heb. 12:28).

The Bible records many examples of God-fearing men and women who courageously obeyed God in the face of death. Obadiah, who feared the Lord from his youth, hid and fed one hundred prophets of God when they were cut off by Jezebel (1 Kings 18:3,4,12). The Hebrew midwives "feared God, and did not as the king of Egypt commanded them, but saved the men children alive" (Ex. 1:17). Peter and the other apostles said to the council, "We ought to obey God rather than men" (Acts 5:29). Believers in heaven who "had gotten the victory over the beast" are marked by the fear of God. Their victory song proclaims, "Who shall not fear thee, O Lord, and glorify thy name?" (Rev. 15:2-4).

Truly, God "will fulfill the desire of them that fear him: he also will hear their cry, and will save them" (Psa. 145:19). "The angel of the Lord encampeth round about them that fear him, and delivereth them" (Psa. 34:7). "It shall be well with them that fear God" (Eccl. 8:12).

Those who put Christ before self and possessions—Jesus linked this truth both with persecution and with His coming in glory: "If any man will come after me, let him deny himself, and take up his cross, and follow me. For whosoever will save his life shall lose it: and whosoever will lose his life for my sake shall find it. For what is a man profited, if he shall gain the whole world, and lose his own soul? or what shall a man give in exchange for his soul? For the Son of man shall come in the glory of his Father with his angels; and then he shall reward every man according to his works" (Matt. 16:24-27).

In summary, the Bible gives many examples of people who prove that it is possible to live an overcoming life in the midst of tribulation. Unfortunately, Christians today do not even want to hear about the coming persecution of the Church, which indicates little or no cross experience on their part and little resolve to walk with God regardless of the cost.

Why does the New Testament frequently urge us to overcome covetousness in view of the Second Coming?

Overcoming the world and denying self include overcoming the spirit of covetousness, which is selfish desire beyond reason. A person can be covetous for acquiring material possessions, money, luxury, food, power, or any number of things. God's Word declares, "Love not the *world*, neither *the things* that are in the *world*. If any man love the *world*, the love of the Father is not in him. For all that is in the *world*, the lust of the flesh, and the lust of the eyes, and the pride of life, is not of the Father, but is of the *world*" (1 John 2:15,16).

The love of money is the root of all evil (1 Tim. 6:10). Here's a list of some of these evils and the biblical characters who perpetrated them:

- theft, Achan (Josh. 7:21)
- betrayal, Judas (Luke 22:4,5)
- religious racketeering, Gehazi (2 Kings 4:15-27)
- fraud, the Jews robbing their brethren (Neh. 5:6-8)
- pride, the rich church of the Laodiceans (Rev. 3:17)
- bribery and injustice, Samuel's sons (1 Sam. 8:3)
- idolatry, Demetrius, the silversmith (Acts 19:24-29)
- lying, Ananias and Sapphira (Acts 5:1-10)
- inconsideration of others, Lot of Abraham (Gen. 13:9-11)
- overreaching, Laban (Gen. 31:7)
- shamelessness, the people in Jeremiah's day (Jer. 8:10-12)
- hatred, the Pharisees (Luke 16:14)
- forsaking the right way, Balaam (2 Pet. 2:15)
- departing from the faith, Demas (2 Tim. 4:10)
- selfishness, the rich fool (Luke 12:15-21)
- domestic problems, he who is greedy of gain (Pro. 15:27)
- witchcraft, the damsel and her masters (Acts 16:16-19)

Scripture also teaches that a covetous person is an idolater (Eph. 5:5; Col. 3:5); an enemy of God (Phil. 3:18,19); cursed (2 Pet. 2:14; Psa. 10:3); sorrowful (1 Tim. 6:10); unqualified for the Lord's service (Phil. 2:20,21; 1 Tim. 3:3; Ex. 18:21); and hell bound (1 Tim. 6:9; 1 Cor. 6:10).

Overcoming the economic implications of the number of the beast (666) will be tremendously difficult because no man will be able to buy or sell. (This includes everything from buying groceries to earning wages.) He will have to take the mark or name of the beast, or the number of his name (666), on his right hand or forehead (Rev. 13:16-18). Living for material possessions will increase the possibility of one's taking the mark of the beast. Therefore, as Christians, we should learn contentment and "seek first the kingdom of God and His righteousness" (Matt. 6:33).

Scripture states, "Let your conversation [manner of life] be without covetousness; and be content with such things as ye have: for he hath said, I will never leave thee, nor forsake thee. So that we may boldly say, The Lord is my helper, and I will not fear what man shall do unto me" (Heb. 13:5,6). The Lord will never forsake us; therefore, we need not live covetously or fear what man can do to us, not even the man of sin. Glory to God!

Jesus emphatically warned, "Take heed, and beware of covetousness: for a man's life consisteth not in the abundance of things which he possesseth" (Luke 12:15); "It is easier for a camel to go through the eye of a needle, than for a rich man to enter into the kingdom of God" (Matt. 19:24); "Remember Lot's wife" (Luke 17:32).

To fight the good fight of faith and to lay hold of eternal life, one must learn contentment and pursue spiritual things. "And having food and raiment let us be therewith content. But they that will be rich fall into temptation and a snare, and into many foolish and hurtful lusts, which drown men in destruction and perdition. For the love of money is the root of all evil: which while some coveted after, they have erred from the faith, and pierced themselves through with many sorrows. But thou, O man of God, flee these things; and follow after righteousness, godliness, faith, love, patience, meekness. Fight the good fight of faith, lay hold on eternal life. . . . I give thee charge in the the sight of God, . . . that thou keep this commandment without spot, unrebukeable, until the appearing of our Lord Jesus Christ" (1 Tim. 6:8-14). "Godliness with contentment is great gain" (1 Tim. 6:6). Contentment is one key to living an overcoming life, especially in these last days when many are carried away by the spirit of materialism and the love of money (2 Tim. 3:2; 2 Pet. 2:1-3).

Who will be able to overcome the beast and his image?

In the last days, all the world must worship the beast and his image or be killed (Rev. 13:14,15). Who will have power to resist? Those whose names are written in the Lamb's book of life

(Rev. 13:8) and who are obeying the apostolic injunctions, "abstain from pollutions of idols" (Acts 15:20) and "keep yourselves from idols" (1 John 5:21). They'll refuse to bow to the beast and his image as Shadrach, Meshach, and Abednego refused to bow to the image of King Nebuchadnezzar (Dan. 3). In other words, one must overcome all forms of idolatry now to have power to resist the seduction of the beast and his image.

The Bible forbids making and revering all visible representations of God. The second commandment states, "Thou shalt *not make* unto thee any graven image. . . . Thou shalt *not bow down* thyself to them, *nor serve them*: for I the Lord thy God am a jealous God" (Ex. 20:4,5). In fact, the Bible contains more references to the second commandment than to any other of the Ten Commandments.

This commandment forbids the worship of the true God with any tangible impression of Him. Aaron took gold from the people and "fashioned it with a graving tool, after he had made it a molten calf: and they said, These be thy gods, O Israel, which brought thee up out of the land of Egypt. And when Aaron saw it, he built an altar before it; and Aaron made proclamation, and said, Tomorrow *is a feast to the Lord*" (Ex. 32:4,5). Aaron tried to represent the Lord with an outward form on which the people could focus their worship.

More than ever, Christianity is filled with so-called pictures of Christ, symbols of the Holy Spirit in the form of a dove, crucifixes, icons, and other images. Many people claim that these are not worshiped but are mere representations. This duplicates Aaron's sin in setting up the golden calf and breaking the second commandment.

The Bible forbids making and revering all visible representations of God for several reasons:

1. They are grossly evil and deceptive.
2. They portray false and destructive impressions of God and, consequently, are a hindrance to approaching Him.
3. They are incompatible with the love of God.
4. They provoke God to anger and to jealousy.

Let's examine each reason in more detail.

1. Visible representations of God are grossly evil and deceptive. The Bible describes idolatry as:

- the vain imaginations of those who reject God (Rom. 1:21-23)
- a teacher of lies (Isa. 44:19,20; Jer. 10:14,15; Hab. 2:18,19; Rom. 1:23,25)
- blasphemy (Ezek. 20:24-31)
- an abomination to God (Deut. 7:25; Isa. 44:19; Ezek. 8:9,10; 16:36; 1 Pet. 4:3)
- a snare (Deut. 7:25; Psa. 106:36)
- a cursed thing (Deut. 7:26)
- that which is vain and unprofitable (2 Kings 17:15,16; Psa. 115:4-8; Isa. 41:29; 44:9,10; 46:5-7; Jer. 8:19; 10:3-5)

The Bible also links the practice of idolatry with:

- turning to "weak and beggarly elements" and "bondage" (Gal. 4:8,9)
- hating God (Ex. 20:5)
- holding fast to deceit (Isa. 44:20; Jer. 8:5; 1 Cor. 12:2)
- having fellowship with devils (Duet. 32:17; 2 Chr. 11:15; Psa. 106:36,37; 1 Cor. 10:20,21; Rev. 9:20)
- practicing witchcraft and offering human sacrifices (2 Kings 17:16,17; 21:6,7; 2 Chr. 33:6,7; Ezek. 23:37-39)
- spiritual adultery and estrangement from God (Ezek. 6:9; 14:5; 23:37; 44:10)
- self-corruption and defilement (Deut. 4:16-18; Ezek. 20:7; 36:18; Acts 15:20)
- unanswered prayer (Ezek. 20:31)
- polluting God's name (Isa. 42:8; Ezek. 20:39)
- ignorance and superstition (Acts 17:16,22,23)
- sodomy, atheism, astrology, and other evils (Acts 7:40-43; Rom. 1:21-32)
- rebellion and unbelief (2 Kings 17:14-16)
- forgetting and virtually forsaking God (2 Kings 22:17; Jer. 2:9-13; Psa. 106:19-21)

2. Visible representations of God portray false and destructive impressions of Him and, consequently, are a hindrance to approaching Him.

- "No man hath seen God at anytime" (John 1:18) and "God is a Spirit: and they that worship him must worship him in spirit and in truth" (John 4:24). Therefore, all representations of Him are false. God commanded the children of Israel, "Take ye therefore good heed unto yourselves; for *ye saw no manner of similitude* on the day that the Lord spake unto you in Horeb out of the midst of the fire: Lest ye corrupt yourselves, and *make* you a *graven image*, the similitude of any figure, the likeness of male or female, the likeness of any beast that is on the earth, the likeness of an winged fowl that flieth in the air, the likeness of any thing that creepeth on the ground, the likeness of any fish that is in the waters beneath the earth" (Deut. 4:15-18).

Likewise, no one has seen the Lord Jesus Christ in the fullness of His glory. "Who only hath immortality, dwelling in the light which no man can approach unto; *whom no man hath seen, nor can see*" (1 Tim. 6:16). "When he shall appear, . . . we shall see him as he is" (1 John 3:2). "For now we see through a glass, darkly; but then face to face" (1 Cor. 13:12). See also 2 Cor. 5:16; 1 Tim. 1:17.

Sadly, many religious groups are revering physical representations of God the Holy Spirit, particularly the symbol of the dove. We need to seriously consider Paul's warning: To change "*the glory of the uncorruptible God* into an image made like to corruptible man, and to *birds*, and four-footed beasts, and creeping things" is to change "the truth of God into a lie" and to worship and serve "the creature more than the Creator" (Rom. 1:23,25). See also Deut. 4:17.

• God has ordained that faith comes by hearing the Word, not by seeing an image (Rom. 10:17). "We walk by faith, not by sight" (2 Cor. 5:7). We love and believe in Jesus, though we have not seen Him. "Whom having *not seen*, ye love; in whom, *though now ye see him not*, yet *believing*, ye rejoice with joy unspeakable and full of glory" (1 Pet. 1:8). By faith Moses esteemed "the reproach of Christ greater riches than the treasures in Egypt" and "forsook Egypt, not fearing the wrath of the king: for he endured, as seeing him who is *invisible*" (Heb. 11:26,27). In contrast to the Egyptians who worshiped hideous, visible gods, Moses saw Christ through the eyes of faith.

• To approach God, a person doesn't need a material object. God has given His Word and Holy Spirit to reveal Christ. By faith, in the name of Jesus, we can go directly to the throne of grace for help in our time of need (Heb. 4:16).

• God cannot be likened to man-made images. "To whom then

will ye liken me, or shall I be equal? saith the Holy One" (Isa. 40:25). In his message at Mars Hill, Paul said, "Forasmuch then as we are the offspring of God, *we ought not to think that the Godhead is like unto* gold, or silver, or stone, graven by art and man's device" (Acts 17:29).

God is omnipresent (everywhere present) (Psa. 139:7-10); idols are in one place at a time and must be carried (Isa. 46:5-7; Jer. 10:5).

God is omniscient (all knowing) (Psa. 44:21); idols are "dumb" (Hab. 2:18).

God, the creator of heaven and earth, is omnipotent (all powerful) (Matt. 28:18); idols are lifeless and helpless. "They have mouths, but they speak not: eyes have they, but they see not: They have ears, but they hear not: noses have they, but they smell not: They have hands, but they handle not: feet have they, but they walk not: neither speak they through their throat. They that make them are like unto them; so is every one that trusteth in them. O Israel, trust thou in the Lord: he is their help and their shield" (Psa. 115:3-9). "The Lord is the true God, he is the living God, and an everlasting king. . . . The gods that have not made the heavens and the earth, even they shall perish from the earth" (Jer. 10:10,11).

3. Visible representations of God are incompatible with His love. "What agreement hath the temple of God [the believer] with idols? for ye are the temple of the living God; as God hath said, I will dwell in them, and walk in them; and I will be their God, and they shall be my people. Wherefore come out from among them, and be ye separate, saith the Lord, and touch not the unclean thing; and I will receive you, and will be a Father unto you, and ye shall be my sons and daughters, saith the Lord Almighty" (2 Cor. 6:16-18). See also Gen. 35:2,3; Josh. 24:14,23; 1 Sam. 7:3; 1 Kings 18:21; 1 Cor. 10:21.

God wants to show His love to us by being with us, but He cannot dwell where idolatry is present. Therefore, God instructs us not to bring idols into our homes (Deut. 7:26); not to covet the monetary or sentimental value of them, but to destroy them utterly (Ex. 34:13; Num. 33:52; Deut. 7:5,25,26; 2 Sam. 5:21); not to partake of the Lord's supper with a brother who is an idolater (1 Cor. 5:11); to repent and turn from idols to serve the living God (Acts 17:29,30; 1 Thess. 1:9); to keep ourselves from idols (Josh. 23:7); and to testify against idolatry though it may bring persecution (Acts 14:15; 19:26).

4. Visible representations of God provoke Him to anger and jealousy. More than any other sin, the hated sin of idolatry provokes God to anger and jealousy. Old and New Testament writers recorded this truth more than fifty times in the Bible. Israel's idolatry so provoked the Lord to anger that He said to Moses, "Now therefore let me alone, that my wrath may wax hot against them, and that I may consume them" (Ex. 32:10). Using Israel's idolatry as an example, Paul warned the Church, "Now these things were our examples, to the intent we should not lust after evil things, as they also lusted. *Neither be ye idolaters*, as were some of them; as it is written, The people sat down to eat and drink, and rose up to play. . . . Wherefore, my dearly beloved, *flee from idolatry* . . . What say I then? that the *idol* is any thing, or that which is offered in sacrifice to *idols* is any thing? But I say, that the things which the Gentiles sacrifice, they sacrifice to *devils*, and not to God: and I would not that ye should have fellowship with *devils*. Ye cannot drink the cup of the Lord, and the cup of *devils*: ye cannot be partakers of the Lord's table, and of the table of *devils*. Do we *provoke the Lord to jealousy*? are we stronger than he?" (1 Cor. 10:6,7,14,19-22).

The New Testament further admonishes, "Be not deceived: neither fornicators, nor *idolaters* . . . shall inherit the kingdom of God" (1 Cor. 6:9,10). "*Idolaters*, and all liars, shall have their part in the lake which burneth with fire and brimstone" (Rev. 21:8). Moreover, with specific reference to those who "worship the beast and his image," God's Word declares, "the same shall drink of the wine of the wrath of God, which is poured out without mixture into the cup of his indignation; and he shall be tormented with fire and brimstone in the presence of the holy angels, and in the presence of the Lamb: And the smoke of their torment ascendeth up for ever and ever: and they have no rest day nor night, who worship the beast and his image" (Rev. 14:9-11).

In addition to making visible representations of God, glorying in men is another form of idolatry. God says, "I am the Lord:

that is my name: and *my glory will I not give to another*, neither my praise to graven images" (Isa. 42:8). Excessive admiration of persons could lead many to worship the beast. The Scripture commands, "Thou shalt worship the Lord thy God, and him only shalt thou serve" (Luke 4:8); "Let no man glory in men" (1 Cor. 3:21); "How can ye believe, which receive honour one of another, and seek not the honour that cometh from God only?" (John 5:44); and "He that glorieth, let him glory in the Lord" (1 Cor. 1:31). Moreover, the Bible says there is "One God and Father of all, who is above all, and through all, and in you all" (Eph. 4:6); "And call no man your father upon the earth: for one is your Father, which is in heaven. Neither be ye called masters: for one is your Master, even Christ" (Matt. 23:9,10).

Rather than worshiping the beast and his image, we should "*fear God*, and give glory to him; . . . and worship him that made heaven, and earth, and the sea, and the fountains of waters" (Rev. 14:7). Resisting all forms of idolatry now will strengthen us to resist worshiping "the beast" and "his image" during the coming days of tribulation. God will give us grace to refuse though threatened with death itself (Dan. 3:18; Rev. 13:14-18; 20:4).

How important is Christian fellowship to living an overcoming life?

Not only should believers assemble to encourage one another, but they should gather "*so much the more*" as they see "the day approaching" (Heb. 10:25). In these last days of apostasy, God-fearing believers increasingly need to encourage one another (Mal. 3:16). Exhortation helps to edify them and keep them from being "hardened through the deceitfulness of sin" (Heb. 3:13). Scripture gives other important reasons for "not forsaking the assembling of ourselves together":

- To bear one another's burdens (Gal. 6:2; Rom. 15:1-7)
- To provoke one another to good works (Heb. 10:24)
- To show Christian love to one another (Col. 2:2; 1 Pet. 3:8)
- To help spread the gospel (Acts 13:2,3; 14:27)
- To comfort one another (1 Thess. 4:18; 5:11)
- To have power in prayer (Matt. 18:19,20)

• To magnify the Lord together (Psa. 34:3)

• To strengthen one another in the faith (Luke 22:32; Acts 18:23)

• To follow righteousness, faith, love, and peace "with them that call on the Lord out of a pure heart" (2 Tim. 2:22).

In these last days of apostasy and persecution, like-minded believers may again have to meet in homes as they did in the early church. Let's look at some New Testament examples:

• The Holy Spirit was first poured out in an "upper room" of a house (Acts 1:13).

• "In every house" the apostles "ceased not to teach and preach Jesus Christ" (Acts 5:42).

• Peter first met with Gentiles in the house of Cornelius (Acts 10:22,27).

• The Lord's table was served in houses (Acts 2:46; 20:7,8).

• Prayer was made without ceasing in the house of Mary (Acts 12:5,12).

• There was prayer for the sick in houses (Acts 9:33,34,39-41).

• Philip's four daughters evidently prophesied in their house (Acts 21:8,9).

• Persecution in the synagogue meant meetings in the house of Justus (Acts 18:7,8).

• Saul entered every house and arrested believers. No doubt they were the houses where the church gathered (Acts 8:3).

• The apostles wrote about the church in the house of Aquila and Priscilla (1 Cor. 16:19); in the house of Nymphas (Col. 4:15); in the house of Philemon (Phile. 1:1,2); and in the house of the elect lady (2 John 1:1,10).

In the early church, the emphasis was on spreading the gospel into all the world (Acts 8:4; 11:19), prayer (Acts 13:3), purity of doctrine (Acts 2:42; 1 Tim. 1:3), and purity of heart (Acts 2:46), not on church buildings or denominations. The New Testament states that our bodies are the temple of the living God (1 Cor. 3:16,17; 6:19,20; 2 Cor. 6:16; Eph. 2:20-22; 1 Pet. 2:5). In fact, church buildings as we know them today did not exist until the third century.

Jesus graciously promises that "if two of you shall agree on earth as touching any thing that they shall ask, it shall be done for them of my Father which is in heaven. For where two or three are gathered together in my name, there am I in the midst of them" (Matt. 18:19,20). Thus, when we fellowship in His name, the Lord Himself is with us, and He helps us to lead an overcoming life.

What are the consequences of not living an overcoming life?

According to Christ's message to the seven churches mentioned in Revelation chapters two and three, the consequences of not living an overcoming life is condemnation when Jesus comes on the Day of Judgment.

Sadly, many teach that believers will not come into judgment and that they can never lose their salvation. While Jesus promised eternal reward to overcomers, He also admonished those who left their "first love" (Rev. 2:4,5); who upheld false teachers and false doctrines (Rev. 2:14,15, 20-23); who were not watchful (Rev. 3:3); and who were "lukewarm" (Rev. 3:16) to repent and overcome lest they be condemned.

Consider, for example, the church at Pergamos. They were upholding false doctrine, which Jesus hates. Therefore, He rebuked them, saying, "*Repent*; or else I will come unto thee quickly, and will fight against them with the *sword* of my mouth" (Rev. 2:16). Scripture affirms that this verse refers to condemnation on the last day: "And out of his mouth goeth a *sharp sword*, that with it he should smite the nations: and he shall rule them with a rod of iron: and he treadeth the winepress of the fierceness and wrath of Almighty God" (Rev. 19:15).

Also, to the church at Sardis, Jesus said, "Remember therefore how thou hast received and heard, and hold fast, and *repent*. If therefore thou shalt not watch, I will come on thee as a *thief*, and thou shalt not know what hour I will come upon thee" (Rev. 3:3). We know that Jesus' coming to us as a thief can only mean eternal condemnation (Matt. 24:43; 1 Thess. 5:2-4). See Chapter Sixteen.

What blessings does Jesus promise to overcomers?

In the Book of Revelation, Jesus promised many blessings to overcomers. Most of these are eternal blessings, not temporal or fleeting pleasures.

- "to eat of the tree of life, which is in the midst of the paradise of God" (2:7)
- to "not be hurt of the second death" (2:11)
- "to eat of the hidden manna" (2:17)
- to receive "a white stone, and in the stone a new name written" (2:17)
- to receive "power over the nations" (2:26)
- to receive "the morning star" (2:28)
- to "be clothed in white raiment" (3:5)
- to have our names kept in the book of life (3:5)
- to have Jesus confess our names before the Father and His angels (3:5)
- to be "a pillar in the temple" of God (3:12)
- to have the name of God, the name of the city of God, and a new name written upon us (3:12)
- to sit with Jesus in His throne (3:21)
- to inherit all things (21:7)
- to be the sons and daughters of God throughout eternity

Thus, the overcomer shall be blessed of God, not condemned.

Worldwide persecution against the Church may lurk just around the corner. The diligent will be prepared for persecution, girding themselves in holy armor. By fellowshiping together, avoiding temptation and covetousness, and resisting idolatry, they will overcome until that glorious day of the Lord's return.

18

Rewards

When will rewards be given to the faithful?

The Bible gives a variety of descriptions of this event, which shows that the faithful will be rewarded at the Second Coming of Christ, immediately after the Great Tribulation.

At the appearing of Jesus Christ—"And when the chief Shepherd shall appear, ye shall receive a crown of glory that fadeth not away" (1 Pet. 5:4). See also Matt. 16:27; 2 Tim. 4:8; 1 Pet. 1:7.

At the resurrection of the just—"And thou shalt be blessed; for they cannot recompense thee: for thou shalt be recompensed at the resurrection of the just" (Luke 14:14).

At the seventh and last trump—"And the seventh angel sounded . . . and there were great voices in heaven, saying, The kingdoms of this world are become the kingdoms of our Lord, and of his Christ; and he shall reign for ever and ever . . . and that thou shouldest give reward unto thy servants the prophets, and to the saints, and them that fear thy name, small and great" (Rev.11:15,18).

At the judgment seat of Christ—"For we must all appear before the judgment seat of Christ; that every one may receive the things done in his body, according to that he hath done, whether it be good or bad" (2 Cor. 5:10). See also Matt. 25:31-46; Rev. 20:11-15; 21:7,8.

On the Day of the Lord, which is the Day of Judgment—"Every man's work shall be made manifest: for *the day* shall declare it, because it shall be revealed by fire; and the fire shall try every man's work of what sort it is. If any man's work abide which he hath built thereupon, he shall receive a reward" (1 Cor. 3:13,14). "Holding forth the word of life; that I may rejoice in the day of Christ, that I have not run in vain, neither laboured in vain" (Phil. 2:16). See also Matt. 7:22; 2 Cor. 1:14.

At the end of the world—"But that which ye have already hold fast till I come. And he that overcometh, and keepeth my works unto the end, to him will I give power over the nations" (Rev. 2:25,26). See also 1 Pet. 1:13-17.

At the time of the new heaven and new earth—"And I saw a new heaven and a new earth: for the first heaven and first earth were passed away; and there was no more sea. . . . He that overcometh shall inherit all things; and I will be his God, and he shall be my son" (Rev. 21:1,7). See also Matt. 25:34; Mark 10:29,30.

What reward will be given to the faithful?

There are many aspects of the reward Jesus will give on that day, some of which are included below. Since God's promises are conditional, note the requirements for receiving them.

To appear with Christ in glory—"Set your affection on things above, not on things on the earth. For ye are dead, and your life is hid with Christ in God. When Christ, who is our life, shall appear, then shall ye also appear with him in glory" (Col. 3:2-4). "For I reckon that the sufferings of this present time are not worthy to be compared with the glory which shall be revealed in us" (Rom. 8:18). See also 2 Cor. 4:17; Phil. 3:20,21; 2 Thess. 1:10; Heb. 10:32-35; 11:35; 1 John 3:2.

To be spared in the day of wrath and to have victory over our enemies—"And they shall be mine, saith the Lord of hosts, in that day when I make up my jewels; and *I will spare them*, as a man spareth his own son that serveth him. . . . For, behold, the day cometh, that shall burn as an oven; and all the proud, yea, and all that do wickedly, shall be stubble: and the day that cometh shall burn them up, saith the Lord of hosts, that it shall leave them neither root nor branch. But unto you that fear my name shall the Sun of righteousness arise with healing in his wings; and ye shall go forth, and grow up as calves of the stall. And ye shall tread down the wicked; for they shall be ashes under the soles of your feet in the day that I shall do this, saith the Lord of hosts" (Mal. 3:17; 4:1-3).

"The righteous shall rejoice when he seeth the vengeance: he shall wash his feet in the blood of the wicked. So that a man shall say, verily there is a reward for the righteous: verily he is a God that judgeth in the earth" (Psa. 58:10,11). See also Isa. 25:8; 51:7,8; Rev. 19:14-21.

To be glad with exceeding joy—"But rejoice, inasmuch as ye are partakers of Christ's sufferings; that, when his glory shall be revealed, ye may be glad also with exceeding joy" (1 Pet. 4:13). See also Psa. 16:11; Isa. 35:10; 51:11; 65:17-19; Matt. 25:21; Rev. 7:17.

To have the Lord confess us before His Father—"Whosoever therefore shall confess me before men, him will I confess also before my Father which is in heaven" (Matt. 10:32,33). See also Mark 8:34-38; Luke 9:23-26.

To have the praise of God—"Therefore judge nothing before the time, until the Lord come, who both will bring to light the hidden things of darkness, and will make manifest the counsels of the hearts: and then shall every man have praise of God" (1 Cor. 4:5).

To receive crowns—An incorruptible crown for those who practice self-denial (1 Cor. 9:25-27); a crown of rejoicing for soul winners (1 Thess. 2:19,20); a crown of righteousness for those who fight the good fight of faith and who love "His appearing" (2 Tim. 4:7,8); a crown of life for those who endure temptation and are "faithful unto death" (James 1:12; Rev. 2:10); and a crown of glory for faithful elders who are not "lords over God's heritage," but are examples to the people (1 Pet. 5:4).

To reap what we have sown in the Lord—"He that soweth to the Spirit shall of the Spirit reap life everlasting. And let us not be weary in well doing: for in due season we shall reap, if we faint not" (Gal. 6:8,9). See also Matt. 13:43; 2 Cor. 1:14; 9:6.

To inherit an eternal kingdom and to enter the city whose builder and maker is God—"Then shall the King say unto them on his right hand, Come, ye blessed of my Father, inherit the kingdom prepared for you from the foundation of the world" (Matt. 25:34). "Blessed are they that do his commandments, that they may have right to the tree of life, and may enter in through the gates into the city" (Rev. 22:14). See also Matt. 8:11; Luke 14:12-15; 22:29,30; Heb. 6:10-12; 9:15; 11:10; 12:28; James 2:5; 1 Pet. 1:4; Rev. 21:7.

To see God—"Blessed are the pure in heart: for they shall see

God" (Matt. 5:8). "Thine eyes shall see the king in his beauty" (Isa. 33:17). See also Psa. 17:15; 1 Cor. 13:12; 1 John 3:2; Rev. 22:4.

To reign with Christ for ever and ever—"If we suffer, we shall also reign with him: if we deny him, he also will deny us" (2 Tim. 2:12). "And there shall be no night there; and they need no candle, neither light of the sun; for the Lord God giveth them light: and they shall reign for ever and ever" (Rev. 22:5).

On what basis will God reward some and punish others?

A careful look at Scripture reveals God's basis for rewards and punishment:

God's righteousness—"The Lord . . . shall judge the world with righteousness, and the people with his truth" (Psa. 96:13).

The Word of God—Jesus said, "The word that I have spoken, the same shall judge him in the last day" (John 12:48).

Our motives—"The Lord is a God of knowledge, and by him actions are weighed" (1 Sam. 2:3). We must ask ourselves if we are doing all from a motive of love for Christ and for the glory of God or from a motive of selfishness and for the glory and praise of men. The Pharisees believed that God would reward their acts of piety and self-denial regardless of their motives. But Jesus said that they who give, pray, or fast to be seen of men will have no eternal reward (Matt. 6:1,5,16). He also asked, "How can ye believe, which receive honour one of another, and seek not the honour that cometh from God only?" (John 5:44).

A person may appear generous and merciful, but really acts from a selfish motive. He may appear happy to give or to show mercy, but he does so only to those of his own family, nationality, church, or denomination. Personal benefit or pride may motivate his actions. A person motivated by the love of God, however, gives freely and compassionately to those in need even though they are not one of his "own." The good Samaritan demonstrated God's love toward his neighbor (Luke 10:27-37).

Paul showed the necessity of doing all from a motive of love for Christ and for the glory of God. "And though I bestow all my goods to feed the poor, and though I give my body to be burned, and have not charity [love], it profiteth me nothing" (1 Cor.

13:3); "Whether therefore ye eat, or drink, or whatsoever ye do, do all to the glory of God" (1 Cor. 10:31). See also 1 Cor. 4:5.

Faithfulness—"And the Lord said, Who then is that faithful and wise steward, whom his lord shall make ruler over his household, to give them their portion of meat in due season? Blessed is that servant, whom his lord when he cometh shall find so doing. Of a truth I say unto you, that he will make him ruler over all that he hath" (Luke 12:42-44). See also Matt. 10:41,42; 25:14-30.

Degree of understanding and privilege—"And that servant, which knew his lord's will, and prepared not himself, neither did according to his will, shall be beaten with many stripes. But he that knew not, and did commit things worthy of stripes, shall be beaten with few stripes. For unto whomsoever much is given, of him shall be much required: and to whom men have committed much, of him they will ask the more" (Luke 12:47,48). With great blessing comes great responsibility.

Our actions, our words, our works—"I the Lord search the heart, I try the reins, even to give every man according to his ways, and according to the fruit of his doings" (Jer. 17:10). "Talk no more so exceeding proudly; let not arrogancy come out of your mouth: for the Lord is a God of knowledge, and by him actions are weighed" (1 Sam. 2:3). See also Eccl. 12:14; 1 Cor. 3:11-15; 2 Cor. 5:10.

God gives special warning to the youth: "Rejoice, O young man, in thy youth; and let thy heart cheer thee in the days of thy youth, and walk in the ways of thine heart, and in the sight of thine eyes: but know thou, that for all these things God will bring thee into judgment" (Eccl. 11:9). God "will render to every man according to his deeds" (Rom. 2:6).

Are believer's works really important?

Yes, believer's works are important, but only if they result from faith. Good works can never be the means of salvation. Some early believers trusted in works to be saved by keeping some of the Mosaic laws of cleansing in addition to their faith in Christ. But Paul clearly stated that we are "justified by the faith of Christ, and not by the works of the law: for by the works of the law shall no flesh be justified" (Gal. 2:16). He also warned,

"Christ is become of no effect unto you, whosoever of you are justified by the law; ye are fallen from grace" (Gal. 5:4).

Others think they will be saved by doing good deeds to outweigh their bad deeds. The apostle Paul emphatically declared that salvation is *not* according to our works, but according to the grace and power of God: "Who hath saved us, and called us with an holy calling, *not according to our works*, but according to his own purpose and grace, which was given us in Christ Jesus before the world began" (2 Tim. 1:9); "*Not by works* of righteousness which we have done, but according to his mercy he saved us, by the washing of regeneration, and renewing of the Holy Ghost; which he shed on us abundantly through Jesus Christ our Saviour" (Titus 3:5,6). On the Day of the Lord, many will boast of their "many wonderful works," but those works will not save them (Matt. 7:22).

On the other hand, works that are the result of faith are important for the following eight reasons—

1. The apostle Paul preached everywhere that men "should repent and turn to God, and *do works* meet for repentance" (Acts 26:20). These "works" were not the means to salvation, but the results of salvation—works that show by the believer's conduct that he had truly repented and turned to God. These works include such things as turning from idolatry to serving the living God (1 Thess. 1:9); from lying to speaking the truth; from stealing to laboring and giving to those in need; from speaking corrupt things to speaking things that are good; and from bitterness and anger to kindness and tenderheartedness (Eph. 4:25-32).

2. Believers are "created in Christ Jesus unto good works" (Eph. 2:10). The Bible says, "For by grace are ye saved through faith; and that not of yourselves: it is the gift of God: *not of works*, lest any man should boast. For we are his workmanship, created in Christ Jesus *unto good works*, which God hath before ordained that we should walk in them" (Eph. 2:8-10). Here we understand that our salvation is "not of works," but rather "unto good works." (Compare 2 Timothy 1:9 with 3:17 and Titus 3:5 with 3:8.)

What are these "good works which God hath before ordained" (Eph. 2:10)? They are an outgrowth of true holiness of heart, holiness that is blameless in the sight of God and that extends to others because of His love: "According as he hath chosen us in him before the foundation of the world, that we should be holy and without blame before him in love (Eph. 1:4). This truth, then, is what Paul meant when he said, "And though I bestow all my goods to feed the poor, and though I give my body to be burned, and have not charity [the love of God], it profiteth me nothing" (1 Cor. 13:3).

In the New Testament, believers are instructed to "be careful to maintain good works" (Titus 3:8,14); to be "fruitful in every good work" (Col. 1:10); to be established "in every good word and work" (2 Thess. 2:17); to follow "diligently . . . every good work" (1 Tim. 5:10); to "be rich in good works" (1 Tim. 6:18); to be "thoroughly furnished unto all good works" (2 Tim. 3:17); to show "a pattern of good works" (Titus 2:7); to be "zealous of good works" (Titus 2:14); "to provoke unto love and to good works" (Heb.10:24); and to be "perfect in every good work" (Heb. 13:21).

3. Faith without works is dead (James 2:14-26). Living faith is born of the Spirit of God and with loving, willing obedience keeps His commandments (1 John 5:3,4), thus bringing forth good works. On the other hand, dead faith is born of the flesh, is "not subject to the law of God," and does not seek to please God (Rom. 8:7,8). It intellectually believes in one God (as the devils do), but does not produce corresponding actions—it merely rests in a profession of Christian faith. It gives assent to God's Word, but it does not obey. "They profess that they know God; but in works they deny him, being abominable, and disobedient, and unto *every good work reprobate*" (Titus 1:16).

4. Jesus stressed the importance of works by saying to each of the seven churches in Revelation chapters two and three, "*I know thy works.*"

5. God gives believers grace to abound to every good work. "And God is able to make all grace abound toward you; that ye, always having all sufficiency in all things, may abound to *every good work*" (2 Cor. 9:8).

6. It's by our *good works* that we let our light shine before men and our heavenly Father is glorified (Matt. 5:16; 1 Pet. 2:12).

7. Our good works will be rewarded. "For God is not unrighteous to forget your work and labour of love, which ye have

shewed toward his name, in that ye have ministered to the saints, and do minister" (Heb. 6:10). "Blessed are the merciful: for they shall obtain mercy" (Matt. 5:7). "Blessed are the dead which die in the Lord from henceforth: yea, saith the Spirit, that they may rest from their labours; and their works do follow them" (Rev. 14:13).

8. Believer's works are important because when Jesus comes "he shall reward every man *according to his works*" (Matt. 16:27). Jesus illustrated this truth in Matthew 25:31-46. Therefore, let us "fear God, and keep his commandments: for this is the whole duty of man. For God shall bring *every work* into judgment, with every secret thing, whether it be good, or whether it be evil" (Eccl. 12:13,14).

What does the Bible say about the rewards of living for Christ?

The rewards of Christ are great (Matt. 5:12), full (Ruth 2:12), sure (Pro. 11:18), satisfying (Psa. 17:15), unspeakable (1 Cor. 2:9), and eternal (Matt. 25:46). They give believers encouragement:

To walk in obedience and the fear of the Lord—"At the name of Jesus every knee should bow, of things in heaven, and things in earth, and things under the earth; and that every tongue should confess that Jesus Christ is Lord, to the glory of God the Father. Wherefore, my beloved, as ye have always obeyed, not as in my presence only, but now much more in my absence, work out your own salvation with fear and trembling" (Phil. 2:10-12). See Rev. 11:18.

To be temperate in all things—"Know ye not that they which run in a race run all, but one receiveth the prize? So run, that ye may obtain. And every man that striveth for the mastery is temperate in all things. Now they do it to obtain a corruptible crown; but we an incorruptible. I therefore so run, not as uncertainly; so fight I, not as one that beateth the air: But I keep under my body, and bring it into subjection: lest that by any means, when I have preached to others, I myself should be a castaway" (1 Cor. 9:24-27).

To be careful—"Look to yourselves, that we lose not those

things which we have wrought, but that we receive a full reward" (2 John 1:8).

To press forward—"I press toward the mark for the prize of the high calling of God in Christ Jesus" (Phil. 3:14).

To bear the reproach of Christ—Moses chose "to suffer affliction with the people of God, than to enjoy the pleasures of sin for a season; esteeming the reproach of Christ greater riches than the treasures in Egypt: for he had respect unto the recompence of the reward" (Heb. 11:25,26). See also Matt. 16:24-27; Luke 6:22,23.

To persuade others of the gospel—"For we must all appear before the judgment seat of Christ. . . . Knowing therefore the terror of the Lord, we persuade men" (2 Cor. 5:10,11). See also Pro. 24:10-12; Isa. 40:9,10; 1 Thess. 2:19; Jude 1:22-24.

To be steadfast in the work of the Lord—"Therefore, my beloved brethren, be ye stedfast, unmovable, always abounding in the work of the Lord, forasmuch as ye know that your labour is not in vain in the Lord" (1 Cor. 15:58). "Cast not away therefore your confidence, which hath great recompence of reward" (Heb. 10:35). "Be thou faithful unto death, and I will give thee a crown of life" (Rev. 2:10).

To love our enemies—"But love ye your enemies, and do good, and lend, hoping for nothing again; and your reward shall be great, and ye shall be the children of the Highest: for he is kind unto the unthankful and to the evil" (Luke 6:35). See also Rom. 14:10-12; Jude 1:21.

To keep the commandments of God—"And, behold, I come quickly; and my reward is with me. . . . Blessed are they that do his commandments, that they may have right to the tree of life, and may enter in through the gates into the city" (Rev. 22:12,14). "The judgments of the Lord are true and righteous altogether. . . . Moreover by them is thy servant warned: and in keeping of them there is great reward" (Psa. 19:9,11).

To be built up in the faith and pray in the Holy Spirit—"But ye, beloved, building up yourselves on your most holy faith, praying in the Holy Ghost. . . . Now unto him that is able to keep you from falling, and to present you faultless before the presence of his glory with exceeding joy, to the only wise God our Saviour, be glory and majesty, dominion and power, both now and ever. Amen" (Jude 1:20,24,25).

Objections Answered

Doesn't the Bible require believers to keep the Mosaic laws of cleansing?

The works of the law should not be confused with good works. We are saved to do good works (Eph. 2:8-10), but not to do the works of the law (Acts 15:1-11). Paul never calls the works of the law "good works." He himself was "dead to the law" that he "might live unto God" (Gal. 2:19). Consider two important reasons why New Testament believers are not required to keep the Mosaic laws of cleansing:

First, the laws of cleansing were intended to serve a temporary purpose—to bring us to Christ. They show us that we are all unclean, that we cannot cleanse ourselves, and that we need a Savior. The "law was our schoolmaster to *bring us unto Christ*, that we might be justified by faith. But after that faith is come, *we are no longer under a schoolmaster* [*the law*]" (Gal. 3:24,25). See also Rom. 7:1-6; Gal. 4:1-7,21-31.

According to the complicated and burdensome laws of cleansing, persons were considered unclean for many reasons, including: being uncircumcised (Ex. 12:43-48; Isa. 52:1; Ezek. 44:7); eating pork or other "unclean" foods (Lev. 11:7,8); having leprosy (Lev. 13:8); having a "running issue out of his flesh"—a scabby sore (Lev. 15:2); issuing a seed of copulation (Lev. 15:16); touching a corpse or entering the tent of a dead person (Num. 19:11-14); touching a grave (Num. 19:16); touching a carcass (Lev. 11:24,39). Also, a woman, after giving birth to a child or having an issue of blood was considered unclean (Lev. 12:2-5; 15:19). Furthermore, anyone accidently touching an "unclean" person or anything he or she came in contact with, such as a bed, a chair, a saddle, clothing, saliva, or food, was also considered unclean (Lev. 15).

An unclean person was disqualified from appearing in worship before God; hence, he was not allowed to mingle in society (Ezek. 44:7,8; Lev. 12:1-4). Some were even put out of the camp—"every leper, and every one that hath a issue, and whosoever is defiled by the dead: both male and female" (Num. 5:2,3).

To be cleansed meant keeping various codes of purification such as bathing the body with water (Lev. 15:5-7,13); washing one's clothes (Lev. 15:5,6); keeping certain days of purification (Lev. chapters 11-15); going to the tabernacle with particular animal sacrifices (Lev. 15:14,15); and being pronounced clean by the Levitical priesthood (Lev. 14:11; Num. 19:7-21).

Thus, because a person was considered "unclean" by being involved in the ordinary things of life such as eating, disease, childbirth, and death, and because the laws of cleansing were complicated, it was almost impossible for a person to ever be sure he was "clean." These laws show us, then, that in the sight of God "we are all as an *unclean thing*, and all our righteousnesses are as filthy rags [Hebrew, *menstrual rags*]" (Isa. 64:6); therefore, we need a Savior.

Second, if a New Testament believer keeps one law of cleansing, he must keep them all (which is literally impossible), or else be cursed. "For I testify again to every man that is circumcised, that he is a debtor to do the whole law" (Gal. 5:3); "Cursed is every one that continueth not in all things which are written in the book of the law to do them" (Gal. 3:10).

Why is it impossible for New Testament believers to keep all the laws of cleansing?

These Mosaic laws were designed to be in force only until Christ's coming (Heb. 9:9,10). They were "a shadow of things to come; but the body is of Christ" (Col. 2:17). He has fulfilled all types and shadows of the ceremonial law (Heb. 8:5; 9:8-14,23; 10:1-14). We are, therefore, no longer under the Old Covenant with its tabernacle, Levitical priesthood, and offering up of animal sacrifices. That has been abolished once and for all by the sacrifice of Jesus Christ. We are now under "a better covenant, which was established upon better promises" (Heb. 8:6).

Jesus Christ cleansed "unclean" people without their keeping the laws concerning days of purification, bathing, washing their clothes, and going to the tabernacle with animal sacrifices. A leper came to Jesus, saying, "Lord, if thou wilt, thou canst make me clean. And Jesus put forth his hand, and touched him, saying, I will; be thou clean. And immediately his leprosy was cleansed" (Matt. 8:2,3). Jesus also healed the women who had an issue of blood for twelve years (Matt. 9:20,21). He also raised the dead—taking the dead girl by the hand (Matt. 9:23-26) and, on another occasion, touching the bier of the widow's son (Luke 7:13,14). Jesus' touching those who were ceremonially unclean showed that His coming put an end to the ceremonial law. His atonement on the cross completed the requirements to keep ceremonial law.

Consider the case of a mother who was considered "unclean" after giving birth to a boy (Lev. 12). The seven laws she had to fulfill for purification do not apply to New Testament believers for two reasons. First, they have already been fulfilled in Christ. Second, the temple in Jerusalem with its priesthood and the offering of animal sacrifices no longer exists.

A Mother Under the Law (Lev. 12)	**A Believer Under Grace (The New Testament)**
1. "If a woman have . . . a manchild: then she shall be *unclean* seven days" (Lev. 12:2).	Never considered ceremonially unclean—"What God hath cleansed, that call not thou common [or unclean]" (Acts 10:15,28). Jesus taught that the sins of the heart make a person unclean (Mark 7:21-23). He also rebuked the Pharisees because they prided themselves in outward ceremonial cleanliness while inwardly they were morally unclean (Matt. 23:27).
2. "The eighth day the flesh of his foreskin shall be *circumcised*" (Lev. 12:3).	As a work of righteousness, physical circumcision is no longer necessary. True circumcision is a spiritual work of Christ in the heart and the spirit (Rom. 2:29; Col. 2:11). See also Gal. 5:2,3.
3. "She shall then continue in the blood of her *purifying* three and thirty days" (Lev. 12:4).	God *purifies* the heart by faith (Acts 15:9). "If we walk in the light, . . . the blood of Jesus Christ his Son *cleanseth* us from all sin" (1 John 1:7).
4. "She shall touch no *hallowed* thing, nor come into the *sanctuary*, until the days of her purifying be fulfilled" (Lev. 12:4). See also Num. 3:13.	One should not assume the *hallowed* thing represents the Bible and the sanctuary a church building. The Bible purifies (John 15:3; 17:17; Eph. 5:26); it should be read everyday (Pro. 8:33,34; Matt. 4:4;

A Mother Under the Law (Lev. 12)	A Believer Under Grace (The New Testament)
	6:11; Acts 17:11,12). The sanctuary was a type of a "greater and more perfect tabernacle, not made with hands. . . . *the presence of God*" (Heb. 9:11,24). Spiritually, believers "enter into the holiest [the sanctuary] by the blood of Jesus" (Heb. 10:19-22).
5. "When the days of her purifying are fulfilled, . . . she shall bring a *lamb* of the first year, . . . and a young pigeon, or a turtledove, . . . unto the door of the *tabernacle*, . . . unto the *priest*" (Lev. 12:6).	Animal sacrifices, the tabernacle, and the Levitical priesthood have all been abolished forever (Heb. 9:12). Jesus, our *High Priest*, is the *Lamb of God* who entered the "greater and more perfect *tabernacle*, . . . now to appear in the presence of God for us" (Heb. 9:11,24).
6. The priest "shall offer it before the Lord, and make *an atonement* for her" (12:7).	Through our High Priest, the Lord Jesus Christ, "we have now received the *atonement*" (Rom. 5:11).
7. "She shall be *cleansed* from the issue of her blood" (Lev. 12:7).	There is "a fountain opened . . . for sin and for *uncleanness*" (Zech. 13:1)— "the precious blood of Christ" (1 Pet. 1:19). It *cleanses* "us from *all sin*" (1 John 1:7).

Thus, we now serve God, not in the literal sense of the laws of cleansing, but in the true sense of their spiritual meaning and fulfillment in Christ.

Is there anything wrong with obligating believers to keep just a few ceremonial laws of cleansing?

Obligating believers to keep some of the ceremonial laws of cleansing was introduced into the early church. Consider the Galatian church. Through faith in Jesus Christ, they experienced salvation, received the Holy Spirit, suffered for their faith, and witnessed the working of miracles (Gal. 3:2-5; 4:5,6). They had begun well, but false brethren who desired "to make a fair shew in the flesh" constrained them "to be circumcised" (Gal. 6:12)

and to "observe days, and months, and times, and years" (Gal. 4:10). Hence, they were influenced to believe that they could be made perfect by adding "the works of the law" to the "the hearing of faith" (Gal. 3:3,5).

Luke described a similar situation in Acts 15. Certain men taught believers, saying, "Except ye be circumcised after the manner of Moses, ye cannot be saved" (Acts 15:1). Paul and Barnabas, knowing the danger of keeping even one law of cleansing, such as circumcision, "had no small dissension and disputation with them" (Acts 15:2).

Consequently, the matter was brought before the apostles and elders in Jerusalem. At the council, "there rose up certain of the sect of the Pharisees which believed, saying, That it was needful to circumcise them, and to command them to keep the law of Moses" (Acts 15:5). After "much disputing," Peter, Barnabas, Paul, and James each spoke in favor of not obligating believers to keep the laws of cleansing. As a result, it pleased "the apostles and elders, with the whole church, to send chosen men of their own company" with letters to the Gentiles saying, "It seemed good to the Holy Ghost, and to us, to lay upon you no greater burden than these necessary things; that ye abstain from meats offered to idols, and from blood, and from things strangled, and from fornication: from which if ye keep yourselves, ye shall do well" (Acts 15:22,28,29).

Paul's response to the Galatian church, and the decision of the apostles and brothers in Jerusalem (Acts 15), illustrate why believers are not obligated to keep any Mosaic law of cleansing:

1. God is primarily concerned with heart purity, not ceremonial uncleanness such as uncircumcision (Acts 15:8).

2. Heart purity comes by faith, not by keeping the ceremonial laws of purification (Acts 15:9).

3. The Gentiles, like the apostles, received salvation by *grace* through *faith*, not by the works of the law (Acts 15:7-12; Gal. 1:6,15; 2:16; 3:2-5,9,14,26). Paul declared the express testimony of the Bible—"*the just shall live by faith*" (Gal. 3:11). See also Hab. 2:4; Rom. 1:17; Heb. 10:38. He also stated that four hundred and thirty years before the law was given, God promised Abraham that He "would justify the heathen [the Gentiles] through *faith*" (Gal. 3:8,17).

4. Keeping the laws of cleansing is of no spiritual benefit to

New Testament believers. They cannot justify (Gal. 2:16); impart the Holy Spirit (Gal. 3:2); bring perfection (Gal. 3:3); impart righteousness (Gal. 2:21); give grace (Gal. 1:3; John 1:17); work miracles (Gal. 3:5); give life (Gal. 3:21); give an inheritance (Rom. 4:14, Gal. 3:18); or give peace of conscience (Heb. 9:9; 10:1,2). These blessings only come by grace through faith in the Lord Jesus.

5. Not once did the apostles command believers to keep the ceremonial law (Acts 15:24). In fact, by *the authority of the Holy Spirit*, they declared that it was unnecessary (Acts 15:28).

6. The apostles, who were "Jews by nature," (Gal. 2:15) did not observe the laws of cleansing (Gal. 2:19); neither, then, is doing so a requirement for Gentiles (Acts 15:28,29).

7. When we try to keep even one part of the ceremonial law, Christ's death, our suffering for Him, and the labor of others on our behalf is in vain (Gal. 2:21; 3:4; 4:9-11).

8. He who troubles converts to keep the ceremonial law "shall bear his judgment" (Gal. 5:10,12; 1:6-9; Titus 1:10,11).

9. Obligating believers to keep even one law of cleansing:

- burdens them (Acts 15:28)
- entangles them in a yoke of bondage (Acts 15:10; Gal. 4:9; 5:1)
- troubles them (Acts 15:19,24; Gal. 1:7; 5:12)
- subverts their souls (Acts 15:24)
- hinders them from obeying the truth (Gal. 5:7)
- makes them zealous for the wrong thing (Gal. 4:17,18)
- causes them to be removed from God to another gospel (Gal. 1:6)
- causes them to fall from grace and to need "Christ to be formed in them again" (Gal. 4:19; 5:4)
- corrupts them, as leaven, in their life and conduct (Gal. 5:9)
- causes the cross to cease to be a stumbling block and is made meaningless (Gal. 5:11)
- perverts the gospel of Christ (Gal. 1:7)
- frustrates the grace of God (Gal. 2:21)
- makes Christ to become of no effect (Gal. 5:4)
- tempts God (Acts 15:10)
- has its roots in phariseeism (Acts 15:5; Gal. 6:12,13) and produces hypocrisy (Matt. 23:25-29)

Therefore, those who insist on adhering to one law of cleansing as necessary for salvation imply that Christ's work to justify us by grace is not enough. Moreover, they exclude themselves from the blessings of the gospel of grace: "I marvel that ye are so soon *removed* from him that called you into the *grace* of Christ unto another gospel" (Gal. 1:6). "Christ is become of no effect unto you, whosoever of you are justified by the law; ye are *fallen from grace*" (Gal. 5:4).

By keeping certain ceremonial laws, won't I be more holy?

According to Scripture, keeping certain Mosaic laws of cleansing is not a help to holiness, but a hindrance. First, it produces self-righteousness (Phil. 3:9), which, in turn, leads to rejecting the righteousness of God (compare Rom. 9:32 with 10:3); to being more concerned with the external appearance rather than with purity of heart (Matt. 23:25-28; Luke 11:39-44); to justifying ourselves before men (Luke 16:15); and to being proud and despising others (Isa. 65:5; Luke 18:9-14; Gal. 6:12,13; Col. 2:16-18).

Observing some of the ceremonial laws of cleansing also leads to self-deception. It makes a person feel religious and holy because he is doing religious things while he is not necessarily humble and godly in his heart. "For if a man think himself to be something, when he is nothing, he deceiveth himself" (Gal. 6:3).

True holiness is attained, not by the works of the law, but by faith in the Lord Jesus Christ: "The Gentiles . . . attained to righteousness, even the righteousness which is of *faith*" (Rom. 9:30). On the other hand, "Israel . . . hath *not* attained to the law of righteousness. Wherefore? Because they sought it not by faith, but as it were by the *works of the law*" (Rom. 9:31,32).

Let's contrast the blessings of living by faith alone with the dangers of living by faith plus the works of the law:

One Living by Faith Alone	One Living by Faith, Plus the Law
Is delivered "from this present evil world"—Gal. 1:4.	Is turning again to the weak and beggarly elements of the world—Gal. 4:3,9.
Has God's grace—Gal. 1:6.	Frustrates and falls from God's grace—Gal. 2:21; 5:4.

One Living by Faith Alone	One Living by Faith, Plus the Law
Continues in the truth—Gal. 2:5.	Is bewitched and hindered from obeying the truth—Gal. 3:1; 5:7.
Believes the gospel—Acts 15:7.	Is removed from God unto another gospel—Gal. 1:6.
Takes Christ's burden, which is light—Matt. 11:30.	Takes the burden of the law, which is heavy—Acts 15:10; Matt. 23:4.
Is in the Spirit—Gal. 3:3.	Seeks perfection in the flesh—Gal. 3:3.
Is free in Christ—Gal. 5:1.	Christ profits him nothing—Gal. 5:2.
Stands fast in the liberty of Christ—Gal. 5:1.	Is entangled with the yoke of bondage—Gal. 5:1; Acts 15:10.
Is under the blessings of the gospel—Gal. 3:8,9,14.	Is under the curse of the law—Gal. 3:10.
Has the Word of God effectually working in him—1 Thess. 2:13.	Christ is become of "no effect" unto him—Gal. 5:4.
Considers one who tells him the truth his friend—Gal. 4:13-15.	Considers one who tells him the truth his enemy—Gal. 4:16.
Is being built up—Jude 1:20.	Is being subverted—Acts 15:24.
Rejoices in God—Acts 15:28-31.	Tempts God—Acts 15:10.
Is "justified by the faith of Christ"—Gal. 2:16.	Is "not justified by the works of the law"—Gal. 2:16.
Glories in the suffering of the cross—Gal. 6:14.	Glories in men—Gal. 6:12,13.
Has the peace of God—Gal. 6:16.	Is troubled—Gal. 1:7; 5:12.
Is from Jerusalem, which is above—freedom—Gal. 4:26.	Is from Jerusalem, which now is—bondage—Gal. 4:26.
As Isaac, is born after the Spirit—Gal. 4:29.	As Ishmael, is born after the flesh—Gal. 4:23,29.
Reaps life everlasting—Gal. 6:8.	Reaps corruption and judgment—Gal. 6:8.

We have seen that adding the "works of the law" to the "hearing of faith" (Gal. 3:5) is a definite hindrance to holiness. It is very dangerous to mix faith in Christ with the works of the law, true Christianity with Judaism. It is like being religious without fearing and knowing God. Only when believers are "*dead to the law*" and "married" to Christ can they "bring forth fruit unto God" (Rom. 7:4).

Doesn't freedom from the Mosaic laws of cleansing give believers a license to sin?

Absolutely not! Living by faith in Christ produces true holy living and the fruit of the Spirit (Gal. 2:20; 5:22,23). While believers are free from the works of the law, they are under "the law of the Spirit of life in Christ Jesus" (Rom. 8:2; Gal. 6:2) and keep His commandments because they love Him (John 14:15).

Paul wrote to the Galatians, "For, brethren, ye have been called unto liberty; only use not liberty for an occasion to the flesh, but by love serve one another. For all the law is fulfilled in one word, even in this; Thou shalt love thy neighbour as thyself. . . . This I say then, Walk in the Spirit, and ye shall not fulfil the lust of the flesh" (Gal. 5:13,14,16). Peter also proclaimed, "As free, and not using your liberty for a cloak of maliciousness, but as the servants of God" (1 Pet. 2:16).

Moreover, "they that are Christ's have crucified the flesh with the affections and lusts" (Gal. 5:24). "For the grace of God that bringeth salvation" teaches us "that, denying ungodliness and worldly lusts, we should live soberly, righteously, and godly, in this present world" (Titus 2:11,12).

In summary, salvation is not a result of our works nor of keeping the Mosaic laws of cleansing in addition to faith in Jesus. Good works as a result of salvation are important, however, because God richly rewards believers for the good works they do in this life out of love for Him.

19

The End of the World

What is meant by the term, "end of the world" (Matt. 24:3)?

The word "end" suggests an entire completion, the consummation of all things, the climax. The end of the world is the great judgment day of God Almighty. The earth shall be destroyed, brought to an end, abolished completely. Therefore, the term, "end of the world" means the last day, the day when time shall be no more!

When will the end of the world take place?

- When the gospel has been preached in all the world for a witness (Matt. 24:14).
- Immediately after the Tribulation (Matt. 24:29,35).
- When Jesus comes to receive His Church (1 Cor. 1:7,8; 1 Pet. 1:13; Rev. 2:25,26; Matt. 24:29-31).
- When the sixth seal is opened (Rev. 6:12).
- When the last trump sounds (1 Cor. 15:51,52; Rev. 11:18).
- On the Day of the Lord (2 Pet. 3:7,10,12).

Did Jesus and the apostles link the gathering of the Church with the end of the world?

Yes. They exhorted believers:

To "endure unto the end"—To endure means to carry on through suffering without yielding or to continue in spite of hardships. As sin and false religion increase in the world, persecution will also increase against true believers. But Jesus said, "He that shall endure unto *the end*, the same shall be saved" (Matt. 24:13).

To preach until the end—"Go ye therefore, and teach all nations. . . . lo, I am with you alway, even unto *the end of the world*" (Matt. 28:19,20). "And this gospel of the kingdom shall be preached in all the world for a witness unto all nations; and then shall *the end* come" (Matt. 24:14). Certainly, Jesus would not expect us to preach the gospel until "the end come" if He were coming to gather us before the end.

To wait until the end—"Waiting for the coming of our Lord Jesus Christ: Who shall also confirm you unto *the end*" (1 Cor. 1:7,8).

To hold fast until the end—"Hold fast the confidence and the rejoicing of the hope firm unto *the end*" (Heb. 3:6). See also Heb. 3:14; 6:11.

To hope to the end—"Gird up the loins of your mind, be sober, and hope to *the end* for the grace that is to be brought unto you at the revelation of Jesus Christ" (1 Pet. 1:13).

To keep the works of Jesus until the end—"But that which ye have already hold fast till I come. And he that overcometh, and keepeth my works unto *the end*, to him will I give power over the nations" (Rev. 2:25,26). Jesus said, "Occupy till I come" (Luke 19:13). To occupy means to persist in doing the work commanded us to do. A false hope only hinders us from doing what we can and must do for God today. Jesus expects us to keep His works "unto the end."

Jesus and the apostles repeatedly relate the hope of the Second Coming to the end of the world. Surely all these exhortations about the end would not be given to the Church if her real hope were a secret rapture some years before the end.

Do any of the parables tell us that Jesus is coming at the end of the world?

Yes, at least one-third of the parables, twelve in all, teach that Jesus is coming at the end of the world. Consider the parables of the wheat and tares and of the draw net. Both teach that believers will remain on the earth until the final separation at the end of the world.

In the parable of the wheat and the tares Jesus stated, "Let *both grow* together until the harvest." When is the harvest? "The harvest is *the end of the world*." Then "the Son of man shall send forth his angels, and they shall gather out of his kingdom all things that offend, and them which do iniquity; and shall cast them into a furnace of fire: there shall be wailing and gnashing of teeth. Then shall the righteous shine forth as the sun in the kingdom of their Father" (Matt. 13:30,39,41-43). See also Rev. 14:14 to 15:4.

In the parable of the draw net (Matt. 13:47-50), Jesus said, "Again, the kingdom of heaven is like unto a net, that was cast into the sea, and gathered of every kind: Which, when it was full, they drew to shore, and sat down, and gathered the good into vessels, but cast the bad away. So shall it be at *the end of the world*: the angels shall come forth, and sever the wicked from among the just, and shall cast them into the furnace of fire: there shall be wailing and gnashing of teeth."

There are four parables found in the context of Matthew 24:29-31: the parable of the householder (24:42-51); the parable of the ten virgins (25:1- 13); the parable of the ten talents (25:14-30); and the parable of the sheep and goats (25:31-46). Each shows (either directly or by implication) the eternal reward of the faithful and the eternal doom of the unfaithful when Christ returns at the end of the world.

This truth is also seen in the parables of the marriage of the king's son (Matt. 22:2-14); the unmerciful servant (Matt. 18:23-35); the wise steward (Luke 12:36-48); the parable of the pounds (Luke 19:12-27); the parable of the unjust judge (Luke 18:1-8); and the parable of the house on the rock (Matt. 7:21-27). The last two parables refer to "the day when the Son of man is revealed" (Luke 17:30) and "that day" (Matt. 7:22), which is the Day of the Lord at the end of the world.

Is there a difference between the end of this age and the end of the world?

There is no difference. The end of this age is the end of this world because Jesus spoke of only two worlds: "this world" and "that world." "The children of *this world* [Greek, age] marry, and are given in marriage: But they which shall be accounted worthy to obtain *that world* [Greek, age], and the resurrection from the dead, neither marry, nor are given in marriage" (Luke 20:34,35). He connects the obtaining of "that world" with "the resurrection," and we have seen that the resurrection is at the end of the world.

That Jesus spoke of two worlds is also seen in Mark 10:30:

"But he shall receive an hundredfold now in this time, houses, and brethren, and sisters, and mothers, and children, and lands, with persecutions; and in *the world to come* eternal life." Here Jesus linked the world to come with "eternal life." By comparing Matthew 25:46 with 24:29-31, we see that the righteous enter eternal life when Jesus returns at the end of the world. The meaning of these two terms, "the end of this age" and "the end of the world," is identical. See also Matt. 12:32; Luke 18:30; Eph. 1:21; 1 Tim. 4:8; Heb. 6:5.

When Jesus comes in glory, what will end?

At the sounding of the seventh and last trump, the brightness of our Lord's coming and the glory of His presence and power will bring an end to:

Babylon—"And after these things I saw another angel come down from heaven, having great power; and the earth was lightened with his glory. And he cried mightily with a strong voice, saying, Babylon the great is fallen, is fallen, . . . she shall be utterly burned with fire: for strong is the Lord God who judgeth her" (Rev. 18:1,2,8).

The ungodly—"In flaming fire taking vengeance on them that know not God, and that obey not the gospel of our Lord Jesus Christ: who shall be punished with everlasting destruction from the presence of the Lord, and from the glory of his power; when he shall come to be glorified in his saints" (2 Thess. 1:8,9,10). See also Psa. 9:3,4; 68:2; 114:7; Isa. 64:2; Ezek. 38:20; Rev. 6:15-17; 14:10.

The man of sin—"And then shall that Wicked be revealed, whom the Lord shall consume with the spirit of his mouth, and shall destroy with the brightness of his coming" (2 Thess. 2:8).

The kingdoms of this world—"And the seventh angel sounded; and there were great voices in heaven, saying, The kingdoms of this world are become the kingdoms of our Lord, and of his Christ; and he shall reign for ever and ever" (Rev. 11:15). "But the judgment shall sit, and they [the Father and the Son] shall take away his [the beast's] dominion, to consume and to destroy it unto the *end*" (Dan. 7:26).

The earth—"The mountains quake at him, and the hills melt, and the earth is burned at his presence, yea, the world, and all that dwell therein" (Nah. 1:5).

Death and Satan—"In a moment, in the twinkling of an eye, at the last trump: for the trumpet shall sound, and the dead shall be raised incorruptible, and we shall be changed. . . . So when this corruptible shall have put on incorruption, and this mortal shall have put on immortality, then shall be brought to pass the saying that is written, *Death* is swallowed up in victory" (1 Cor. 15:52,54). See also Isa. 25:8; Hos. 13:14. "Then cometh the end . . . He must reign, till he hath put all enemies under his feet. The last enemy that shall be destroyed is death" (1 Cor. 15:24-26). Satan, who wields the power of death, will also be destroyed (Heb. 2:14). See also Rev. 20:14; 21:4.

Time—"The angel which I saw stand upon the sea and upon the earth lifted up his hand to heaven, and sware by him that liveth forever and ever, . . . that *there should be time no longer*: but in the days of the voice of the seventh angel, when he shall begin to sound [the last trump], the mystery of God should be finished, as he hath declared to his servants the prophets" (Rev. 10:5-7).

Will the earth be completely destroyed?

Jesus Himself declared, "After that tribulation, the sun shall be darkened, and the moon shall not give her light, and the stars of heaven shall fall, and the powers that are in heaven shall be shaken. . . . Heaven and earth shall pass away" (Mark 13:24,25,31). See also Matt. 24:29,35; Luke 21:33.

The apostle John added, "And I beheld when he had opened the sixth seal, and, lo, there was a great earthquake; and the sun became black as sackcloth of hair, and the moon became as blood; and the stars of heaven fell unto the earth, even as a fig tree casteth her untimely figs, when she is shaken of a mighty wind. And the heaven departed as a scroll when it is rolled together; and every mountain and island were moved out of their places" (Rev. 6:12-14). "And I saw a new heaven and a new earth: for the first heaven and the first earth were passed away; and there was no more sea" (Rev. 21:1). See also Rev. 16:20.

Peter described the same destruction of the earth: "But the

heavens and the earth, . . . [are] reserved unto fire against the day of judgment and perdition of ungodly men. . . . But the day of the Lord will come as a thief in the night; in the which the heavens shall pass away with a great noise, and the elements shall melt with fervent heat, the earth also and the works that are therein shall be burned up. . . . all these things shall be dissolved. . . . the heavens being on fire shall be dissolved, and the elements shall melt with fervent heat" (2 Pet. 3:7,10-12).

The writer of Hebrews described the removing and destruction of this earth with fire: "Now he hath promised, saying, Yet once more I shake not the earth only, but also heaven, and this word, yet once more, signifieth the removing of those things that are shaken, as of things that are made, that those things which cannot be shaken may remain . . . For our God is a consuming fire" (Heb. 12:26,27,29). See also Heb. 1:10-12.

Nahum prophesied, "The mountains quake at him, and the hills melt, and the earth is burned at his presence, yea, the world, and all that dwell therein" (Nahum 1:5)

Isaiah also prophesied, "The earth is utterly broken down, the earth is clean dissolved, the earth is moved exceedingly. The earth shall reel to and fro like a drunkard, and shall be removed like a cottage; and the transgression thereof shall be heavy upon it; and it shall fall, and not rise again" (Isa. 24:19,20). See also Isa. 13:9,10,13; 24:4; 34:4; 51:6; 64:1-3; 65:17.

These and many other passages plainly state that the earth will be destroyed when Jesus comes "and [will] not rise again" (Isa. 24:20).

Why will God destroy the earth?

Just as God will "punish the inhabitants of the earth for their iniquity" (Isa. 26:21), so He will destroy the earth because it has been cursed (Gen. 3:17) and is defiled by sin and innocent blood.

"The earth also is defiled under the inhabitants thereof; because they have transgressed the laws, changed the ordinance, broken the everlasting covenant. Therefore hath the curse devoured the earth. . . . the transgression thereof shall be heavy upon it; and it shall fall, and not rise again" (Isa. 24:5,6,20).

"And shed innocent blood, even the blood of their sons and of their daughters, whom they sacrificed unto the idols of Canaan:

and the land [the earth] was polluted with blood" (Psa. 106:38). See also Gen. 4:9-12; Lev. 18:25; Jer. 16:18.

How will "the meek inherit the earth" (Matt. 5:5) if there isn't one?

The Bible teaches that the inheritance of believers is "a new heaven and a new earth." First, in two of the other Beatitudes, Jesus promised heaven to "the poor in spirit" and to "the persecuted for righteousness' sake" (Matt. 5:3,10,12). In addition, He promised that "the pure in heart . . . shall see God" (v. 8). According to Revelation 22:4 and 21:1, the pure in heart will "see his face" in "a new heaven and a new earth." Therefore, "the earth" that Jesus promised to the meek will be the new earth.

Second, consider Psalm thirty-seven:

"But the meek shall *inherit* the earth; and shall delight themselves in the abundance of peace" (v. 11).

"For such as be blessed of him shall *inherit* the earth; and they that be cursed of him shall be cut off" (v. 22).

"The Lord knoweth the days of the upright: and their *inheritance* shall be for ever" (v. 18).

"The righteous shall *inherit* the land, and dwell therein for ever" (v. 29).

Each of these four verses speaks of our inheritance. Verses 11 and 22 speak of inheriting the earth. Verses 18 and 29 state that this inheritance is forever. Thus, we see again that the meek shall inherit the new earth.

Third, consider Isaiah 60:19 and 21: "The sun shall be no more thy light by day; neither for brightness shall the moon give light unto thee: but the Lord shall be unto thee an everlasting light, and thy God thy glory. . . . Thy people also shall be all righteous: they shall inherit the land *for ever*." We know "for ever" is speaking of the new heaven and earth because verse 19 describes the new heaven and earth in a similar way to the description in Revelation 21:23; 22:5.

Finally, the inheritance of believers is not this earth, but "an eternal inheritance" (Heb. 9:15) and "an inheritance incorruptible, and undefiled, and that fadeth not away, reserved in heaven" (1 Pet. 1:4). When Jesus comes, they will "inherit the kingdom prepared . . . from the foundation of the world" (Matt. 25:34).

Objection Answered

Doesn't Revelation 21:1 teach the destruction and renovation of heaven, God's dwelling place, and the destruction and renovation of this earth?

Revelation 21:1 reads, "And I saw a new heaven and a new earth: for the first heaven and the first earth were passed away; and there was no more sea."

"The first heaven and the first earth" is a compound name for this universe. Therefore, "the first heaven" is not heaven, the home of God, as some suppose, but the firmament or the sky. The following verses show that it will be destroyed together with "the first earth": "*Heaven* and earth shall pass away" (Matt. 24:35). "The stars of *heaven* fell . . . *heaven* departed as a scroll . . . every mountain and island were moved out of their places" (Rev. 6:13,14); "The *heavens* shall pass away with a great noise, . . . the earth also and the works that are therein shall be burned up" (2 Pet. 3:10); "The *heavens* being on fire shall be dissolved" (2 Pet. 3:12) and "the earth also . . . shall be burned up" (2 Pet. 3:10). Will the earth be renovated? The Bible teaches that it "shall pass away" (Matt. 24:35), that "it shall fall, and not rise again" (Isa. 24:20), and that it "shall be burned up" and "be dissolved" (2 Pet. 3:10,11). Moreover, what would be the purpose of a renovated earth? At the coming of Jesus, the righteous will inherit everlasting life and the wicked everlasting punishment (Matt. 25:46).

On the other hand, the term "a new heaven and a new earth" is a compound name for heaven, the home of God. It will never be destroyed because there's no sin there (Isa. 57:15; 2 Pet. 3:13; Rev. 21:27); the will of God is always carried out there (Matt. 6:10); the saints' inheritance is reserved there (1 Pet. 1:4); and it is everlasting (Psa. 145:13; Isa. 57:15; 2 Pet. 1:11). When Jesus comes, His people will "inherit the kingdom prepared . . . *from the foundation of the world*" (Matt. 25:34).

In summary, when Jesus returns in glory, He shall completely destroy this world. He will gather His Church, those who have hoped and endured to the end. They shall inherit a new heaven and a new earth, which refers to God's eternal kingdom.

20

Heaven

Will believers inherit heaven when Jesus comes?

Some people teach that when Jesus comes, the Church will rule on earth for a thousand years before they enter heaven to spend eternity. However, the following verses show that at the Second Coming, the saints will inherit heaven.

Consider the promises of Jesus: "I will come again, and receive you unto myself; that where I am [heaven], there ye may be also" (John 14:3). At the resurrection, "they which shall be accounted worthy" shall obtain "*that world* [heaven]" (Luke 20:35). See also Mark 10:30. When Jesus returns, "many shall come from the east and west, and shall sit down with Abraham, and Isaac, and Jacob, in *the kingdom of heaven*" (Matt. 8:11; Luke 13:25-29). "When the Son of man shall come in his glory," then shall "the King say unto them on his right hand, Come, ye blessed of my Father, inherit the kingdom prepared for you from the foundation of the world," which is heaven—"life eternal" (Matt. 25:31,34,46). See also John 5:28,29.

According to the apostle Paul, when the Lord Himself shall "descend from heaven," believers will be "caught up . . . to meet the Lord in the air: and so shall we ever be with the Lord [in heaven]" (1 Thess. 4:16,17). He also wrote, "When Christ, who is our life, shall appear, then shall ye also appear with him in glory [heaven]" (Col. 3:4). See also Heb. 12:28.

Consider also three examples in Revelation that associate the coming of the Lord with the saints in heaven:

1. "Hide us from the face of him that sitteth on the throne. . . . the great day of his wrath is come" (Rev. 6:16,17). "After this I beheld, and, lo, a great multitude, which no man could number, of all nations, and kindreds, and people, and tongues, stood before the throne, and before the Lamb, clothed with white

robes, and palms in their hands. . . . And all the angels stood round about the throne" (Rev. 7:9,11).

2. "And upon the cloud one sat like unto the Son of man, having on his head a golden crown, and in his hand a sharp sickle. . . . for the harvest of the earth is ripe" (Rev. 14:14,15). "And I saw another sign in heaven. . . . And I saw as it were a sea of glass mingled with fire [a metaphor that refers to heaven]: and them that had gotten the victory over the beast, and over his image, and over his mark, and over the number of his name, stand on the sea of glass, having the harps of God" (Rev. 15:1,2). See also Matt. 13:29,30,37-43.

3. "And I saw a great white throne, and him that sat on it, from whose face the earth and the heaven fled away. . . . And I saw the dead, small and great, stand before God" (Rev. 20:11,12). "And I saw a new heaven and a new earth: for the first heaven and the first earth were passed away. . . . And God shall wipe away all tears from their eyes" (Rev. 21:1,4).

These passages prove that when Jesus comes to gather believers, they will go to heaven to ever be with Him.

Where is heaven?

The Bible suggests that heaven is beyond the sky. "Elijah went *up* by a whirlwind into heaven" (2 Kings 2:11). When praying to His Father, Jesus "lifted *up* his eyes to heaven" (John 17:1). When returning to heaven, "he was taken *up*" (Acts. 1:9) and, when Jesus comes again, the Church will be "caught *up* together . . . in the clouds to meet the Lord in the air: and so shall we ever be with the Lord" (1 Thess. 4:17).

What is heaven like?

Heaven is a place of such delight that the thought of it gives comfort and joy in tribulation. Jesus said, "Let not your heart be troubled: ye believe in God, believe also in me. In my Father's house are many mansions: if it were not so, I would have told you. I go to prepare a place for you" (John 14:1,2). When facing death on the cross, Jesus Himself was strengthened as He thought of heaven and its glories. "For the *joy* that was set before him endured the cross" (Heb. 12:2). Persecuted believers received comfort with encouragements about heaven: "For ye had compassion of me in my bonds, and took joyfully the spoiling of your goods, knowing in yourselves that ye have in *heaven* a better and an enduring substance. Cast not away therefore your confidence, which hath great recompence of reward" (Heb. 10:34,35). See also Matt. 5:10-12.

Heaven is a place where we will have glorified, immortal bodies. "We know that, when he [Jesus] shall appear, we shall be like him; for we shall see him as he is" (1 John 3:2). "Who shall change our vile body, that it may be fashioned like unto his glorious body" (Phil. 3:21). "The dead shall be raised incorruptible, and we shall be changed. For this corruptible must put on incorruption, and this mortal must put on immortality" (1 Cor. 15:52,53).

Heaven is a place where we will behold the glory of the Lord. Jesus prayed, "Father, I will that they also, whom thou hast given me, be with me where I am; that they may behold my *glory*, which thou hast given me" (John 17:24).

Heaven is a place of everlasting joy where sorrow and sighing shall flee away. "And the ransomed of the Lord shall return, and come to Zion with songs and everlasting joy upon their heads: they shall obtain joy and gladness, and sorrow and sighing shall flee away" (Isa. 35:10). "With gladness and rejoicing shall they be brought: they shall enter into the king's palace" (Psa. 45:15). If believers on earth are able to "rejoice with joy unspeakable and full of glory" even when they are "tried with fire" (1 Pet. 1:7,8), how much more will they rejoice in heaven? See also Isa. 62:4,5; 65:17-19; Rev. 19:6,7.

Heaven will be a wonderful place—no more sorrow, nor crying (Rev. 21:4); no more pain (Rev. 21:4); no more tears (Rev. 7:17); no more curse (Rev. 22:3); no more night (Rev. 22:5); no more death (Rev. 21:4); no more corruption (1 Cor. 15:42,50); and no more hunger or thirst (Rev. 7:16). We won't experience conflicts with sin because Satan, the tempter, will have been cast "into the lake of fire and brimstone" (Rev. 20:10). We won't fear anything or anyone because "there shall in no wise enter into it any thing that defileth, neither whatsoever worketh abomination, or maketh a lie: but they which are written in the Lamb's book of life" (Rev. 21:27). See also 1 Cor. 6:9,10; Gal. 5:19-21; Eph. 5:5; Rev. 22:15.

Heaven is a place of perfect understanding. "For we know in part, and we prophesy in part. But when that which is perfect is come, then that which is in part shall be done away. . . . For now we see through a glass, darkly; but then face to face: now I know in part; but then shall I know even as also I am known" (1 Cor. 13:9,10,12).

Heaven is an everlasting place. God's people will have an abundant entrance into "the *everlasting kingdom* of our Lord and Saviour Jesus Christ" (2 Pet. 1:11) and will reign for ever and ever (Rev. 22:5). They will enjoy everlasting life (John 3:16); everlasting salvation (Isa. 45:17); everlasting joy (Isa. 51:11); everlasting kindness (Isa. 54:8); everlasting righteousness (Dan. 9:24); everlasting love (Jer. 31:3); God's everlasting covenant (Heb. 13:20); and everlasting consolation (2 Thess. 2:16). See also Psa. 145:13; Rom. 2:7; 2 Cor. 5:1; 1 Pet. 5:10; Rev. 11:15.

Heaven is a holy place for a holy people. The Bible refers to heaven as God's "holy dwelling place" (2 Chr. 30:27); "the holy city" (Rev. 21:2); "the holy Jerusalem" (Rev. 21:10); and as a place "wherein dwelleth righteousness" (2 Pet. 3:13). Only the pure in heart will go there. "Who shall ascend into the hill of the Lord? or who shall stand in his holy place? He that hath clean hands, and a pure heart; who hath not lifted up his soul unto vanity, nor sworn deceitfully" (Psa. 24:3,4).

What are other terms used to describe heaven?

- Father's house (John 14:2)
- The kingdom (Matt. 25:34), the kingdom of heaven (Matt. 19:23), the kingdom of God (Matt. 19:24), His heavenly kingdom (2 Tim. 4:18)
- New heavens and a new earth (2 Pet. 3:13; Rev. 21:1; Isa. 65:17; 66:22)
- The city of the living God (Heb. 12:22), the city of the great king (Psa. 48:2)
- Mount Zion; Zion (Heb. 12:22; Psa. 48:2,11,12; Isa. 33:20)
- The heavenly Jerusalem (Heb. 12:22); the new Jerusalem (Rev. 21:2)
- Paradise (Luke 23:43; Rev. 2:7)
- Life eternal (Matt. 25:46)

- The world (or age) to come (Mark 10:30)
- A heavenly country (Heb. 11:16)
- A better country (Heb. 11:16)

Why is heaven referred to as "a better country"?

The writer of Hebrews compares "that country," which Abraham and Sara left in answer to the call of God, with "a better country, that is, an heavenly," which they desired (Heb. 11:15,16). Similarly, we receive "the heavenly calling" when we hear and obey the gospel. As a result, we should no longer desire to be "conformed to this world" (Rom. 12:2); to love the "things that are in the world" (1 John 2:15); or to have "the friendship of the world" (James 4:4). That is, we should no longer "mind the things of the flesh," but "the things of the Spirit" (Rom. 8:5). As with Abraham and Sara, we should set our affections on things above, not on things on the earth because when Christ shall appear, then shall we also appear with him in glory (Col. 3:2,4).

The following comparisons show some ways in which heaven is "a better country":

On earth, life is short and uncertain as a vapor (James 4:14), a flower (Job 14:2), a shadow (Job 14:2), and a tale that is told (Psa. 90:9); in heaven, life is forever and ever (Rev. 22:5).

On earth, life is full of trouble (Job 14:1); in heaven, life is full of joy and pleasures forevermore (Psa. 16:11).

On earth, our belongings and property can be plundered and confiscated for Christ's sake; in heaven, we have "a better and an enduring substance" (Heb. 10:34)—an "inheritance incorruptible, and undefiled, and that fadeth not away" (1 Pet. 1:4).

On earth, the cities are built by man; heaven itself is "a city . . . whose builder and maker is God" (Heb. 11:10). On earth, life is insecure because of thieves and the corruption of moth and rust; heaven is a place where "neither moth nor rust doth corrupt, and where thieves do not break through nor steal" (Matt. 6:20).

Indeed, heaven is a better country. God promises, "And my people shall dwell in a peaceable habitation, and in sure dwellings, and in quiet resting places" (Isa. 32:18).

Will we recognize one another in heaven?

Yes, we will. King David expected to recognize his baby who had died (2 Sam. 12:23). The disciples recognized Moses and Elijah on the Mount of Transfiguration (Matt. 17:3,4). Jesus says that "many shall come from the east and west, and shall sit down with Abraham, and Isaac, and Jacob, in the kingdom of heaven" (Matt. 8:11). This verse implies that we will recognize one another when we get there.

Here is an appropriate poem about heaven:

I dreamt death came the other night.
Heavens gates swung open wide
And there an angel stood.
God ushered me inside,
And there to my astonishment
Stood folks I had known before.
Some I judged and labeled as unfit for heaven's door.
Indignant words rose to my lips,
But never were set free,
Cause every face showed stunned surprise—
No one expected me!

Author unknown

What will we do in heaven?

In heaven we will see God face to face. "And they shall see his face; and his name shall be in their foreheads" (Rev. 22:4). God is pure and holy; none but the pure and holy shall see Him. "Blessed are the pure in heart: for they shall see God" (Matt. 5:8). "Follow peace with all men, and holiness, without which no man shall see the Lord" (Heb. 12:14). "We shall see him as he is. And every man that hath this hope in him purifieth himself, even as he is pure" (1 John 3:2,3). Believers purify themselves by fearing God and obeying His Word (John 15:3; 17:17; 1 Pet. 1:14-17).

God promises the one who "walketh righteously, and speaketh uprightly; . . . that despiseth the gain of oppressions, that shaketh his hands from holding of bribes, that stoppeth his ears from hearing of blood, and shutteth his eyes from seeing evil. . . . Thine eyes shall see the king in his beauty" (Isa. 33:15,17).

In heaven we will sing unto the Lord a new song. "And I heard a voice from heaven, as the voice of many waters, and as the voice of a great thunder: and I heard the voice of harpers harping with their harps: and they sung as it were *a new song* before the throne" (Rev. 14:2,3). See also Rev. 15:2-4.

In heaven we will fall down and worship the Lord, casting our crowns before Him. "The four and twenty elders fall down before him that sat on the throne, and worship him that liveth for ever and ever, and cast their crowns before the throne, saying, Thou art worthy, O Lord, to receive glory and honour and power: for thou hast created all things, and for thy pleasure they are and were created" (Rev. 4:10,11). See also Rev. 5:8-14; 7:9-12; 14:1-3; 15:2-4; 19:1-7.

In heaven we will rest from our labors. "And I heard a voice from heaven saying unto me, Write, Blessed are the dead which die in the Lord from henceforth: Yea, saith the Spirit, that they may *rest* from their labours; and their works do follow them" (Rev. 14:13).

In heaven we will serve the Lord. "And there shall be no more curse: but the throne of God and of the Lamb shall be in it; and his servants shall serve him" (Rev. 22:3). See also Psa. 102:22; Matt. 25:21; Rev. 7:15.

In heaven we will enjoy holy fellowship. This fellowship will be with Jesus and our heavenly Father as well as with all the saints. They "shall come from the east and west, and shall sit down with Abraham, and Isaac, and Jacob, in the kingdom of heaven" (Matt. 8:11)

Will this fellowship include eating and drinking?

Yes. With regard to heaven, Jesus spoke of "the marriage supper of the Lamb" (Rev. 19:9). He also said, "Blessed is he that shall eat bread in the kingdom of God" (Luke 14:15); "To him that overcometh will I give to eat of the hidden manna" (Rev. 2:17); and "I will not drink henceforth of this fruit of the vine, until that day when I drink it new with you in my Father's kingdom" (Matt. 26:29).

For the following reasons, however, eating and drinking in heaven will probably be in a spiritual sense, which, of course, will be more glorious.

1. The apostle Paul said that "the kingdom of God is not meat and drink; but righteousness, and peace, and joy in the Holy Ghost" (Rom. 14:17).

2. Jesus stressed the importance of spiritual food over natural food. He said, "I have meat to eat that ye know not of" (John 4:32); "Labour not for the meat which perisheth, but for that meat which endureth unto everlasting life, which the Son of man shall give unto you: for him hath God the Father sealed" (John 6:27). See also Isa. 55:2.

3. Jesus often spoke of eating and drinking in a spiritual sense, especially in John, chapter six. He said, "He that eateth my flesh, and drinketh my blood, dwelleth in me, and I in him. As the living Father hath sent me, and I live by the Father: so he that eateth me, even he shall live by me" (John 6:56,57).

How did Jesus live by the Father, by physically eating His flesh and drinking His blood? Of course not! But by hearing and obeying His Word (John 5:19,20,30; 8:28,29; 12:49,50; 14:10). Likewise, believers dwell in Christ and live by Him through having His Word abiding in them: "If ye abide in me, and *my words abide in you*, ye shall ask what ye will, and it shall be done unto you" (John 15:7).

The Bible often typifies the Word of God as something that we eat and drink. "Man shall not live by bread alone, but by every word that proceedeth out of the mouth of God" (Matt. 4:4). The angel of the Lord gave the apostle John "the little book" and said, "Take it, and *eat* it up" (Rev. 10:9). Jeremiah praised God saying, "Thy words were found, and I did eat them; and thy word was unto me the joy and rejoicing of mine heart" (Jer. 15:16). David declared, "How sweet are thy words unto my taste! yea, sweeter than honey to my mouth" (Psa. 119:103). Peter said, "As newborn babes, desire the sincere milk of the the word, that ye may grow thereby: If so be ye have *tasted that the Lord is gracious*" (1 Pet. 2:2,3). Notice that we taste the graciousness of the Lord by feasting on His Word.

To further emphasize the spiritual meaning of eating His flesh and drinking His blood, Christ added, "It is the spirit that quickeneth; the flesh profiteth nothing: *the words that I speak unto you, they are spirit, and they are life*" (John 6:63). The flesh, or natural meat and drink, profits nothing. The words of Christ, however, give *life.* Peter received the revelation of this truth; he associated the words of Jesus with eternal life. "Lord, to whom shall we go? thou hast the words of eternal life" (John 6:68).

Thus, eating the bread and the hidden manna, and drinking the new fruit of the vine in heaven could represent our continuing to partake of Christ and His benefits of salvation. Throughout eternity, His wonderful salvation will be the theme of our praise (Rev. 5:9; 19:1).

4. The Bible speaks of the water of life and the tree of life in a spiritual sense, which supersedes the natural. Heaven is described as having "a pure river of *water of life*, clear as crystal" and "*the tree of life*, which bare twelve manner of fruits, and yielded her fruit every month: and the leaves of the tree were for the healing of the nations" (Rev. 22:1,2).

Jesus associated the water of life with everlasting life and His Spirit. He said to the woman at the well, "Whosoever drinketh of this water shall thirst again: but whosoever drinketh of the water that I shall give him shall never thirst; but the water that I shall give him shall be in him a well of water springing up into everlasting life" (John 4:13,14). On another occasion, He said, "If any man thirst, let him come unto me, and drink. He that believeth on me, as the scripture hath said, out of his belly shall flow rivers of living water. (But this spake he of the Spirit)" (John 7:37-39). See also Psa. 36:8,9; Isa. 33:21; Rev. 21:6; 22:17.

Solomon associated the tree of life with wisdom and understanding: "Happy is the man that findeth wisdom, and the man that getteth understanding. . . . She is a *tree of life* to them that lay hold upon her: and happy is every one that retaineth her" (Pro. 3:13,18). No doubt the tree of life represents Christ "in whom are hid all the treasures of wisdom and knowledge" (Col. 2:3). See also Rev. 2:7; 22:14.

Will there be many people in heaven?

One of the disciples asked the Master a similar question. "Lord, are there few that be saved?" Jesus answered, "Strive to enter in at the strait gate: for many, I say unto you, will seek to enter in, and shall not be able" (Luke 13:23,24). Verse 25 explains why many will not be able to enter when Jesus comes; it will be too late—the door will be shut.

In spite of the testimony of Christians and in spite of the tender pleading of the Holy Spirit, many persist on the broad, popular way that leads to destruction. Therefore, comparatively few will enter the narrow way that leads to life eternal (Matt. 7:13,14).

Still, as God promised Abraham, heaven will be filled with the redeemed of all ages, who are as many as the stars of heaven and as the sand that is upon the seashore (Gen. 22:17). In the parable of the great banquet, the king commanded his servants, "Go out into the highways and hedges, and compel them to come in, that *my house may be filled*" (Luke 14:23). In Revelation, John saw "*a great multitude, which no man could number*, . . . before the throne and before the Lamb" (Rev. 7:9). He also "heard a great voice of *much people* in heaven, saying, Alleluia: Salvation, and glory, and honour, and power, unto the Lord our God" (Rev. 19:1).

On the other hand, hell is very large in order to receive the millions going there. "Hell hath enlarged herself, and opened her mouth without measure: and their glory, and their multitude, and their pomp, and he that rejoiceth, shall descend into it" (Isa. 5:14).

Souls are perishing, and the "night cometh, when no man can work" (John 9:4). Therefore, let us do the works of God while there is still time to spread the gospel everywhere. Paul said, "Woe is unto me, if I preach not the gospel" (1 Cor. 9:16).

Can a person know that he is going to heaven?

Yes! Having the assurance of sins forgiven and eternal life is indeed God's greatest blessing to man.

Paul wrote, "*We know* that if our earthly house of this tabernacle were dissolved, we have a building of God, an house not made with hands, *eternal* in the heavens" (2 Cor. 5:1). John added, "These things have I written unto you that believe on the name of the Son of God: that *ye may know that ye have eternal life*" (1 John 5:13).

In addition, Jesus assured His followers, "Rejoice, because

your names *are written in heaven*" (Luke 10:20). "I go to prepare *a place for you.* And if I go and prepare *a place for you*, I will come again, and receive *you* unto myself; that where I am, there *ye may be also*" (John 14:2,3). "Verily, verily, I say unto you, he that heareth my word, and believeth on him that sent me, *hath everlasting life*" (John 5:24).

Salvation is the gift of eternal life that God gives by grace through faith. Those who receive this gift can *know* that they are saved and have eternal life. "For by grace are ye *saved* through faith; and that not of yourselves: it is the gift of God" (Eph. 2:8). "For the wages of sin is death; but the *gift of God is eternal life* through Jesus Christ our Lord" (Rom. 6:23).

The epistle of First John emphasizes our assurance of these spiritual truths. The phrase "we know" is repeated at least ten times:

We do know that we know him (2:3).

We know that . . . we shall be like him (3:2).

We know that we have passed from death unto life (3:14).

We know that we are of the truth (3:19).

We know that he abideth in us (3:24).

We know that he hears us (5:15).

We know that we have the petitions that we desired of him (5:15).

We know that whosoever is born of God sinneth not (5:18).

We know that we are of God (5:19).

We know that the Son of God is come, and hath given us an understanding, that we may *know him* that is true, and *we are in him* that is true, even in his Son Jesus Christ. This is the true God, and *eternal life* (5:20).

How can a person know he is really saved and has eternal life?

The assurance of salvation rests in a person, the Lord Jesus Christ. He is the only Savior. "Neither is there salvation in any other: for there is none other name under heaven given among men, whereby we must be saved" (Acts 4:12). Many today base their hope of salvation in water baptism, in church membership, in religion, in good works, in sacraments, in keeping the traditions of men, or in the Lord's supper. But Paul testified, "I know *whom* I have believed" (2 Tim. 1:12). He trusted in Christ and Christ alone. John stated, "And this is the record, that God hath given to us eternal life, and this life *is in his Son*" (1 John 5:11).

Salvation is a gift of God that is received when one, with godly sorrow and faith, repents and turns from every known sin, idol, and evil association, and completely surrenders to Jesus Christ to live wholly for Him. "For godly sorrow worketh repentance to salvation" (2 Cor. 7:10). God promises, "Wherefore come out from among them, and be ye separate, saith the Lord, and touch not the unclean thing; and I will receive you, and will be a Father unto you, and ye shall be my sons and daughters, saith the Lord Almighty" (2 Cor. 6:17,18).

A person's greatest assurance of salvation is the reality of knowing that his life is completely changed from the love of self to the love of Jesus. Christ does not save a person in his sins, but from his sins (Matt. 1:21). Someone has said, "No change, no conversion." The Bible says, "If any man *be in Christ*, he is a new creature: old things are passed away; behold, *all things* are become new" (2 Cor. 5:17). Here are ten biblical results of salvation whereby a person can know that he is saved:

1. *Freedom from the power of sin*—"If the Son therefore shall make you free, ye shall be free indeed" (John 8:36). "Sin shall not have dominion over you" (Rom. 6:14). "*We know* that whosoever is born of God sinneth not; but he that is begotten of God keepeth himself, and that wicked one toucheth him not" (1 John 5:18).

When a person has real salvation, he is set free from sin and avoids it. If he should slip and fall, he will be miserable and will not remain in sin. He will repent and go on with the Lord (1 John 2:1,2). When a sheep falls into the mud, he struggles to get out; it is not his environment and he's not happy there. It is not so with a hog. When he falls into the mud, he likes it and wants to stay there. A saved person behaves like the sheep; a lost person behaves like the hog. See 1 John 3:5-10.

2. *Peace with God*—"Therefore being justified by faith, we have peace with God through our Lord Jesus Christ" (Rom. 5:1).

3. *A love for brothers in Christ*—"*We know* that we have passed from death unto life, because we love the brethren" (1 John 3:14).

4. *The joy of salvation and a desire to tell others about Jesus*—

When a person is a new creature in Christ, God commits to him the ministry or the word of reconciliation, making him an ambassador for Christ (2 Cor. 5:17-20). David said, "Restore unto me the joy of thy salvation; and uphold me with thy free spirit. Then will I teach transgressors thy ways; and sinners shall be converted unto thee" (Psa. 51:12,13).

5. *The witness of the Spirit and a desire to pray*—"And hereby *we know* that he abideth in us, by the Spirit which he hath given us" (1 John 3:24). "Hereby *know we* that we dwell in him, and he in us, because he hath given us of his Spirit" (1 John 4:13). "The Spirit itself beareth witness with our spirit, that *we are the children of God*" (Rom. 8:16). "And because *ye are sons*, God hath sent forth the Spirit of his Son into your hearts, crying, Abba, Father" (Gal. 4:6). When Ananias visited Paul, the new convert, he said, "Behold, he prayeth" (Acts 9:11).

6. *A desire for the Word of God*—"As newborn babes [in Christ], desire the sincere milk of the word, that ye may grow thereby" (1 Pet. 2:2). "He that is of God heareth God's words" (John 8:47). See also Matt. 5:6; Luke 6:21,25; Psa. 42:2.

7. *Keeping the Word of God*—"And hereby *we do know that we know him*, if we keep his commandments. He that saith, I know him, and keepeth not his commandments, is a liar, and the truth is not in him. But whoso keepeth his word, in him verily is the love of God perfected: hereby *know we that we are in him*" (1 John 2:3-5).

8. *Doing good works*—"My little children, let us not love in word, neither in tongue; but in deed and in truth. And hereby *we know that we are of the truth, and shall assure our hearts* before him" (1 John 3:18,19). See Heb. 6:9,10.

9. *Being persuaded of Christ's keeping power*—"For *I know whom* I have believed, and *am persuaded* that he is able to keep that which I have committed unto him against that day" (2 Tim. 1:12). See Heb. 7:25.

10. *Having the hope of our Lord's Second Coming*—"Beloved, *now are we the sons of God*, and it doth not yet appear what we shall be: but *we know* that, when he shall appear, we shall be like him; for we shall see him as he is. And every man that hath this *hope* in him purifieth himself, even as he is pure" (1 John 3:2,3). See also Titus 2:11-13.

Do you know that you are in Christ Jesus and have everlasting life? If not, salvation can be yours. Come to Jesus in repentance and trust Him to forgive you of all your sins and to save you now. Confess your sins directly to Him: "If we confess our sins, he is faithful and just to forgive us our sins, and to cleanse us from all unrighteousness" (1 John 1:9). Jesus promised, "Him that cometh to me I will in no wise cast out" (John 6:37) and "He that heareth my word, and believeth on him that sent me, hath everlasting life, and shall not come into condemnation; but is past from death unto life" (John 5:24).

Heaven	**Hell**
A place of eternal joy and bliss—Matt. 25:23.	A place of immeasurable suffering, of "everlasting burnings" (Isa. 33:14), without hope of escape—Mark 9:43-48.
A place where men drink the new fruit of the vine with Christ—Matt. 26:29.	A place where men drink the wine of the wrath of God—Rev. 14:10.
A place inhabited by God, Jesus, the angels, and the righteous—Heb. 12:22-24.	A place inhabited by the devil and his angels, the beast, the false prophet, and the ungodly—Rev. 20:10,15.
A place where the inhabitants will not suffer any heat—Rev. 7:16.	A place where the inhabitants will suffer intense heat, fire, and brimstone—Rev. 21:8.
A place of light. Jesus is the light; there's no darkness—Rev. 22:5.	A place of "blackness of darkness for ever"—Jude 1:13.
A place of life eternal—Matt. 25:46; Dan. 12:2.	A place of everlasting punishment, shame, and contempt—Matt. 25:46; Dan. 12:2.
A place of beautiful mansions—John 14:1-3.	A prison house of endless despair—Luke 16:26,28.
A place of eternal comfort—Luke 16:25.	A place of eternal torment—Luke 16:24,25,28; Rev. 14:11.
A place of everlasting joy where sorrow and sighing shall flee away—Isa. 35:10.	A place of sorrow where there's weeping, wailing, and gnashing of teeth—Matt. 8:12; 13:42.

Heaven	Hell
A place where there's a "blessed . . . holy" crowd (Matt. 25:34; Rev. 22:11). The poor in spirit, the meek, the merciful, the pure, and the peacemakers—Matt. 5:3-9.	A place where there's a "cursed . . . filthy" crowd (Matt. 25:41; Rev. 22:11). The fearful, and unbelieving, and the abominable, and murderers, and whoremongers, and sorcerers, and idolaters, and all liars—Rev. 21:8.
A place of eternal rest—Rev. 14:13.	A place where there is "no rest day nor night"—Rev. 14:11.
A place of eternal fellowship with the Lord and His people—Matt. 8:11.	A place of utter loneliness in "outer darkness"—Matt. 8:12.
A place prepared for a prepared people—John 14:1-3; Rev. 21:2.	A place prepared for the devil and his angels—Matt. 25:41.
The destiny of those on the narrow way—Matt. 7:14.	The destiny of those on the broad, easy way—Matt. 7:13.
A place with "a pure river of water"—Rev. 22:1.	A place without one drop of water of to cool the tongue—Luke 16:24.

Is heaven closed to the unsaved dead?

Scripture indicates that men have no chance of getting saved and entering heaven after death. Now is the time to repent. After death, a person cannot pass from heaven to hell, nor from hell to heaven because "there is a great gulf fixed" between the two (Luke 16:26).

God says, "It is appointed unto men once to die, but after this the judgment" (Heb. 9:27). "Repent, . . . For I have no pleasure in the death of him that dieth, saith the Lord God: wherefore turn yourselves, and live ye" (Ezek. 18:30,32).

Jesus said, "I tell you, Nay: but, except ye repent, ye shall all likewise perish" (Luke 13:3). "Then said Jesus again unto them [those who would not repent], I go my way, and ye shall seek me, and shall die in your sins: whither I go, *ye cannot come*" (John 8:21).

The angel who showed John the glories of heaven said, "He that is unjust, let him be unjust still: and he which is filthy, let him be filthy still: and he that is righteous, let him be righteous still: and he that is holy, let him be holy still" (Rev. 22:11).

Will our Christian conduct in this life make a difference in heaven?

Yes! The Bible teaches that:

- Greatness in heaven will be measured according to genuine conversion and childlike humility (Matt. 18:4) It is also related to our obeying the Lord's commandments and teaching them to others (Matt. 5:19; Dan. 12:3).
- The mercy we receive will be based on the mercy we have shown to others (Matt. 5:7; Luke 6:35,36).
- Rewards and glory will be measured according to the suffering and losses we have endured for Christ's sake (Matt. 5:10-12; Mark 10:29,30; Rom. 8:18; 2 Cor. 4:17; 1 Tim. 4:8-10; Heb. 10:32-35).
- Degrees of authority and rule will be measured according to our faithfulness to Christ, even in little things (Matt. 25:14-30; Luke 12:48; 19:12-27).
- Treasure in heaven will depend upon our laying up treasure there through faithfulness in giving and in doing kind deeds as unto Christ (Matt. 6:19,20; Luke 12:20,21,33; 1 Tim. 6:19).
- To have an abundant entrance into "the everlasting kingdom our Lord and Saviour Jesus Christ" (2 Pet. 1:11) we must obey God's Word, which says, "giving all diligence, add to your faith virtue; and to virtue knowledge; and to knowledge temperance; and to temperance patience; and to patience godliness; and to godliness brotherly kindness; and to brotherly kindness charity" (2 Pet. 1:5-7).

How should the prospect of our inheriting heaven make us better Christians?

The prospect of heaven should motivate believers to do the following:

To rejoice when hated and ostracized for Christ's sake—"Blessed are ye, when men shall hate you, and when they shall separate you from their company, and shall reproach you, and cast out your name as evil, for the Son of man's sake. Rejoice ye in that day, and leap for joy: for, behold, your reward is great in heaven:

for in the like manner did their fathers unto the prophets" (Luke 6:22,23).

To be free from worry, and to seek first the kingdom of God—"Therefore take no thought, saying, What shall we eat? or, What shall we drink? or, Wherewithal shall we be clothed? (For after all these things do the Gentiles seek:) for your heavenly Father knoweth that ye have need of all these things. But seek ye first the kingdom of God, and his righteousness; and all these things shall be added unto you" (Matt. 6:31-33). See also Col. 3:1-3; Phil. 3:7-21.

To serve God in practical holiness—"But now being made free from sin, and become servants to God, ye have your fruit unto holiness, and the end everlasting life" (Rom. 6:22). See also 1 Tim. 4:8.

To be unselfish and free from covetousness—"And I will say to my soul, Soul, thou hast much goods laid up for many years; take thine ease, eat, drink, and be merry. But God said unto him, Thou fool, this night thy soul shall be required of thee: then whose shall those things be, which thou hast provided? So is he that layeth up treasure for himself, and is not rich toward God" (Luke 12:19-21). See also Matt. 19:21.

To be faithful to Jesus no matter the cost—To the disciples who left all to follow Jesus, He said, "Ye are they which have continued with me in my temptations. And I appoint unto you a kingdom, as my Father hath appointed unto me" (Luke 22:28,29). "When the Son of man shall sit in the throne of his glory, ye also shall sit upon twelve thrones, judging the twelve tribes of Israel. And everyone that hath forsaken houses, or brethren, or sisters, or father, or mother, or wife, or children, or lands, for my name's sake, shall receive an hundredfold, and shall *inherit everlasting life*" (Matt. 19:28,29). See also Mark 10:29,30.

In conclusion, consider the faithfulness and usefulness of other great men and women who were motivated by heaven:

Abraham, Isaac, and Jacob lived as pilgrims and strangers on the earth because they "*looked for a city* which hath foundations, whose builder and maker is God" (Heb. 11:10).

Moses "refused to be called the son of Pharaoh's daughter; choosing rather to suffer affliction with the people of God, than to enjoy the pleasures of sin for a season; esteeming the reproach of Christ greater riches than the treasures in Egypt: for *he had respect unto the recompence of the reward*" (Heb. 11:24-26).

"Women received their dead raised to life again: and others were tortured, not accepting deliverance; that they might obtain a *better resurrection*" (Heb. 11:35).

The apostle Paul willingly suffered the loss of all things for Christ's sake; he was a true citizen of heaven. "But what things were gain to me, those I counted loss for Christ. . . . for whom I have suffered the loss of all things, and do count them but dung, that I may win Christ. . . . If by any means I might attain unto *the resurrection* of the dead. . . . For our conversation is in *heaven*; from whence also we look for the Saviour, the Lord Jesus Christ" (Phil. 3:7,8,11,20).

As Christians, we should also deny ourselves and take up our cross to follow Jesus—ever looking for that city and refusing to set our hearts on earthly things. The Scripture says, "And the world passeth away, and the lust thereof: but he that doeth the will of God abideth for ever" (1 John 2:17). "Let us go forth therefore unto him without the camp, bearing his reproach. For here have we no *continuing city*, but *we seek one to come*" (Heb. 13:13,14)—"the city of God, the holy place of the tabernacles of the most High" (Psa. 46:4).

21

The Final Battle

When will the final battle be fought?

We know it will be fought when Jesus comes at the end of the world because the events described in the context of this battle all occur on the Day of the Lord:

- The resurrected saints are with Christ (1 Thess. 4:16-5:2; Rev. 19:7-9,14; 20:9).
- Fire comes down from heaven (2 Thess. 1:7-10; Rev. 20:11).
- All the wicked are destroyed (1 Thess. 5:2,3; Rev. 19:14-21; 20:9).
- Satan, the beast, and the false prophet are destroyed (2 Thess. 2:1-3,8; Rev. 19:20; 20:10).
- The earth is destroyed (Isa. 13:3-10; 34:1-10; Joel 2:1-11; 3:9-16; 2 Pet. 3:10; Rev. 16:14-21). There can be no other battle after this one because all men, including "the remnant," will be slain in that day (Rev. 19:18,21).

Is there a thousand year interval between the battle of Armageddon and the battle of Gog and Magog, or are they the same battle?

They are the same battle; therefore, there is not a thousand year interval between them. Students of end-time prophecy must realize that the events of Revelation 20:1-10, which include the battle of Gog and Magog, do not follow chronologically the events of chapter nineteen (the battle of Armageddon). If they did, there would be no nation left for Satan to deceive (20:8) because all would have already been slain in the battle described in Revelation 19:17-21.

Moreover, the nations of the earth are seen as coming against Christ and His Church not only in chapters 19 and 20, but also in chapters 16 and 17. Does this mean, then, that there are four battles fought by Christ and His Church in the end time? No, a close examination of the details shows that each passage speaks of the same battle that will be fought at the coming of Jesus.

The term "Gog and Magog" occurs in Revelation 20:8 and in Ezekiel 38 and 39. The events of these two portions of Scripture agree with each other and with the description of the battle of Armageddon that is given in Revelation 16:12-16; 17:13,14 and 19:14-21. Therefore, they are the same battle.

The Events of Battle	**Gog and Magog**	**Armageddon**
Satan loosed from the pit	Rev. 20:7	Rev. 17:8,13,14
Satan deceives and gathers the nations to battle	Rev. 20:8	Rev. 16:13,14; 19:19,20
Nations come against Christ and His Church	Ezek. 38:15,16; Rev. 20:9	Rev. 16:14; 17:13,14; 19:19,20
The sword of the Lord	Ezek. 38:21	Rev. 19:15,21
Fire, hailstone, and brimstone fall from heaven	Ezek. 38:19,22; 39:6; Rev. 20:9	Rev. 16:18-21
Mountains are thrown down	Ezek. 38:20	Rev. 16:20
The wicked are destroyed	Ezek. 38:20-22; Rev. 20:9	Rev. 19:18-21
The fowls eat slain men	Ezek. 39:4,17-20	Rev. 19:17,18
Satan, the beast, and the false prophet are destroyed	Rev. 20:10	Rev. 19:19,20
God proclaims, "It is done," which speaks of the end of the world.	Ezek. 39:8	Rev. 16:17; 21:6

When will Christ rule the nations with a rod of iron?

To understand Christ's rule with a rod of iron, we must realize that it will *not* mean peace, but war. The rod of iron will *not* merely be used to subdue the nations and force them into obedience for a thousand years of peace, as some teach. The Bible alludes to the rod of iron in several ways:

- A two edged sword (Psa. 149:6)
- The sword of Jesus' mouth (Rev. 2:12,16; 19:15,21)

- The spirit of His mouth (2 Thess. 2:8)
- The rod of His strength (Psa. 110:2)
- The rod of His mouth (Isa. 11:4)
- The breath of His lips (Isa. 11:4)

These terms for the rod of iron show that the weapon of warfare is the Word of God, which is the sword of the Spirit (Eph. 6:17; Heb. 4:12; Rev. 1:16). Jesus said, "He that rejecteth me, and receiveth not my words, hath one that judgeth him: *the word* that I have spoken, the same shall judge him in the last day" (John 12:48).

The following passages reveal that the rod of iron will be used by Christ and His Church to break the nations to shivers and to dash them to pieces like an earthen vessel during the final battle, on the Day of the Lord.

Jesus promised His people power to rule with a rod of iron. "And he that overcometh, and keepeth my works unto the end, to him will I give power over the nations: and he shall rule them with *a rod of iron*; as the vessels of a potter shall they be broken to shivers: even as I received of my Father" (Rev. 2:26,27).

"Let the saints be joyful in glory. . . . Let the high praises of God be in their mouth, and *a two-edged sword* in their hand; to execute vengeance upon the heathen, and punishments upon the people; to bind their kings with chains, and their nobles with fetters of iron; to execute upon them the judgment written: this honour have all his saints. Praise ye the Lord" (Psa. 149:5-9).

"Arise and thresh, O daughter of Zion: for I will make *thine horn iron*, and I will make thy hoofs brass: and thou shalt beat in pieces many people: and I will consecrate their gain unto the Lord, and their substance unto the Lord of the whole earth" (Micah 4:13).

God said to His Son, "Ask of me, and I shall give thee the heathen for thine inheritance, and the uttermost parts of the earth for thy possession. Thou shalt break them with *a rod of iron*; thou shalt dash them in pieces like a potter's vessel" (Psalm 2:8,9). See also Rev. 12:5.

The apostle John described the final battle when the nations are smitten with the rod of iron. "And I saw heaven opened, and behold a white horse; and he that sat upon him was called

Faithful and True, and in righteousness he doth judge and make war. His eyes were as a flame of fire, and on his head were many crowns; and he had a name written, that no man knew, but he himself. And he was clothed with a vesture dipped in blood: and his name is called *The Word of God.* And the armies which were in heaven followed him upon white horses, clothed in fine linen, white and clean. And out of his mouth goeth *a sharp sword*, that with it he should smite the nations: and he shall rule them with *a rod of iron*: and he treadeth the winepress of the fierceness and wrath of Almighty God. And he hath on his vesture and on his thigh a name written, King of kings, and Lord of lords.

"And I saw an angel standing in the sun; and he cried with a loud voice, saying to all the fowls that fly in the midst of heaven, Come and gather yourselves together unto the supper of the great God; that ye may eat the flesh of kings, and the flesh of captains, and the flesh of mighty men, and the flesh of horses, and of them that sit on them, and the flesh of all men, both free and bond, both small and great. And I saw the beast, and the kings of the earth, and their armies, gathered together to *make war* against him that sat on the horse, and against his army. And the beast was taken, and with him the false prophet that wrought miracles before him, with which he deceived them that had received the mark of the beast, and them that worshipped his image. These both were cast alive into a lake of fire burning with brimstone. And the remnant were slain with *the sword* of him that sat upon the horse, which *sword proceeded out of his mouth*: and all the fowls were filled with their flesh" (Rev. 19:11-21).

We've shown that the King of kings and Lord of lords and His army, the Church, have triumphed gloriously. They've defeated the kings of the earth, their armies, and the beast and false prophet. All have been destroyed with the rod of iron; not even a remnant remains. See also Isa. 34:1-5. Since all the wicked are destroyed and the beast is slain, we know that this occurs on the Day of the Lord (1 Thess. 5:3; 2 Thess. 1:7-10; 2:8).

What happens after the final battle is fought?

The following chart shows that after the final battle, Christ and His Church are seen in God's eternal kingdom, which is heaven.

The Final Battle	A Heavenly Reign Forever
He shall smite the earth: with the rod of his mouth, and with the breath of his lips shall he slay the wicked—Isa. 11:4.	The wolf also shall dwell with the lamb . . . and a little child shall lead them—Isa. 11:6. (Isaiah 65:17, 25 shows this to be in the new heaven and earth.)
The Lord shall punish the host of the high ones that are on high, and the kings of the earth—Isa. 24:21.	The Lord of hosts shall reign in mount Zion, and in Jerusalem—Isa. 24:23. (That is, the heavenly Mount Zion and Jerusalem, see Heb. 12:22.)
God will come with vengeance, even God with a recompence—Isa. 35:4.	And the ransomed of the Lord shall return, and come to Zion with songs and *everlasting* joy—Isa. 35:10.
The Lord will come with fire. . . . the slain of the Lord shall be many—Isa. 65:15,16.	The new heavens and the new earth—Isa. 66:22.
And he shall judge among many people, and rebuke strong nations afar off—Micah 4:3.	And the Lord shall reign over them in *mount Zion* from henceforth, even *for ever*—Micah 4:7.
I beheld even till the beast was slain, and his body destroyed, and giving to the burning flame—Dan. 7:11.	His [the Lord's] dominion is an *everlasting* dominion, which shall not pass away, and *his kingdom that which shall not be destroyed*—Dan. 7:14.
The day of the Lord . . . sudden destruction cometh . . . they shall not escape—1 Thess. 5:2,3.	Caught up . . . to meet the Lord in the air: and so shall we ever be with the Lord—1 Thess. 4:17.
The Lord Jesus shall be revealed . . . in flaming fire taking vengeance on them that know not God, and that obey not the gospel: . . . who shall be punished with everlasting destruction—2 Thess. 1:7-9.	When he shall come to be glorified in his saints—2 Thess. 1:10. (Since the wicked will be punished with "everlasting destruction," the saints will be rewarded with everlasting life. Also, glorification is linked with heaven in Phil. 3:20,21.)
[At the sound of the seventh and last trumpet] the nations were angry, and thy wrath is come—Rev. 11:18.	The kingdoms of this world are become the kingdoms of our Lord . . . and he shall reign for ever and ever—Rev. 11:15.

When will Satan be loosed to deceive the nations and gather them to battle?

The following Scriptural reasons show that Satan will be loosed "a little season" *before* the final battle:

1. The final battle occurs when Jesus returns at *the end* of the world.

2. The events of Revelation 20:1-10 do not follow chronologically the events of chapter nineteen.

3. Revelation 20:1-10 cannot be interpreted to be a series of events happening in chronological order when Jesus returns because other passages of Scripture show that some of the events occur before then. Let's examine two events concerning the loosing of Satan that must unfold before Jesus returns and the final battle is fought:

• Satan loosed from the bottomless pit (20:3,7). John described Satan, in the person of the Antichrist, as "the beast that ascendeth out of the bottomless pit" or "the sea" who shall make war with the saints (Rev. 11:7; 13:1; 17:8,13,14). Paul wrote that Satan's power to work through the Antichrist is restrained until a short time before Christ's coming (2 Thess. 2:1-10).

• Satan deceives and gathers the nations to battle (20:3,8). The New Testament shows Satan performing signs and lying wonders through the Antichrist and the false prophet. They will work as a trinity to deceive the nations and gather them to battle against Christ and His Church.

"And I saw three unclean spirits like frogs come out of the mouth of the dragon, and out of the mouth of the beast, and out of the mouth of the false prophet. For they are the spirits of devils, working miracles, which go forth unto the kings of the earth and of the whole world, to gather them to the battle of that great day of God Almighty" (Rev. 16:13,14).

"And I saw the beast, and the kings of the earth, and their armies, gathered together to make war against him that sat on the horse [Jesus Christ], and against his army [the Church]. And the beast was taken, and with him the false prophet that wrought miracles before him, with which he deceived them that had received the mark of the beast, and them that worshipped his image. These both were cast alive into a lake of fire burning with brimstone" (Rev. 19:19,20). See also 2 Thess. 2:9-12.

In summary, Satan, in the person of the Antichrist, will be loosed before the coming of Jesus to deceive and gather the nations to battle. How and when will he accomplish these purposes? By working miracles through the Antichrist and the false prophet, Satan will deceive the nations into making an image of the beast; into worshiping the beast's image; into receiving the beast's mark; and finally, into gathering them to battle against the Lord Jesus Christ.

Does Scripture show many similarities between Satan and the Antichrist?

Yes, definitely! In fact, the following twelve descriptions of Satan (the dragon) and the Antichrist (the man of sin or the beast) show that they are one:

- Both have seven heads and ten horns (Rev. 12:3; 13:1).
- Both are called wicked (1 John 5:18; 2 Thess. 2:8).
- Both are red or scarlet (Rev. 12:3; 17:3).
- Both are restrained (Rev. 20:3; 2 Thess. 2:6-8).
- Both ascend from the bottomless pit (Rev. 20:3,7; 17:8).
- Both are worshiped (Rev. 13:4).
- Both make war with the saints (Rev. 12:17; 20:7-9; 13:7).
- Both have unclean spirits and work miracles (Rev. 16:13,14).
- Both deceive the nations (Rev. 20:8; 19:20; 2 Thess. 2:10).
- Both gather the nations to battle (Rev. 20:8; 19:19; 16:13,14).
- Both are defeated in battle (Rev. 20:9; 19:14-18,21).
- Both are judged with the wicked (2 Thess. 1:8,9; 2:8; Rev. 19:20,21; 20:9,10).
- Both are cast into the lake of fire (Rev. 20:10; 19:20).

There can be no doubt, then, that Satan, in the person of the Antichrist, is loosed to deceive the nations into making war against Christ and His Church before the coming of Jesus.

When was Satan bound?

Revelation 20:1,2 states, "And I saw an angel come down from heaven, having *the key of the bottomless pit* and a great chain in his hand. And he laid hold on the dragon, that old serpent, which is the Devil, and Satan, and bound him a thousand years." When does this occur? The New Testament shows that Jesus has *the keys of hell and death* and that He bound Satan at His first coming.

Jesus himself declared:

"How can one enter into a strong man's house, and spoil his goods, except he first *bind* the strong man? and then he will spoil his house" (Matt. 12:29).

"When a strong man armed keepeth his palace, his goods are in peace: But when a stronger than he shall come upon him, and *overcome him*, he taketh from him all his armour wherein he trusted, and divideth his spoils" (Luke 11:21,22). See also Mark 3:27.

"*Now* is the judgment of this world: *now* shall *the prince of this world* [*Satan*] *be cast out*. And I, if I be lifted up from the earth, will draw all men unto me" (John 12:31,32).

"Of judgment, because *the prince of this world is judged*" (John 16:11).

"I am he that liveth, and was dead; and, behold, I am alive for evermore, Amen; and *have the keys of hell and of death*" (Rev. 1:18).

"And *I will give unto thee the keys of the kingdom* of heaven: and whatsoever thou shalt *bind* on earth shall be bound in heaven: and whatsoever thou shalt loose on earth shall be loosed in heaven" (Matt. 16:19). See also Matt. 18:18-20.

"I beheld Satan as lightning fall from heaven. Behold, I give unto you power to tread on serpents and scorpions, and over *all the power of the enemy*: and nothing shall by any means hurt you" (Luke 10:18,19).

The apostles wrote:

"And having *spoiled principalities and powers*, he [Jesus] made a shew of them openly, *triumphing over them* in it" (Col. 2:15).

"For this purpose the Son of God was manifested, that he might *destroy* the works of the devil" (1 John 3:8).

Jesus (Eve's seed) bruised the head of Satan. God said to Satan, the serpent, "And I will put enmity between thee and the woman, and between thy seed and her seed; it shall *bruise thy head*, and thou shalt bruise his heel" (Gen. 3:15).

These verses show that Satan is bound, overcome, cast out, judged, fallen, spoiled, bruised, and triumphed over by our Lord Jesus Christ. His works are destroyed. Furthermore, our Lord has the keys of hell and death and has given believers "the keys of the kingdom" and power over all the power of the enemy.

Because Jesus Christ cast out Satan, all nations can be blessed by hearing and receiving the gospel. "Now is the judgment of this world: now shall the prince of this world [Satan] be cast out. And I, if I be lifted up from the earth, *will draw all men unto me*" (John 12:31,32). John saw in heaven the redeemed "out of every kindred, and tongue, and people, and nation" (Rev. 5:9).

Our resurrected Lord, "having spoiled principalities and powers," said, "Thus it is written, and thus it behooved Christ to suffer, and to rise from the dead the third day: And that repentance and remission of sins should be preached in his name among *all nations*, beginning at Jerusalem" (Luke 24:46,47). He commissioned His disciples with these words: "*All power* is given unto me in heaven and in earth. Go ye therefore, and teach *all nations*" (Matt. 28:18,19). See also Luke 10:18,19.

Jesus Christ has been given all power over Satan; therefore, Jesus' servants can go forth into Satan's territory and preach the gospel so that they "in whom the god of this world hath blinded the minds" might see "the light of the glorious gospel of Christ" (2 Cor. 4:4). Through Christ's victory, all who believe in Him are delivered "from the power of darkness" and are translated into "the kingdom of his [God's] dear Son" (Col. 1:13). See also Acts 26:17,18 and Chapter Twenty-two.

If Satan is already bound, why are there so many problems in the world?

We know that Satan's power is not totally limited. Paul shows that even though Satan is restrained until a time before the coming of the Lord, "the mystery of iniquity doth *already work*" (2 Thess. 2:7). John, when speaking of the "Spirit of antichrist," said, "even now already is it in the world" (1 John 4:3).

Satan is a deceiver, and his spirit of deception will increase as we near the end. But his power "to deceive the nations" and "to gather them together to battle" to make war with the Lord Jesus Christ and His people is restrained by the power of God until he is loosed, in the person of the man of sin, for "a little season" before the coming of the Lord (Rev. 20:3,8). See also 2 Thess. 2:3-12; Rev. 16:13-16; 19:19.

Then unprecedented tribulation, deception, and persecution will be unleashed upon the world. Undoubtedly, that will be the season Jesus spoke of when He said, "the night cometh, when no man can work" (John 9:4). With the great apostasy already upon us and the rise in drug and alcohol use, witchcraft, immorality, pornography, divorce and remarriage, rock and roll music, abortion, violence, and an Antichrist spirit as seen in the New Age Movement, we may be much closer to that time than we realize.

Objection Answered

Doesn't the statement "they shall beat their swords into plowshares" (Micah 4:3) imply a peaceful millennium?

Micah 4:3 states, "And he shall judge among many people, and rebuke strong nations afar off; and they shall beat their swords into plowshares, and their spears into pruninghooks: nation shall not lift up a sword against nation, neither shall they learn war any more."

This statement is about the "daughter of Zion" (the Church) who, together with her Lord, will "beat in pieces many people" when He comes to "judge among many people, and rebuke strong nations afar off" (Micah 4:3,13). Then, after fighting the last battle, they will not "learn war anymore" because "the Lord shall reign over them in mount Zion from henceforth, even *for ever*" (Micah 4:3,7).

Before this final battle, the Lord's command will be, "Beat your plowshares into swords, and your pruninghooks into spears: let the weak say, I am strong" (Joel 3:10). But afterwards, the command will be to do the reverse, "beat their swords into plowshares, and their spears into pruninghooks" (Isa. 2:4; Micah 4:3).

Micah 4:3 cannot be applied to a peaceful millennium on earth because in that final battle the "fierceness and wrath of Almighty God" will be poured out. As a result, "all men, both free and bond, both small and great" will be slain; not even a remnant will be spared (Rev. 19:15,18,21). They will be "broken to shivers" (Rev. 2:27; Psa. 2:9), ground "to powder" (Matt. 21:44), and burned up; "neither root nor branch" will be left (Mal. 4:1; 2

Thess. 1:8; 2 Pet. 3:10). God will take vengeance on all who have persecuted His people (Deut. 32:39-43; Isa. 34:1-8; 35:4; 41:11,12; 60:14; 65:13,14; Jer. 46:10; 1 Thess. 2:14-16; 2 Thess. 1:4-9). All "shall drink of the wine of the wrath of God" because all worshiped the beast, except those whose names are written in the book of life (Rev. 13:8; 14:9-11). Believers will be eternally saved and unbelievers eternally lost (Matt. 25:46).

In summary, Satan, who has been defeated at Calvary, will be loosed for a short while to deceive the nations and to gather them in a final battle against Jesus, the coming King. With fiery indignation, Christ, together with His glorious Church, will completely destroy Satan and all the wicked on the last day and reign forever in heaven—the new Jerusalem.

22

A Literal Millennium? (Part I)

What is meant by the term "literal millennium"?

Millennium is a Latin word meaning a thousand years. Revelation 20:1-10 speaks of a thousand year period six times. Some interpret this to mean that after Christ returns, He will reign on earth for a thousand years with peace and prosperity for all. In other words, there will be a literal millennium.

Is this thousand year period literal or symbolic? Will it occur before or after Christ's return?

The best way to know if a scripture is symbolic or not is to examine it in the light of the rest of the Bible. Here are five significant reasons why this thousand year period symbolizes a long period of time *before* Christ's return:

1. An examination of the four events that are associated with the millennium, in light of the rest of the Bible, indicates that the thousand year period occurs before Christ returns.

• *The binding of Satan for a thousand years so that "he should deceive the nations no more" (Rev. 20:2,3).* Since Jesus bound Satan at His first coming and will destroy all the nations at His second coming, the thousand year period occurs before Christ returns (Matt. 12:28,29; Rev. 19:15,21).

• *The loosing of Satan for a short while to deceive the nations when the thousand years are fulfilled (Rev. 20:7,8).* Since Satan is loosed in the person of the Antichrist to deceive the nations and since he will be judged with the nations at the Second Coming (2 Thess. 2:1-8; Rev. 19:18-21; 20:8-10), the thousand year period occurs before Christ returns. See Chapter Twenty-one.

• *Believers living and reigning as priests of God for a thousand years (Rev. 20:4,6).* Since, by a spiritual resurrection, believers are presently living and reigning as priests (John 5:24,25; 1 Pet.

2:5,9) and will inherit heaven at the Second Coming (Matt. 25:34,46), the thousand year period occurs before Christ returns.

• *The resurrection of "the rest of the dead" after the thousand years are finished (Rev. 20:5).* Since all the dead will be raised and judged at the Second Coming (John 5:28,29; Matt. 13:30,39-43), the thousand year period occurs before Christ returns.

Since these four events show that the thousand year period occurs before the Second Coming and the impossibilities of them being fulfilled in a literal millennium, we know that the thousand years symbolizes a long period of time before Jesus returns.

2. The exact term "a thousand years" (Rev. 20:2,4,6) is used four other times in Scripture—not once literally, but each time symbolically.

• "Yea, though he live *a thousand years* twice told, yet hath he seen no good: do not all go to one place?" (Eccl. 6:6).

• "For *a thousand years* in thy sight are but as yesterday when it is past, and as a watch in the night" (Psa. 90:4).

• "One day is with the Lord as *a thousand years*, and *a thousand years* as one day" (2 Pet. 3:8).

3. The number "thousand" is often used symbolically in Scripture:

• The apostle John mentions "ten thousand times ten thousand, and thousands of thousands" of angels (Rev. 5:11). We know this is a symbolic figure because Hebrews 12:22 says, "an innumerable company of angels."

• "For every beast of the forest is mine, and the cattle upon *a thousand* hills" (Psa. 50:10). Clearly, there are many more than a thousand hills; therefore, the Lord was speaking symbolically.

• "*A thousand* shall fall at thy side, and *ten thousand* at thy right hand; but it shall not come nigh thee" (Psa. 91:7). Obviously, "a thousand" and "ten thousand" do not denote an exact number of people, but many and a great multitude.

• "He hath remembered his covenant *for ever*, the word which he commanded to *a thousand* generations" (Psa. 105:8). Note, "a thousand generations" is symbolic of "for ever."

4. Other symbolic terms are also used in Revelation 20: the bottomless pit and its key, a great chain, the dragon, that old serpent, and Satan's prison. For example, "the dragon" and "that old serpent" symbolize Satan. Also, "the bottomless pit" is

referred to as Satan's "prison" (20:3,7). It is also referred to as "the sea": John saw the beast ascending out of the bottomless pit in Revelation 11:7 and rising up out the sea in Revelation 13:1. Thus, Satan being cast into the bottomless pit is another way of saying that his power is bound or restrained until he is loosed.

5. Nowhere does the Bible specifically mention a literal millennium. In summary, the four events associated with the thousand years occur before the Second Coming. In addition, "thousand" is often used symbolically in Scripture, and other symbolic terms are also used in Revelation 20. Moreover, when interpreted in context, Scripture does not support the teaching of a literal millennium. Clearly, then, the thousand year period is not literal, but symbolizes a long period of time before Christ's return.

Are there a thousand years between the resurrection of the righteous and the resurrection of the wicked?

Revelation 20:5 states, "But the rest of the dead lived not again until the thousand years were finished." This verse implies a thousand years difference between the two resurrections, but Daniel 12:2 gives no such indication: "And many of them that sleep in the dust of the earth shall awake, some to everlasting life, and some to shame and everlasting contempt." The Bible teaches that *all* the dead will be raised when Jesus returns to gather His Church, at the end of the world.

Serious Bible students should interpret the Book of Revelation, which contains much symbolic language, in the light of scriptures that are plainly understood, such as the gospels and the epistles, not vice versa. With this in mind, consider the following fifty-four clear biblical references. They show the righteous and the wicked will be resurrected at the same time. Although some have been cited previously, they are very important and merit repeating here.

First, there is only one bodily resurrection of the dead. When the Scripture speaks of "the resurrection," it's always singular. Hebrews 6:2 records the doctrine of the "resurrection of the dead." Martha mentioned "the resurrection at the last day" (John 11:24). Jesus spoke of "the resurrection" and "the resurrection of the dead" (Matt. 22:30,31; Luke 20:35). Moreover,

Paul emphatically stated, "there shall be *a resurrection of the dead*, both of the just and unjust" (Acts 24:15). See also Acts 17:32; 24:21. "Resurrection" is never mentioned in the plural, thus implying one bodily resurrection.

Scripture clearly shows that the resurrection of *all the dead* occurs when Jesus comes to gather His Church. When will both the righteous and the wicked be raised?

- When all that are in the graves shall hear Jesus' voice—"Marvel not at this: for the hour is coming, in the which *all* that are in the graves shall hear his voice. And shall come forth; they that have done good, unto the resurrection of life; and they that have done evil, unto the resurrection of damnation" (John 5:28,29).
- At the appearing of Jesus—"The Lord Jesus Christ . . . shall judge the quick [the living] and the dead at his appearing and his kingdom" (2 Tim. 4:1).
- On the last day—"And this is the will of him that sent me, that every one which seeth the Son, and believeth on him, may have everlasting life: and I will raise him up at the last day" (John 6:40). "He that rejecteth me, and receiveth not my words, hath one that judgeth him: the word that I have spoken, the same shall judge him in the last day" (John 12:48). Obviously, the righteous will not be raised a thousand years before the wicked, but on the last day.
- At the end of the world—"So shall it be at the end of the world: the angels shall come forth, and sever the wicked from among the just, and shall cast them into the furnace of fire: there shall be wailing and gnashing of teeth" (Matt. 13:49,50). See also Matt. 13:39-43.
- At the seventh and last trump, which is "the time of the dead" when both the wicked and the saints will come forth—"The seventh angel sounded . . . And the nations were angry, and thy wrath is come, and *the time of the dead*, that they should be judged, and that thou shouldest give reward unto thy servants the prophets, and to the saints, and them that fear thy name [the just], small and great; and shouldest destroy them [the unjust] which destroy the earth" (Rev. 11:15,18).
- On the Day of the Lord when the righteous are "caught up"

to meet the Lord and the wicked face "sudden destruction" (1 Thess. 4:17; 5:3). See also 2 Thess. 1:7-10; 2 Pet. 3:7-10; Luke 17:26-30; Psa. 50:3-5; Isa. 26:19-21.

In summary, the coming of Jesus is "the time of the dead" (Rev. 11:18) when "all that are in the graves" (John 5:28) shall come forth. "All" includes all nations (Matt. 25:32); every man (Rom. 2:6); the living and the dead (2 Tim. 4:1); the just and the unjust (Acts 24:15; Matt. 13:49); the small and great (Rev. 20:12); they that have done good and they that have done evil (John 5:29).

On that day, the divine verdict will be either life or damnation (John 5:29); life eternal or everlasting punishment (Matt. 25:46); eternal life or wrath (Rom. 2:5-7); inherit all things or be cast into the lake of fire (Rev. 20:15; 21:7,8); everlasting life or shame and everlasting contempt (Dan. 12:2).

These scriptures show that the resurrection of the righteous and resurrection of the wicked are not separated by a thousand years.

What is meant by "the first resurrection" (Rev. 20:5)?

This term is found only in Revelation 20:5,6: "This is the first resurrection. Blessed and holy is he that hath part in *the first resurrection*: on such *the second death* hath no power, but they shall be priests of God and of Christ, and shall reign with him a thousand years." Since the Bible tells us that "the second death" is everlasting death in the lake of fire (Rev. 20:14), we know "the first resurrection" represents the opposite, that is, everlasting life.

Furthermore, they who have the assurance of everlasting life by believing on the Lord Jesus Christ are blessed and holy (Rom. 4:7,8; Heb. 3:1) and are priests of God on whom the second death has no power (1 Pet. 2:5,9; Rev. 2:11). The first resurrection, therefore, is a metaphor representing the believer's resurrection from eternal spiritual death. In other words, it is the experience of salvation—being saved, converted, born again, regenerated.

The first resurrection, which "now is," and the bodily resurrection, which "is coming," are two definite resurrections made possible by the quickening word of Jesus (John 5:24-29).

1. A spiritual resurrection raises us from the deadness of sin

to the life of God and His righteousness, and from the second death to everlasting life. "Verily, verily, I say unto you, He that heareth my word, and believeth on him that sent me, hath everlasting life, and shall not come into condemnation; but is passed from *death* unto *life*. Verily, verily, I say unto you, The hour is coming, and *now is*, when *the dead* shall hear the voice of the Son of God [the gospel]: and they that hear *shall live* [everlasting life]" (verses 24,25). Indeed, this is the first resurrection!

2. The bodily resurrection involves "all that are in the graves." "Marvel not at this: for the hour *is coming* [when Christ returns], in the which all that are in the graves shall hear his voice, and shall come forth; they that have done good, unto the resurrection of life; and they that have done evil, unto the resurrection of damnation" (verses 28,29). According to John 5:24 and Revelation 20:6, only those who had part in the first resurrection will come forth unto "the resurrection of life." The rest of the dead will come forth unto "the second death," which is "the resurrection of damnation."

Here are some other scriptures that relate to the believer's first or spiritual resurrection from the deadness of sins.

"And you hath he *quickened* [to make alive], who were *dead* in trespasses and sins. . . . But God, . . . even when we were *dead* in sins, hath *quickened* us together with Christ, (by grace ye are saved;) and hath *raised* [resurrected] us up together, and made us sit together in heavenly places in Christ Jesus" (Eph. 2:1,4-6).

"And you, being *dead* in your sins . . . hath he *quickened* together with him, having forgiven you all trespasses" (Col. 2:13).

"For this my son was *dead*, and is *alive* again; he was lost, and is found" (Luke 15:24,32)—a parable that speaks of spiritual resurrection.

"If ye then be *risen* [resurrected] with Christ, seek those things which are above, where Christ sitteth on the right hand of God" (Col. 3:1).

"For the wages of sin is *death* [the second death]; but the gift of God is *eternal life* through Jesus Christ our Lord" (Rom. 6:23).

Jesus said, "I am the resurrection, and the life: he that believeth in me, though he were *dead*, yet shall he *live*: and whosoever liveth and believeth in me *shall never die.* Believest thou this? (John 11:25,26). See also John 8:51.

"Wherefore he saith, Awake thou that sleepest, and arise from the dead, and Christ shall give thee light" (Eph. 5:14).

"But if the Spirit of him that raised up Jesus from the dead dwell in you, he that raised up Christ from the dead shall also quicken your mortal bodies by his Spirit that dwelleth in you" (Rom. 8:11). Our spiritual resurrection now is the pledge of our bodily resurrection to glory hereafter.

What is meant by the statement, "and they lived and reigned with Christ a thousand years" (Rev. 20:4)?

This statement is given in the context of *the souls* whom John saw in heaven. "And I saw *the souls of them* that were beheaded for the witness of Jesus, and for the word of God, and which had not worshipped the beast, neither his image, neither had received his mark upon their foreheads, or in their hand; and they lived and reigned with Christ a thousand years" (Rev. 20:4). For the following reasons, we know that John referred to the continuance of spiritual resurrection life that believers enjoy even after death, not to the bodily resurrection of the dead:

- As in the fifth seal, John saw in heaven *the souls* of martyrs *before* the coming of Jesus and the bodily resurrection (Rev. 6:9-11).
- We have already seen that the dead will *not* be bodily resurrected until after the thousand years are finished, that is, at the Second Coming on the last day.
- Abraham, Isaac, and Jacob are also seen as risen and living in heaven before the bodily resurrection of the dead. Jesus said, "And as touching the dead, that they *rise*: have ye not read in the book of Moses, how in the bush God spake unto him, saying, I am the God of Abraham, and the God of Isaac, and the God of Jacob? He is not the God of the dead, but the God of the *living*" (Mark 12:26,27).
- Paul indicated that believers live in heaven before the bodily resurrection of the dead. "It is a faithful saying: for if we be dead with him, we shall also *live* with him" (2 Tim. 2:11); "We are confident, I say, and willing rather to be *absent from the body*, and to be *present with the Lord*" (2 Cor. 5:8). "For to me to live is

Christ, and to die is gain. . . . For I am in a strait betwixt two, having a desire to depart, and to be *with Christ*; which is far better" (Phil. 1:21,23).

• Jesus declared that believers live on after death. "I am the resurrection, and the life: he that believeth in me, though he were dead, yet shall he live: And whosoever liveth and believeth in me shall never die. Believest thou this?" (John 11:25,26).

Thus, the statement, "and they lived and reigned with Christ a thousand years" refers to *the souls* of those who died in Christ. They are living and reigning in heaven awaiting the bodily resurrection of the dead.

Who are the "rest of the dead" in Revelation 20:5?

In contrast with the souls who "lived and reigned with Christ" (verse 4), or those who had part in "the first resurrection" (verse 5), the "rest of the dead" are the unconverted dead who have not passed from spiritual death to spiritual life by believing on the Lord Jesus. They will be physically resurrected on the last day only to face the judgment and the second death, which is the lake of fire burning with brimstone (Rev. 20:14,15; 21:8).

When will believers reign as priests of God (Rev. 20:6)?

Revelation 20:6 says, "Blessed and holy is he that hath part in the first resurrection: . . . they shall be priests of God and of Christ, and shall reign with him a thousand years." All who experience the first resurrection have the wonderful privilege of reigning as priests of God during the period of time from Christ's first coming to His Second Coming.

Peter wrote to "*lively* stones," who "are built up a spiritual house, *an holy priesthood*, to offer up spiritual sacrifices, acceptable to God by Jesus Christ. . . . Ye are a chosen generation, a *royal priesthood*" (1 Pet. 2:5,9). John wrote that we have been made "*kings and priests* unto God" (Rev. 1:5,6). That believers have been made "*a royal* priesthood" and "*kings*" indicates they are now *reigning* as priests.

As a holy and royal priesthood, believers are clothed with the garments of salvation, righteousness, and humility (Psa. 132:9,16; 1 Pet. 5:5). They also have the blessings and responsibilities of approaching God in prayer, offering up of spiritual sacrifices, keeping God's commandments, and interceding for others. Since Calvary, every believer has access to God at all times. In the Old Testament this was not so; only the high priest could enter "the holy of holies," and that only once a year with a blood sacrifice. But now, every believer is a priest and should have "boldness to enter into the holiest by the blood of Jesus" (Heb. 10:19). See also Rom. 5:2; Eph. 2:18; 3:12; Heb. 4:16.

As a holy priesthood, believers "offer up spiritual sacrifices, acceptable to God by Jesus Christ" (1 Pet. 2:5). These sacrifices include "the sacrifice of praise to God continually, that is, the fruit of our lips giving thanks to his name" (Heb. 13:15); sacrificial gifts as "an odour of a sweet smell" (Phil. 4:18); doing good to others (Heb. 13:16); ministering the gospel (Rom. 15:16; 2 Cor. 5:17-20; Isa. 61:6; 66:20,21); showing mercy and having the knowledge of God (Hos. 6:6); and, most demanding, the giving of our own selves as a living sacrifice, holy and acceptable to God (Rom. 12:1; Phil. 2:17).

As a holy priesthood, believers also have the responsibility to keep the commandments of God by obeying His Word (1 Pet. 1:14-16; 2:1,2). Also, they must intercede before God for men (1 Tim. 2:1; Rev. 5:8; 8:3,4; Mal. 1:11) and before men for God (Matt. 28:19,20; Rom. 15:16). After the Second Coming, however, believers will no longer need to intercede and to evangelize souls. Then, it will be too late for unbelievers to be converted; the door will be shut (Matt. 25:10; Luke 13:25).

The New Testament proclaims that believers are already in "the kingdom of his dear Son" (Col. 1:13), reigning "in heavenly places in Christ Jesus" (compare Eph. 1:20 with 2:6). (The following verses show that Christ is reigning now: Acts 2:33-36; 3:22; 5:31; 1 Cor. 15:25; Eph. 1:20-23; Phil. 2:9; Col. 1:16-19; 1 Tim. 1:17; Heb. 1:8; 7:1-3 and 1 Pet. 3:22.)

Revelation 1:5,6 states, "Unto him that loved us, and washed us from our sins in his own blood, and *hath made us kings and priests* unto God and his Father; to him be glory and dominion for ever and ever. Amen."

Who or what do believers reign over?

Through Christ, believers are "more than conquerors" over every trial of life, whether it be "tribulation, or distress, or persecution, or famine, or nakedness, or peril, or sword" (Rom. 8:35,37). They also reign victoriously over sin. "For if by one man's offence death reigned by one; much more they which receive abundance of grace and of the gift of righteousness shall *reign* in life by one, Jesus Christ. . . . That as sin hath reigned unto death, even so might grace *reign* through righteousness unto eternal life by Jesus Christ our Lord" (Rom. 5:17,21); "Let not sin therefore reign in your mortal body. . . . For *sin shall not have dominion* over you" (Rom. 6:12,14). See also 1 John 5:1-5,18.

Believers also reign victoriously over Satan because it is written, "Greater is he that is in you, than he that is in the world" (1 John 4:4) and "Behold, I give unto you power to tread on serpents and scorpions, and over all the power of the enemy: and nothing shall by any means hurt you" (Luke 10:19). By God's grace, believers will reign victoriously until the end, even having victory "over the beast, and over his image, and over his mark, and over the number of his name" (Rev. 15:2).

When will judgment be given unto the saints (Rev. 20:4)?

The Bible teaches that the saints will judge the wicked when Jesus comes (Rev. 19:14,15; Dan. 7:22). Jesus also promised that those who continue with Him in His temptations now will eat and drink at His table in His heavenly kingdom and "sit on thrones judging the twelve tribes of Israel" (Luke 22:29,30).

Moreover, in this present day, all who have the life of Jesus are given grace, authority, and wisdom by the power of the Holy Spirit and the instruction of the Word to "abound yet more and more in knowledge and in all *judgment*" (Phil. 1:9). "Zion [the Church] shall be redeemed with *judgment*, and her converts with righteousness" (Isa. 1:27). "The Lord is exalted; for he dwelleth on high: he hath filled Zion with *judgment* and righteousness. And wisdom and knowledge shall be the stability of thy times, and strength of salvation: the fear of the Lord is his treasure" (Isa. 33:5,6). See also Psa. 119:66; Pro. 2:1-9; Matt. 12:17-21; Heb. 8:10. Believers are given judgment or spiritual insight for the following purposes:

- To "prove all things" (1 Thess. 5:21)
- To "try the spirits" (1 John 4:1; 1 Cor. 14:29)
- To judge ourselves (1 Cor. 10:29; Rom. 14:13)

- To "discern both good and evil" (Heb. 5:14)
- To "judge righteous judgment" (John 7:24)
- To speak "wisdom" (Psa. 37:30)
- To be "comforted" (Psa. 119:52)
- To be revived (Psa. 119:156)
- To be helped (Psa. 119:175)
- To "mark" and "avoid" those who are false (Rom. 16:17,18)
- To settle disputes (Matt. 18:15-17; 1 Cor. 6:4)
- To maintain proper church discipline (1 Cor. 5:12,13)

Paul declared, "He that is spiritual *judgeth* all things" (1 Cor. 2:15). The Lord Jesus spoke of "the weightier matters of the law, *judgment*, mercy, and faith" (Matt. 23:23). When believers "approve things that are excellent," they will "be sincere and without offence till the day of Christ" (Phil. 1:10). See Isa. 56:1. They will also have a purifying influence in the earth. "When thy judgments are in the earth, the inhabitants of the world will learn righteousness" (Isa. 26:9). Unfortunately, believers often fail to judge with righteous judgment. When we slip from this responsibility, worldliness, spiritual darkness, wickedness, apostasy, and desolation follow.

"Therefore is *judgment* far from us . . . we walk in darkness. . . . We are in desolate places as dead men. . . . Our sins testify against us: . . . in transgressing and lying against the Lord, and departing away from our God. . . . And *judgment* is turned away backward, and justice standeth afar off: for truth is fallen in the street, and equity cannot enter. Yea, truth faileth; and he that departeth from evil maketh himself a prey: and the Lord saw it, it displeased him that there was no *judgment*" (Isa. 59:9,10,12,14,15). "For the time is come that *judgment* must begin at the house of God" (1 Pet. 4:17). "Blessed are they that keep *judgment*, and he that doeth righteousness at all times" (Psa. 106:3). See also Jer. 5:1-9.

What assumptions do many make about Revelation 20?

We will consider fourteen false assumptions about this often misunderstood chapter and will endeavor to show from God's Word its true meaning. Since much of this chapter is written in symbolic speech, we must interpret it in the light of the books that we understand such as the gospels and the epistles.

1. Many assume that when Jesus returns, Satan will be bound a thousand years "that he should deceive the nations no more" (Rev. 20:1-3).

Not once do the gospels and epistles teach the binding of Satan for a thousand years as an event of the Second Coming, but that he is already bound (Matt. 12:29; Col. 2:15). Further, they show that when Jesus returns, He will judge the nations, therefore, none will be left for Satan to deceive (Matt. 13:39-43; 25:31-34,41,46; Luke 17:27-30; 1 Thess. 5:3; 2 Thess. 1:7-9; 2 Pet. 3:7-12). In fact, Revelation 19:18-21 shows that even the remnant will be slain.

2. Many assume that Satan will be loosed to "deceive the nations" and "gather them together to battle"(Rev. 20:3,7,8) after a literal millennium.

The gospels and epistles teach that Satan, in the person of the Antichrist, will be loosed to deceive the nations a short time *before* the Second Coming. (Compare Matt. 24:24 with 2 Thess. 2:6-12.) See also Rev. 17:8,13,14; 19:18-20; and Chapter Twenty-one. The thousand years symbolizes a long period of time *before* Christ's return.

3. Many assume that verse four speaks of earthly thrones.

Whenever the gospels and epistles speak of thrones with reference to the Church, they are heavenly thrones. All who are "quickened . . . together with Christ" are seated in "heavenly places" (Eph. 2:5,6).

Moreover, Jesus promised, "To him that overcometh will I grant to sit with me in *my throne*, even as I also overcame, and am set down with my Father *in his throne*" (Rev. 3:21); "And I appoint unto you a kingdom, as my Father hath appointed unto me; that ye may eat and drink at my table in *my kingdom*, and sit on *thrones* judging the twelve tribes of Israel" (Luke 22:29,30). According to Revelation 19:1 and 9, this eating and drinking takes place in heaven. In addition, thirty-one verses in the Book of Revelation depict our Lord's throne as being in heaven, never once on earth (Rev. 1:4; 3:21; 4:2-6,9,10; 5:1,6,7,11,13; 6:16; 7:9-11,15,17; 8:3; 12:5; 14:3,5; 16:17; 19:4,5; 20:11; 21:5; 22:1,3). The New Testament makes no mention of believers sitting on earthly thrones.

4. Many assume that the statement, "and judgment was given

unto them" (Rev. 20:4) means that the Church will be given authority to rule on the earth during a literal millennium.

The gospels and epistles teach that judgment and authority is given to the saints now (Luke 10:19; 1 Cor. 2:15; Phil. 1:9), at Christ's coming to judge the world (1 Cor. 6:2-4; Rev. 2:26,27; 19:14-21; Dan. 7:22), and in heaven (Matt. 19:28; Luke 22:29,30). See Chapter Twenty-one.

5. Many assume that the verse, "And I saw *the souls of them* that were beheaded for the witness of Jesus, . . . and they lived and reigned with Christ a thousand years" (Rev. 20:4) refers to the bodily resurrection of the righteous when Jesus returns and to their reigning in a literal millennium.

The gospels and epistles teach that when Jesus returns, the righteous are resurrected and reign in heaven (Matt. 25:34,46; John 14:1-3; 1 Thess. 4:16-18; 2 Pet. 3:10-13). Revelation 20:4 refers to spiritual resurrection life after death and to believers reigning with Christ in heaven *before* His return and the bodily resurrection. As in Revelation 6:9, John saw in heaven "*the souls* [not resurrected bodies] of them that were beheaded for the witness of Jesus." These believers died physically, but their never dying souls lived on in heaven awaiting the bodily resurrection. See Mark 12:26,27; John 11:25,26; Phil. 1:21-23; 2 Tim. 2:11,12.

6. Many assume that "the first resurrection" (Rev. 20:5) is the bodily resurrection of the saints.

The gospels and epistles teach that "the first resurrection" is a spiritual resurrection that occurs when those who are dead in their sins hear the voice of the Son of God and live (John 5:24,25). It is called "the first resurrection" because Jesus referred to two resurrections for everyone who hears the gospel and believes—the spiritual resurrection that "now is" and the bodily resurrection that "is coming" (John 5:25,28). A spiritual and a bodily resurrection are also seen in John 11:24-26 and Colossians 3:1,4.

7. Many assume that the statement, "The rest of the dead lived not again until the thousand years were finished" (Rev. 20:5), speaks of a thousand years between the resurrection of the righteous and the resurrection of the wicked.

The gospels and the epistles teach that *all* the dead will be raised at the same time, namely at the Lord's coming, at the end of the world. Clearly, there's no day after the end of the world. See John 5:28,29; Matt. 13:30,39-43; 25:31,32; Rev. 11:18.

8. Many assume that believers will be priests of God in a literal millennium (Rev. 20:6).

The gospels and epistles teach that believers are already in the spiritual kingdom of God on earth (Luke 17:21; Rom. 14:17; Col. 1:13) and that they are priests of God offering up spiritual sacrifices to Him (1 Pet. 2:5,9). Moreover, they are not seeking a temporary city in a future, earthly kingdom, but "one to come"—an eternal city, namely, heaven. "For here have we no continuing city, but we seek one to come. By him therefore let us [as priests of God] offer the sacrifice of praise to God continually, that is, the fruit of our lips giving thanks to his name" (Heb. 13:14,15).

9. Many assume there are two battles described in Revelation: the battle of Armageddon, which is fought when Jesus comes (Rev. 16:14-16; 19:11-21), and the battle of Gog and Magog, which is supposed to be fought a thousand years later (Rev. 20:8).

The gospels and the epistles teach that when Jesus comes, all the wicked will be destroyed by fire sent down from heaven (Luke 17:29,30; 2 Thess. 1:7-9; 2 Pet. 3:10-12), just as is described in the battle of Gog and Magog (Rev. 20:8,9). Thus, there is not a thousand years between the battle of Armageddon, which is fought when Jesus comes, and the battle of God and Magog. The battles described in Revelation 16, 19, and 20 are three accounts of the same battle. See Chapter Twenty-one.

10. Many assume that Satan will be destroyed a thousand years after the coming of Jesus and the destruction of the beast (Rev. 20:10).

The gospels and epistles teach that the man of sin (the beast) and *the wicked* are destroyed at the coming of Jesus (2 Thess. 1:7-9; 2:8). Similarly, Revelation 20:9,10 reveals that Satan and *the wicked* are destroyed at the same time. Therefore, both the beast and Satan are destroyed when the wicked are destroyed. That is, at the coming of Jesus, at the end of the world. Thus, there is not a thousand year lapse between the destruction of the beast and Satan.

11. Many assume that the great white throne judgment follows a literal millennium.

The gospels and the epistles teach that the throne judgment occurs at the Second Coming, not a thousand years later (Matt. 24:42-51; 25:31-46; 1 Cor. 4:5; 2 Cor. 5:10). It is important to realize that the events of Revelation 20:11-15 do not follow the events of Revelation 20:1-10 in chronological order. Verse 10 comes to a climax with the destruction of the wicked and Satan. Verses 11 to 15 begin with another description of the Second Coming:

- Jesus returning on His throne of glory (compare Rev. 20:11 with 6:16,17; Matt. 25:31).
- Heaven and earth passing away (compare Rev. 20:11 with 6:12-14; 16:20; Matt. 24:29,35; 2 Pet. 3:10-12).
- No place for sinners to hide (compare Rev. 20:11 with 16:15,16; Luke 21:35; 1 Thess. 5:3).
- The resurrection of the dead and the judgment (compare Rev. 20:12 with 11:18; John 5:28,29; Matt. 13:48,49; 25:31-33).
- The righteous inherit heaven (compare Rev. 21:7 with 7:9-17; 15:2-4; 19:1-9; Matt. 25:34,46).
- The wicked receive the wrath of God (compare Rev. 20:15 and 21:8 with 6:15-17; 11:18; 14:14-20; 16:18-21; 19:14-21; 20:9; 2 Thess. 1:7-10).

12. Many assume that believers will not be present at the white throne judgment (Rev. 20:11-15).

The gospels and epistles teach that they will be present. See Matt. 12:36,37; 24:44-51; 25:14-30; 25:31-46; Luke 12:47,48; Rom. 2:4-11; 14:10-12; 1 Cor. 3:11-17; 4:4,5; 2 Cor. 5:9-11; Phil. 2:10-12; Col. 3:23-25; 1 Pet. 1:16,17. Further, Revelation 21:7,8 shows the righteous rewarded and the wicked damned into the lake of fire. See also Chapter Sixteen.

13. Many assume that Revelation 20 teaches a literal millennium of peace on earth.

The gospels and epistles teach that Jesus gives His peace *now* to all who make peace with God and are born again into His spiritual kingdom. "*Peace* I leave with you, my *peace* I give unto you: not as the world giveth, give I unto you" (John 14:27). "Therefore being justified by faith, we have *peace* with God through our Lord Jesus Christ" (Rom. 5:1). "For the kingdom of God is . . . righteousness, and *peace*, and joy in the Holy Ghost" (Rom.

14:17). Moreover, peace is promised in heaven—there will be no more death, sorrow, crying, or pain (Rev. 21:4).

14. Many assume that after His coming, Christ will reign on earth for a thousand years (Rev. 20:2-7).

We have already seen that according to the gospels and the epistles, Christ will not reign on earth for a thousand years after His coming because:

- There is *not* a thousand years between Christ's coming and Satan being loosed out of prison.
- There is *not* a thousand years between the bodily resurrection of the righteous and the wicked.
- There is *not* a thousand years between Christ's coming and the great white throne judgment.
- There is *not* a thousand years between the battles mentioned in Revelation 19 and 20.
- There is *not* a thousand years between the destruction of Antichrist and the destruction of Satan.
- There is *not* a thousand years between Christ's coming and the end of the world.

The gospels and epistles teach that at Christ's coming, the righteous will inherit God's eternal kingdom, the wicked will reap everlasting punishment (Matt. 25:34,41; Luke 13:24-29; John 5:28,29), and the earth will be destroyed (Matt. 24:29,35; 2 Pet. 3:10-12). Who, then, will be left for Christ to reign over? And how will Jesus reign on earth for a thousand years if it has been dissolved?

In summary, many make three major assumptions about the order of events in Revelation 20:1-10.

1. Satan will be bound when Jesus returns the second time.
2. The saints, with new glorified bodies, will reign for a thousand years in a literal, earthly kingdom after Jesus returns.
3. Satan will be loosed to deceive the nations and to gather them to battle after a literal millennium.

In other words, many assume the events of Revelation 20:1-10 begin after the Second Coming of Christ and extend for a thousand years until the great white throne judgment.

By carefully studying Scripture, we've found these truths:

1. Satan has already been bound at Christ's first coming.

2. Those who have had part in "the first resurrection" are now priests reigning with Christ in His spiritual kingdom on earth.

3. "For a little season" before the Second Coming, Satan will be loosed to deceive the nations and to gather them to battle against the Lord and His people when He returns.

In other words, the events of Revelation 20:1-10 begin at the first coming of Christ and extend until His Second Coming.

23

A Literal Millennium? (Part II)

What is the meaning of Old Testament prophecies that seem to depict a literal millennium?

Isaiah 65:25 states, "The wolf and the lamb shall feed together, and the lion shall eat straw like the bullock." This and other Old Testament prophecies are often quoted as teaching a literal millennium of peace when really they are speaking symbolically of the new heaven and the new earth. In this case, the context clearly says, "For, behold, I create new heavens and a new earth: and the former shall not be remembered, nor come into mind" (65:17).

Another verse commonly quoted to prove a thousand year reign on earth is in the same passage of Scripture: "There shall be no more thence an infant of days, nor an old man that hath not filled his days: for the child shall die an hundred years old; but the sinner being an hundred years old shall be *accursed*" (65:20). This metaphor is also in the context of the "new heavens and a new earth" (65:17) and teaches that there will be neither death nor sinners there. In fact, verse fifteen shows that the sinner will be accursed and slain prior to the "new heavens and a new earth." "And ye shall leave your name for a *curse* unto my chosen: for the Lord God shall *slay thee*, and call his servants by another name." It may seem odd to some that "the sinner" is mentioned in the context of heaven. But Revelation 21:8 also mentions the wicked in the context of the new heaven and earth, and shows that they are damned.

That the above verses (Isaiah 65:25,20) concern the "new heavens and a new earth" and not a thousand year reign on this earth can also be seen by understanding the similarities between Isaiah 65:17,19 and Revelation 21:1-4:

Isaiah 65:17,19—"For, behold, I create new heavens and a new earth. . . . And I will rejoice in Jerusalem, and joy in my people: and the voice of weeping shall be no more heard in her, nor the voice of crying."

Revelation 21:1,2,4—"And I saw a new heaven and a new earth. . . . the holy city, new Jerusalem. . . . And God shall wipe away all tears from their eyes; and there shall be no more . . . sorrow, nor crying."

Isaiah 11:6 also speaks symbolically of heaven but is said to prove a literal millennium: "The wolf also shall dwell with the lamb . . . and a little child shall lead them." The context, however, shows all the wicked being slain with none left to enter a supposed peaceful millennium: "And he shall smite the earth: with *the rod* of his mouth, and with the breath of his lips shall he slay the wicked" (Isa. 11:4).

Old Testament prophecies (such as portions of Isaiah chapters 2, 11, 35, 65) used to teach a literal millennium really describe the new heaven and the new earth as revealed in the following chart.

The New Heaven and the New Earth as Described in the Old Testament	**The New Heaven and the New Earth as Described in Revelation**
Mount Zion, Jerusalem—Isa. 24:23; 35:10; 65:17,18,25; Joel 3:17; Micah 4:7.	Mount Zion, the new, holy, or heavenly Jerusalem—Rev. 3:12; 14:1; 21:2,10,23; 22:14,19. See also Heb. 12:22,28.
A tabernacle—Isa. 33:20.	The tabernacle of God—Rev. 21:3.
The substance of the nations—Micah 4:13.	Bring the glory and honour of the nations into it—Rev. 21:24-26.
All flesh worship before me—Isa. 66:22,23.	All nations come and worship—Rev. 15:4; 7:9-11.
Neither shall they learn war any more—Isa. 2:4; Micah 4:3.	Neither shall there be any more pain—Rev. 21:4.
The unclean shall not pass over it—Isa. 35:8; 52:1; Joel 3:17.	There shall in no wise enter into it any thing that defileth—Rev. 21:7,8,27; 22:14,15.
Sorrow and sighing shall flee away—Isa. 35:10; 51:11; 65:18,19.	No more sorrow, nor crying; only joy and gladness—Rev. 7:17; 19:7; 21:4.

The New Heaven and the New Earth as Described in the Old Testament	The New Heaven and the New Earth as Described in Revelation
The eyes of the blind shall be opened—Isa. 35:5-7.	Healing of the nations—Rev. 22:2.
The redeemed shall walk there—Isa. 35:9.	Redeemed us to God by thy blood—Rev. 5:9; 14:3,4.
The Lord, an everlasting light—Isa. 60:20.	The glory of the God is the light of it—Rev. 21:23,25.
The Lord shall reign over them . . . for ever—Isa. 24:23; Micah 4:7.	He shall reign for ever and ever—Rev. 11:15.

What difficult questions arise when one tries to prove a literal millennium?

When Jesus comes to gather His saints on the Day of the Lord, at least thirteen events will occur simultaneously. Since Scripture affirms that they will happen *before* a supposed millennium, some perplexing questions arise if one tries to prove a literal thousand years after these events occur. Consider these thirteen events:

1. At the last trump, the saints will receive new and glorified bodies (1 Cor. 15:51,52). Since "this mortal must put on immortality" and "*death* is swallowed up in victory," they must of necessity enter heaven where there is "*no more death*" (1 Cor. 15:54; Rev. 21:4). Jesus said the children of the resurrection "neither marry, nor are given in marriage: *neither can they die any more*: for they are equal unto the angels" (Luke 20:35,36). See also 2 Cor. 5:1-4. Therefore, two questions arise: How and why will immortals, with glorified bodies as the angels, mingle with mortals for a thousand years on earth before entering heaven? How does a supposed thousand years on earth fit between the destruction of death and the saints going to heaven?

2. The door of salvation will be closed forever (Matt. 7:22,23; 25:10-13). Surely, the Lord would not have delayed His coming for the sake of the unsaved if they had an additional thousand years in which to repent (2 Pet. 3:9; James 5:7). So this raises another question: Since there is no further opportunity for the unconverted to repent after the Second Coming, what will be the purpose of a literal millennium?

3. The wicked will be destroyed. With a rod of iron Christ will smite the nations and "all men, both free and bond, both small and great" will be slain, not even a remnant will be spared (Rev. 19:18-21). This raises several questions:

• Who will be left of the ungodly for the righteous to reign over for a thousand years?

• Who will be left for Satan to deceive no more? (Rev. 20:3).

• Who will be left to rebel and to go to war after a supposed thousand years? (Rev. 20:8,9).

4. When Jesus comes, the man of sin and the kingdoms of this world will be destroyed. During the final battle, the man of sin will be slain (Dan. 7:11; Rev. 19:19,20). As a result, the saints will take away his dominion "to consume and to destroy it" and be given "*an everlasting kingdom*" (Dan. 7:26,27). See also Dan. 7:18; Rev. 11:15. This raises another question: How can a temporal thousand year reign occur between the destruction of the man of sin and the saints' possessing an *everlasting kingdom*?

5. Christ will come on His throne of glory, not to usher in a thousand years of peace and prosperity, but to reward the righteous with an eternal inheritance and the wicked with everlasting fire (Matt. 25:31-46; Rev. 6:16,17; 20:11-15; 21:7,8).

Two more questions arise: Since the final judgment had already taken place, what would be the purpose of a millennium? and Since all will enter their eternal destinies when Jesus comes to gather His Church and to judge the world, who will be left to enter an earthly kingdom?

6. Heaven and earth will pass away on the Day of the Lord (Matt. 24:29,35; 2 Pet. 3:10; Rev. 6:12-14; 16:18-20). How can there be a literal millennium on earth if it has been dissolved?

7. All will be fulfilled when Jesus comes (Luke 21:32). See also Rev. 10:7; 16:17; 21:6. What purpose would an additional thousand years serve?

8. At the resurrection, "this world" will end and "that world" will begin (Luke 20:34,35). What world will be between "this world" and "that world" for a thousand years?

9. At the appearing of Jesus, the saints will receive their reward (2 Tim. 4:8). Jesus said to those who are persecuted for righteousness' sake, "great is your reward in heaven" (Matt. 5:12; Luke 6:23). Will the saints have to wait another thousand years after the coming of Jesus to enter into their reward?

10. When Christ shall appear, then shall we also appear with Him in glory [heaven] (Col. 3:4). The Bible teaches that our Father is in heaven (Matt. 6:9); our Savior is in heaven (Eph. 1:20); our guardian angels are in heaven (Matt. 22:30); our citizenship is in heaven (Phil. 3:20); our reward is in heaven (Matt. 5:12); our treasures are in heaven (Matt. 19:21); our names are recorded in heaven (Luke 10:20); our hope is in heaven (Col. 1:5); our inheritance is in heaven (1 Pet. 1:4); and that when Jesus comes, we will enter heaven (Matt. 25:34,46; John 14:1-3).

Moreover, in light of the Second Coming and heaven, believers are admonished, "If ye then be risen with Christ, seek those things which are above. . . . Set your affection on things above, *not on things on the earth*" (Col. 3:1-3); "For what is a man profited, if he shall gain *the whole world*, and lose his own soul?" (Matt. 16:26). See also Phil. 3:19-21.

Since the Bible clearly teaches that the hope of believers is *not* to gain the *world*, but to gain *heaven*, why would God promise a future thousand year reign in this world? In addition, believers are seen in heaven after the resurrection. How can they be on earth for a thousand years before entering heaven?

11. On the Day of the Lord, Jesus will come with all His holy, mighty angels (Matt. 25:31; 2 Thess. 1:7). They shall come with "a great sound of a trumpet" (Matt. 24:31); they shall ascend and descend upon the Lord Jesus (John 1:51); they shall reap the harvest (Matt. 13:39); they shall gather together Christ's elect to the kingdom of the Father (Matt. 24:31; 13:30,43); they shall gather the tares and cast them into a furnace of fire (Matt. 13:38-42); and they shall spend eternity with the "great multitude" worshiping God in heaven (Rev. 7:9-11).

How does a literal millennium fit between the angels coming with Christ and worshiping God in heaven? Where will the angels be during a supposed literal millennium?

12. Time will be no more at the sounding of the seventh and last trump. (Compare Rev. 10:6,7 with 11:15-19.) That day will be the last day, not a thousand years before the last day; the end of the world, not a thousand years before the end of the world (John 6:39; Matt. 24:29-31). Therefore, since Christ is coming on the last day, at the end of the world when time is no more, how can a thousand years be added?

13. Also, at the sounding of the seventh and last trump, "the

kingdoms of this world are become the kingdoms of our Lord, and of his Christ; and he shall reign *for ever and ever*" (Rev. 11:15). Is there a single scripture to suggest that Jesus' eternal reign "for ever and ever" is a divided reign for a thousand years here on earth and for the rest of eternity in heaven? No, there is not.

In summary, after the events of the Day of the Lord, a literal millennium will be impossible because there will be no more people to reign over; no more battles to be fought; no more earth left to inhabit; no more time—only eternity.

Do you believe that we are in the millennium now?

It depends what you mean by "millennium." If you mean a millennium with literal wolves and lambs feeding together; with literal lions eating straw like bullocks; with a literal throne of David; with a restored Temple; with restored Jewish sacrifices and all Jews converted; and with Christ reigning with a literal rod of iron—our answer is no! Jesus Himself said, "My kingdom is not of this world: if my kingdom were of this world, then would my servants fight, that I should not be delivered to the Jews: but now is my kingdom not from hence" (John 18:36).

On the other hand, if by the term "millennium" you mean that Christ has already defeated Satan, that all who hear and obey the gospel are born into the kingdom of God, and that they are spiritual priests who are reigning with Christ in a spiritual kingdom until He returns—our answer is yes!

When Jesus "was demanded of the Pharisees, when the kingdom of God should come, he answered them and said, The kingdom of God cometh not with observation: Neither shall they say, Lo here! or, lo there! for, behold, *the kingdom of God is within you*" (Luke 17:20,21). In other words, Jesus taught that His kingdom is spiritual and that it is already come.

The New Testament says, the kingdom of God is come (Matt. 12:28; 3:2; 4:17; 10:7); that the kingdom of David is come (Mark 11:10); that the Father has "translated us unto the kingdom of his dear Son" (Col. 1:13); that we should seek "first the kingdom of God, and his righteousness" (Matt. 6:33); that believers have the keys of the kingdom (Matt. 16:19; 18:18); that "the kingdom of God is . . . righteousness, and peace, and joy in the Holy

Ghost" (Rom. 14:17); and that Christ's kingdom is not of this world (John 18:36).

The New Testament also reveals the growth of God's kingdom on earth: "The kingdom of heaven is like to a grain of mustard seed, which a man took, and sowed in his field: which indeed is the least of all seeds: but when it is grown, it is the greatest among herbs, and becometh a tree, so that the birds of the air come and lodge in the branches thereof" (Matt. 13:31,32).

What are the dangers of misunderstanding Revelation 20 and the thousand years?

1. To misunderstand this vital chapter is to misunderstand the following doctrines and how they relate to believers and unbelievers now and in the future: the binding and loosing of Satan (20:1-3,7-10); the first resurrection (20:4-6); the priesthood of believers (20:4,6); the Second Coming (20:11); the resurrection of the dead (20:12); the final battle (20:8,9); the judgment (20:11-15); the destruction of the world (20:11); heaven (20:9); and the lake of fire (20:15).

2. As previously cited, to believe that Revelation 20:1-10 teaches a literal millennium raises many unanswerable questions and contradicts the rest of the Bible. It even contradicts verses 11 through 21:8, which describes the events of the Second Coming with no mention of a thousand year interval—Jesus coming on a throne, heaven and earth passing away, the general resurrection of all the dead, the throne judgment when Christ will judge "every man according to his works," and all men entering their eternal destinies. (Compare with 6:12-17 and Matt. 24:29-31,35; 25:31-46; 16:27.)

3. To teach a literal millennium gives the unconverted a sense of peace when actually "sudden destruction" is coming (1 Thess. 5:3).

4. To believe in a literal millennium hinders believers from preaching the same gospel that the prophets and the apostles preached—that sinners should repent and prepare for the coming judgment (Zeph. 2:2,3; Matt. 3:7; Acts 17:30,31).

5. To teach a literal millennium is to teach lies almost too numerous to mention and to align believers with many false religious groups.

6. To support the teaching of a literal millennium, one has to distort many precious passages of Scripture. For example, the metaphor of "the wolf and the lamb shall feed together" is often used to teach a literal millennium when actually, according to the context, it is describing peace in the "new heavens and a new earth" (Isa. 65:25,17).

7. To teach a literal millennium is to add to the Word of God. Jesus and the apostles taught about the signs of the Second Coming and of the end of the world with no mention of a glorious thousand year reign (Matt. 24 and 25; 2 Thess. 1:7-10; 2:1-8; 2 Pet. 3:10-14).

Objections Answered

Didn't Paul speak of attaining to the "first resurrection"?

No, he did not. The term, "first resurrection," which is a spiritual resurrection, is found only in Revelation 20:5,6. Paul, however, did speak of attaining to the bodily "resurrection of the dead" in Philippians 3:11. He referred to the spiritual resurrection in Romans 6:4; Ephesians 2:1-6; Colossians 2:12,13; 3:1.

Won't survivors of the Day of the Lord go into a literal millennium—those men whom God makes "more precious than fine gold" (Isa. 13:12)?

Isaiah 13:12 says, "I will make a man more precious than fine gold; even a man than the golden wedge of Ophir."

Certain Bible teachers say that some ungodly men, those whom God makes "more precious than fine gold," will survive the Day of the Lord and enter a literal millennium. The following reasons illustrate that Isaiah 13 does not teach any such thing:

1. Isaiah 13 doesn't say anything about a thousand years of peace, but that the Day of the Lord "shall come as destruction from the Almighty" and as "cruel both with wrath and fierce anger, to lay the land desolate" (13:6,9).

2. Isaiah 13 teaches that there will be no survivors on the Day of the Lord.

- "*All* hands [shall] be faint, and *every man's* heart shall melt" (13:7).

• "They shall be in pain as a woman that *travaileth*: . . . their faces shall be as *flames*" (13:8). (Compare with 1 Thess. 5:3; 2 Thess. 1:7,8.)

• "He shall *destroy the sinners* thereof out of it [the earth]" (13:9).

• "And I will *punish the world* for their evil, and the wicked for their iniquity" (13:11). The following passages of Scripture affirm that all sinners, including the remnant, will be destroyed on the Day of the Lord: Zeph. 1:18; Mal. 4:1; Luke 17:26-30; 2 Pet. 3:10-12; Rev. 19:11-21.

3. Isaiah 13 shows that the earth itself will be destroyed.

"They come from a far country, from the end of heaven, even the Lord, and the weapons of his indignation, *to destroy the whole land*. . . . For the stars of heaven and the constellations thereof shall not give their light: the sun shall be darkened in his going forth, and the moon shall not cause her light to shine. I will shake the heavens, and *the earth shall remove out of her place*, in the wrath of the Lord of hosts, and in the day of his fierce anger" (Isa. 13:5,10,13). Isaiah further prophesied that the earth "shall fall, and not rise again" (Isa. 24:20). See also Matt. 24:29-31,35; 2 Pet. 3:10-12; Rev. 6:12-17; 16:18-21.

4. Isaiah 13:12 doesn't say anything about "men" but "a man." "I will make *a man* more precious than fine gold; even *a man* than the golden wedge of Ophir." This verse implies that not even *fine gold* and *the golden wedge of Ophir* will help in the Day of the Lord. This is in accordance with the truth that "riches profit not in the day of wrath" (Pro. 11:4). See also Isa. 2:20; 13:17; Ezek. 7:19; Zeph. 1:18. Therefore, a man who can help will be more precious than fine gold, and that man is the Lord Jesus Christ.

Isaiah prophesied about the uselessness of gold and silver in that day, and the preciousness of our Lord Jesus Christ as a hiding place. "For in *that day* every man shall cast away his idols of *silver*, and his idols of *gold*. . . . Behold, a king shall reign in righteousness, and princes shall rule in judgment. And *a man* shall be as an hiding place from the wind, and a covert from the tempest; as rivers of water in a dry place, as the shadow of a great rock in a weary land" (Isa. 31:7; 32:1,2). For further illustrations of Jesus as our hiding place during the destruction of the Day of the Lord, refer to these passages: Psa. 2:8-12; 145:20; Isa. 26:20,21; Nahum 1:5-7; Zeph. 2:3; Mal. 4:1,2; Luke 17:26-30.

In summary, Isaiah 13 does not teach a peaceful millennium, but the Day of the Lord when all sinners and the earth itself will be destroyed. In that fearful day, silver and gold will not help anyone. Our only hope is in knowing the man Christ Jesus—He is our hiding place.

Doesn't the Bible teach that sinners will enter God's millennial kingdom of peace before being turned into hell?

If the wicked would "not have this man [Jesus] to reign over" them when He was on earth—why would they do so in a literal millennium? (Luke 19:14). Furthermore, God's Word does not promise a future millennial kingdom of peace on earth to anyone, let alone to unrepentant sinners. The Bible says, "There is no peace, saith the Lord, unto the wicked" (Isa. 48:22); "The wicked shall be cut off from the earth, and the transgressors shall be rooted out of it" (Pro. 2:22). They shall be destroyed (Psa. 145:20) and "turned into hell" (Psa. 9:17).

Jesus said, "Except a man be born again, he cannot see *the kingdom of God*" and "He that believeth not the Son shall not see life; but the *wrath* of God abideth on him" (John 3:3,36).

Moreover, Paul declared: "Know ye not that *the unrighteous shall not inherit the kingdom of God? Be not deceived*: neither fornicators, nor idolaters, nor adulterers, nor effeminate, nor abusers of themselves with mankind, nor thieves, nor covetous, nor drunkards, nor revilers, nor extortioners, shall inherit the kingdom of God" (1 Cor. 6:9,10). Those who promise a future millennium of peace on earth, which God has never promised, deceive the ungodly.

God also warns, "If any man worship the beast and his image, and receive his mark in his forehead, or in his hand, the same shall drink of the wine of the wrath of God, which is poured out without mixture into the cup of his indignation; and he shall be tormented with fire and brimstone in the presence of the holy angels, and in the presence of the Lamb" (Rev. 14:9,10). Even if there were a literal millennial kingdom of God on earth, God has not promised unbelievers entrance into it.

Doesn't the "third day," as recorded in Hosea 6:2 and Luke 13:32, signify that a literal millennium will begin the year 2,000 A. D.?

No, it does not. In fact, neither of these verses says anything about the Second Coming or a millennium. Backslidden Israel is promised spiritual revival and rain if she will return to the Lord. "Come, and let us return unto the Lord. . . . After two days will he revive us: in the third day he will raise us up, and we shall live in his sight. . . . And he shall come unto us as the rain, as the latter and former rain unto the earth" (Hosea 6:1-3). Referring to His death, Jesus said, "Go ye, and tell that fox [Herod], Behold, I cast out devils, and I do cures today and tomorrow, and the third day I shall be perfected" (Luke 13:32).

Moreover, Jesus taught that He will come on the "last day," at "the end of the world" (John 6:39; Matt. 13:30,39). The "end" clearly implies that there can be no literal millennium after the end. Jesus also warned against setting dates (Matt. 24:36).

God rested on the seventh day; therefore, won't a literal millennium of rest begin in the year 2,000 A. D. since that completes six thousand years since creation?

This is mere speculation and a teaching of the Mormon Church. Besides, the seventh millennium as a Sabbath has little significance for New Testament believers. They do not observe the seventh day, but the first day of the week:

- Our Lord rose from the dead on the first day of the week (Mark 16:9).
- He first met with His disciples on the first day of the week (John 20:19).
- Jesus again met with His disciples and Thomas on the first day of the week (John 20:26).
- The Holy Spirit was poured out on the first day of the week (Acts 2:1). The day of Pentecost was fifty days after the feast of the Passover, specifically, the day after the seventh Sabbath (Lev. 23:15,16).
- "The disciples came together to break bread [and] Paul preached unto them" on the first day of the week (Acts 20:7).
- Believers gathered the collection for the saints on the first day of the week (1 Cor. 16:2).

Further, the Bible does not teach a sabbatical or a literal millennium and, as already stated, Jesus warned against setting dates (Matt. 24:36).

Isn't a literal millennium the last dispensation of time?

Jesus and the apostles called this present age—not a coming thousand years after this age—the last time. "Little children, it is *the last time*: and as ye have heard that antichrist shall come, even now are there many antichrists; whereby we know that it is *the last time*" (1 John 2:18). See also Acts 2:16,17; 1 Cor. 10:11; Eph. 1:10; 1 Tim. 4:1; 2 Tim. 3:1; Heb. 1:1,2; 9:26; James 5:3; 1 Pet. 1:20; Jude 1:18.

Doesn't the Bible teach that during a literal millennium there will be a restored temple in Jerusalem with all nations bringing offerings to the Lord?

Some Christians hold a future literal interpretation to Isaiah 66:20. They use this passage to support the idea that at the Second Coming, Christ will set up His earthly kingdom and rule with His saints from a throne in Jerusalem. They believe that nations will come up to Jerusalem to keep feast days, new moons, and Sabbaths. Reinstituting temple worship with a Levitical priesthood and animal sacrifices, however, is not in accordance with God's Word for the following seven reasons:

1. Old Testament prophecies of bringing an offering to the Lord, such as Isaiah 66:20, are fulfilled by believers now. We can see this truth by comparing the following two verses:

"And they shall *bring all your brethren for an offering unto the Lord* out of all nations upon horses, and in chariots, and in litters, and upon mules, and upon swift beasts, to my holy mountain Jerusalem, saith the Lord, as the children of Israel bring an offering in a clean vessel into the house of the Lord" (Isa. 66:20).

Paul wrote, "That I should be the minister of Jesus Christ to the Gentiles, ministering the gospel of God, that the *offering up of the Gentiles* might be acceptable, being sanctified by the Holy Ghost" (Rom. 15:16).

Notice that the Old Testament prophecy, which illustrates bringing converts from all nations as an acceptable offering to

God, is fulfilled when believers minister the gospel and win souls for the Lord Jesus Christ.

2. God does not dwell in temples made with hands, but in the hearts of His people (Acts 7:48; 17:24; 1 Cor. 3:16; 6:19). Believers are the temple of the Lord and priests of God offering up spiritual sacrifices (1 Pet. 2:5).

From His throne in heaven, Jesus, our High Priest, is building His temple in the hearts of His people. "Behold the man whose name is The Branch; and he shall grow up out of his place, and he shall build the temple of the Lord: even he shall build the temple of the Lord; and he shall bear the glory, and shall sit and rule upon his throne; and he shall be a priest upon his throne: and the counsel of peace shall be between them both" (Zech. 6:12,13). See also Matt. 16:18; Eph. 2:17-22; Heb. 3:1,3; 8:2.

3. The New Testament does not associate believers with the Old Jerusalem, which is in bondage, but with the New Jerusalem, which is free. "For this Agar is mount Sinai in Arabia, and answereth to [is in the same rank with] Jerusalem which now is, and is in bondage with her children. But Jerusalem which is above is free, which is the mother of us all" (Gal. 4:25,26). "For ye are not come unto the mount that might be touched [Mount Sinai]. . . . But ye are come unto mount Sion, and unto the city of the living God, the heavenly Jerusalem" (Heb. 12:18,22).

4. Jesus pronounced judgment on the temple in Jerusalem and did not later revoke these words or prophesy a restored temple (Matt. 24:1,2; Luke 19:43,44).

5. Jerusalem is not the center of true worship. Jesus said, "The hour cometh, when ye shall neither in this mountain, nor yet at Jerusalem, worship the Father. . . . But the hour cometh, and now is, when the true worshippers shall worship the Father in spirit and in truth: for the Father seeketh such to worship him" (John 4:21,23).

6. Jesus Christ is the true temple (John 1:14; 2:19; Heb. 8:2; 9:11), our high priest (Heb. 3:1), and the Lamb of God—our Passover who was sacrificed for us (1 Cor. 5:7). Thus, He fulfilled the Old Covenant with its temple, priesthood, and animal sacrifices. The Bible, therefore, refers to the Old Covenant as that which is abolished (2 Cor. 3:13), done away (2 Cor. 3:7), cast out (Gal. 4:30), taken away (Heb. 10:9), and blotted out (Col. 2:14-17).

Therefore, to go back to the old Mosaic temple is to resist the Holy Spirit (Acts 7:46-51) and to go in reverse:

- From the New Testament, back to the Old Testament (Heb. 9:15).
- From grace which came by Christ, back to the law which came by Moses (John 1:17).
- From Christ's own blood, back to the blood of animals (Heb. 9:12).
- From an eternal priest (Heb. 7:17), back to temporary priests (Heb. 7:23).
- From an eternal atonement (Heb. 10:14), back to yearly atonements (Heb. 10:3).
- From a heavenly tabernacle (Heb. 9:11), back to an earthly tabernacle (Heb. 9:2,24).
- From that which makes perfect (Heb. 10:14), back to that which makes nothing perfect (Heb. 7:19).
- From serving the living God, back to serving dead works (Heb. 9:13,14).
- From Mount Zion (Heb. 12:22-24), back to Mount Sinai (Gal. 4:24; Heb. 12:18-21).
- From the liberty of Christ, back to the yoke of bondage (Gal. 5:1).
- From the new and living way (Heb. 10:16-20), back to the old way (Heb. 8:13).
- From that which is everlasting (Heb. 13:20), back to that which is abolished (2 Co. 3:11,13).
- From that which ministers life (2 Cor. 3:6,8), back to that which ministers death (2 Cor. 3:7).
- From living by faith (Gal. 3:11), back to living by the works of the law (Gal. 3:10).
- From that which is perfect (James 1:25), back to that which is faulty (Heb. 8:7).
- From worshiping God in the Spirit (John 3:23,24), back to worshiping God in the flesh (John 4:21,22; Gal. 3:3).

7. The Bible tells us that when Jesus returns, all nations will be judged (Matt. 25:31-33).

The righteous will inherit the everlasting kingdom (Matt. 25:34). The apostle John wrote that "*the nations of them which are saved* shall walk in the light of it [the New Jerusalem, heaven]:

and the kings of the earth do bring their glory and honour into it. And the gates of it shall not be shut at all by day: for there shall be no night there. And they shall bring the glory and honour of *the nations* into it. And there shall in no wise enter into it any thing that defileth" (Rev. 21:24-27).

On the other hand, the wicked will be cursed into everlasting fire, prepared for the devil and his angels (Matt. 25:41,46). They will be cast "into a furnace of fire: there shall be wailing and gnashing of teeth" (Matt. 13:42).

In summary, the Bible teaches neither a literal millennium nor restored temple worship with all nations making pilgrimages to a temple in Old Jerusalem and bringing offerings to the Lord. But that when Jesus returns, the nations who are saved will "serve him [Jesus] day and night in his temple" in the New Jerusalem, which is heaven (Rev. 7:15; 21:22-27) and "all the nations that forget God" will be "turned into hell" (Psa. 9:17). See Chapter Twenty-one.

24

Repentance and the Second Coming

Will there be a chance for sinners to repent at the Second Coming of Jesus?

God gives sinners that opportunity now. "Behold, *now* is the accepted time; behold, *now* is the day of salvation" (2 Cor. 6:2). "Now [God] commandeth all men every where to *repent*: Because he hath appointed a day, in the which he will judge the world in righteousness" (Acts 17:30,31). He's even delaying His coming because He's longsuffering and "not willing that any should perish, but that all should come to *repentance*" (2 Pet. 3:9). But at the coming of Jesus it will be too late to repent because that day will come "as a snare" with "sudden destruction" (Luke 21:35; 1 Thess. 5:3). The verdict will then be "He that is unjust, let him be unjust still: and he which is filthy, let him be filthy still: and he that is righteous, let him be righteous still: and he that is holy, let him be holy still" (Rev. 22:11).

Now is the time to repent! "*Today* if ye will hear his voice, harden not your hearts" (Heb. 3:7). Jesus warned, "Except ye repent, ye shall all likewise perish" (Luke 13:5). With such eternal consequences, a person would be unwise to wait until it's too late.

What is repentance?

First, consider briefly what repentance is not. It is *not* merely being dedicated as a baby; nor is it "accepting Christ" without having a change of heart. Repentance is not merely joining a church. Many rejoice to have their names on a church roll, but Jesus said, "Rejoice, because your names are written in heaven" (Luke 10:20).

In addition, repentance is *not* just promising to do better; nor is it doing good deeds in hopes they'll outweigh bad deeds, such as offering gifts to God or to the poor. Also, it is *not* doing penance or performing certain religious duties; nor is it mere cultural refinement or outward correctness of life. Jesus told the parable of two men who went up to the temple to pray. The Pharisee trusted in and boasted of his own righteousness, but the publican "would not lift up so much as his eyes unto heaven, but smote upon his breast, saying, God be merciful to me a sinner." Jesus said, "I tell you, this man went down to his house justified rather than the other" (Luke 18:9-14).

Moreover, repentance is not being baptized without having confessed and forsaken sins (Acts 2:38). Simon the sorcerer was baptized, yet his heart was "not right in the sight of God." Admonishing him to repent of his wickedness, Peter said he was "in the gall of bitterness, and in the bond of iniquity" (Acts 8:13-23).

Finally, repentance is *not* partaking of the Lord's supper. Paul warned, "Wherefore whosoever shall eat this bread, and drink this cup of the Lord, unworthily, shall be guilty of the body and blood of the Lord. But let a man examine himself, and so let him eat of that bread, and drink of that cup. For he that eateth and drinketh unworthily, eateth and drinketh damnation to himself, not discerning the Lord's body. For this cause many are weak and sickly among you, and many sleep" (1 Cor. 11:27-30). Clearly, true repentance must precede water baptism and partaking of the Lord's supper.

What, then, is true repentance? Repentance is having a deep godly sorrow for sin that causes a person to confess it to God and to forsake it (Pro. 28:13). It is a sense of shame and humiliation for having indulged in sin. It is completely exposing one's heart before the Lord so that nothing is held back or covered (2 Cor. 7:10,11). It is turning from Satan to Christ, from the old sinful life to a new life of righteousness, and from idols to serve the living and true God (Ezek. 14:6; 1 Thess. 1:9).

Repentance is also confessing our sins directly to Jesus Christ, *believing* that He will forgive us according to His promises (Acts 4:12; 5:31; 1 Tim. 1:15). Without this faith, confession is meaningless. We must believe that God saves us by His grace and not by our good works, or our own righteousness: "For by grace are ye saved through faith; and that not of yourselves: it is the gift of God: not of works, lest any man should boast" (Eph. 2:8,9).

Repentance is also a willingness to make restitution, wherever possible (Luke 19:8,9). It is a complete change of mind, a change of heart, and a change of action. "For godly sorrow worketh repentance to salvation not to be repented of: but the sorrow of the world worketh death. For behold this selfsame thing, that ye sorrowed after a godly sort, what carefulness it wrought in you, yea, *what clearing of yourselves*, yea, what indignation, yea, what fear, yea, what vehement desire, yea, what zeal, yea, what revenge! In all things ye have approved yourselves to be clear in this matter" (2 Cor. 7:10,11). "Therefore if any man be in Christ, he is a new creature: old things pass away; behold, all things are become new" (2 Cor. 5:17).

True repentance includes conviction, contrition, faith, confession, restitution, and obedience to God's Word.

Why is repentance necessary?

Repentance is necessary because only by repentance can a person experience:

Eternal life—"God also to the Gentiles granted *repentance* unto life" (Acts 11:18).

True conversion and the forgiveness of sins—"*Repent ye* therefore, and be *converted*, that your *sins may be blotted out*" (Acts 3:19). See also Acts 26:18-20.

Saving faith—Jesus came preaching, "The time is fulfilled, and the kingdom of God is at hand: *repent ye*, and *believe* the gospel" (Mark 1:15). Paul also preached "repentance toward God, and faith toward our Lord Jesus Christ" (Acts 20:21). See also Matt. 21:31,32.

The joy of salvation—"I say unto you, that likewise *joy* shall be in heaven over one sinner that *repenteth*, more than over ninety and nine just persons, which need no repentance" (Luke 15:7).

The gift of the Holy Spirit—"Then Peter said unto them, *Repent*, and be baptized every one of you in the name of Jesus Christ for the remission of sins, and ye shall receive *the gift of the Holy Ghost*" (Acts 2:38).

Readiness for the Second Coming—"Now [God] commandeth all men every where to *repent*: because he hath appointed *a day*, in the which he will judge the world in righteousness" (Acts 17:30,31).

To be saved, must repentant sinners confess their sins to someone besides the Lord Jesus?

Absolutely not. The Bible teaches us to come to Christ for forgiveness and salvation: "In whom we have redemption through his blood, the forgiveness of sins, according to the riches of his grace" (Eph. 1:7). Consider the following reasons:

1. *Jesus is the only mediatory priest or advocate recognized in the New Testament.* "For there is one God, and *one mediator* between God and men, the man Christ Jesus" (1 Tim. 2:5).

Jesus Christ Himself said, "I am the way, the truth, and the life: *no man cometh unto the Father, but by me*" (John 14:6).

John exhorted believers, "My little children, these things write I unto you, that ye sin not. And if any man sin, we have an *advocate* with the Father, Jesus Christ the righteous: And he is the propitiation for our sins: and not for ours only, but also for the sins of the whole world" (1 John 2:1,2). See also Heb. 4:15,16; 7:24,25; 8:1,6; 9:24; 10:15-22; 12:24.

2. *When preaching repentance and salvation, the apostles did not instruct their hearers to confess their sins to them or to any other man.* Rather, they instructed them to "repent and turn to God" (Acts 26:20). They made it clear that we should confess our sins to Him who is "faithful and just to forgive us our sins, and to cleanse us from all unrighteousness" (1 John 1:9).

When Simon the sorcerer sinned, Peter commanded him to repent and *pray to God*: "Repent therefore of this thy wickedness, and *pray God*, if perhaps the thought of thine heart may be forgiven thee" (Acts 8:22). The following verses also show that we should turn to the Lord, not to man: Isa. 55:6,7; Hosea 14:2; Joel 2:12,13; Ezra 10:11; 2 Chr. 30:22; Acts 11:21.

3. *Jesus instructs us to come directly to Him.* "Come unto me . . . I will give you rest" (Matt. 11:28); "I am the bread of life: he that *cometh to me* shall never hunger" (John 6:35); "Him that *cometh to me* I will in no wise cast out" (John 6:37). "I am the way, the truth, and the life: *no man cometh unto the Father, but by me*" (John 14:6).

4. *Only the Lord Jesus Christ is exalted by God to give repentance*

and forgiveness of sins. "Him hath God exalted with his right hand to be a Prince and a Saviour, for to give *repentance* to Israel, and *forgiveness* of sins" (Acts 5:31).

Jesus Christ is the only begotten, sinless Son of God (John 3:16; Heb. 4:15) who died for our sins and rose from the dead for our justification (Rom. 4:24,25). Therefore, He is the only one whom God exalted to give repentance and the forgiveness of sins (Acts 5:31; Matt. 9:6) and to be a meditator between God and man (1 John 2:1,2). Jesus Christ is faithful and just not only to forgive us our sins, but to do that which man could never do—that is, to cleanse us with His precious blood (1 John 1:7,9); to deliver us from sin and the powers of darkness (Col. 1:13); to heal our broken hearts (Luke 4:18); to give us peace (Luke 7:48,50); to transform our lives (2 Cor. 5:17); to make intercession for us (Heb. 7:25); and to keep us from falling (Jude 1:24). In other words, only the Lord Jesus Christ is able to save "to the uttermost [them] that come unto God by him" (Heb. 7:25).

5. *Since we find complete forgiveness and salvation through repentance and confessing our sins directly to the Lord, confession to man is unnecessary and unscriptural.* The Bible gives examples of those who confessed to the Lord and found forgiveness: King David (Psa. 32:5; 51; 2 Sam. 24:10); the woman who "was a sinner" (Luke 7:48,50); the prodigal son (Luke 15:20-24); and the publican (Luke 18:13,14).

6. *Only the Lord knows all our sins, including secret sins that we would be too ashamed to tell anyone else (John 4:16-18; Psa. 19:12; 90:8; Rom. 6:21).* If one confessed his sins to God through a man, his confession would not be complete because he would not recall long forgotten deeds of the past. Also, he would be too ashamed to admit some sins to another. But God knows all things and searches the hearts of men (1 Kings 8:38,39; 1 Chr. 28:9; Psa. 44:21; Jer. 17:9,10; Acts 1:24).

7. *Faith in Christ saves us, not just confessing our sins.* True salvation includes faith in the Lord Jesus Christ and His grace giving repentance and the forgiveness of sins (Acts 5:31; 11:18; 2 Tim. 2:25). When the woman who "was a sinner" came to Jesus in tearful repentance, He said to her, "Thy sins are forgiven. . . . *Thy faith* hath saved thee; go in peace" (Luke 7:48,50).

8. *The Bible promises that when we repent and believe on the Lord*

Jesus Christ, our sins are gone forever. The Lord washes our sins away with His precious blood (1 John 1:7; Rev. 1:5); blots them out (Isa. 44:22); removes them as far as the east is from the west (Psa. 103:12); casts them all into the depths of the sea (Mic. 7:19); and remembers them no more (Isa. 43:25; Heb. 10:17). Therefore, it is unscriptural for us to dig up our past sins and reconfess them to an individual or before a group to find forgiveness from the Lord.

9. The Bible says it is a shame even to speak of those things that were done in secret (Eph. 5:12). New converts should not be pressured into publicly confessing that which they should be ashamed of (Rom. 6:21). This practice only serves the purposes of gossip and feeding the evil curiosity of carnal persons.

Rather, new converts should be encouraged to confess, that is, to publicly acknowledge God's wonderful grace in saving them from sin. We believe this is the meaning of the word confess as used in Matthew 3:6 and Acts 19:18. (According to *Strong's Concordance*, confess means to acknowledge, to profess, to promise. In Matthew 11:25 and Luke 10:21, it is translated as giving thanks.)

10. James 5:16 is written to believers, not to repentant sinners at conversion. It says, "Confess your faults one to another, and pray one for another, that ye may be healed." If a believer knows that some sin in his life has caused his sickness, then he should confess that particular sin to God and to the one whom he has offended. See also Matt. 5:24.

As a means to obtaining salvation, what are the evils of confessing all our sins to a man?

The evil of being condemned by one who may be unmerciful— After realizing he had sinned by taking a census of the population, King David said, "Let us fall now into the hand of the Lord; for his mercies are great: and let me not fall into the hand of man" (2 Sam. 24:14). Man is not always merciful and forgiving.

Simon, the Pharisee, showed his scorn for the repentant woman when he said, "She is a sinner" (Luke 7:39). No doubt he thought that her sins were too great to be forgiven. But Jesus, who is rich in mercy, said to her, "Thy sins are forgiven. . . . Thy faith hath saved thee; go in peace" (vs. 48,50).

The evil of doubting God's mercy and grace—To make it compulsory for anyone to confess their sins to an individual or a group is to make them doubt the sufficiency of God's mercy and grace. Thus, instead of walking in newness of life with the joy of the Lord, they often become spiritually crippled and lack the assurance of sins forgiven.

The evil of exalting man—The New Testament teaches that every believer is a priest of God, even newborn babes in Christ (compare 1 Pet. 2:2 with 2:5). Church leaders who encourage and receive confessions are exalting themselves in an unscriptural way (Acts 5:31). Moreover, they show that they could be given to a curious fascination for wickedness.

The evil of temptation—A person hearing all the morbid details of someone else's past sins could become defiled and be led into temptation. See 1 Cor. 15:33.

The evil of shameful speaking—The Bible says, "And have no fellowship with the unfruitful works of darkness, but rather reprove them. For it is a shame even to speak of those things which are done of them in secret" (Eph. 5: 11,12). "What fruit had ye then in those things whereof ye are now ashamed? for the end of those things is death" (Rom. 6:21).

The evil of trusting in man—God says, "There is none righteous, no, not one. . . . For all have sinned, and come short of the glory of God" (Rom. 3:10,23). If one confesses his sins to a man, to whom does that man confess his sins? Moreover, why should one reveal to another that which does not concern him? What good purpose would it serve?

The evil of bondage to man—Usually, a person comes in bondage to the one who hears his confession of sins.

The evil of someone gossiping your confidential confession—"A faithful man who can find?" (Pro. 20:6). But God is "faithful and just to forgive us our sins, and to cleanse us from all unrighteousness" (1 John 1:9).

My sins are great. How can I be sure that God will forgive me?

Be assured that God's Word promises mercy, pardon, and cleansing to all who call upon Him:

"Seek ye the Lord while he may be found, call ye upon him while he is near: Let the wicked forsake his way, and the unrighteous man his thoughts: and let him return unto the Lord, and he will have mercy upon him; and to our God, for *he will abundantly pardon*" (Isa. 55:6,7).

"For thou, Lord, art good, and ready to forgive; and plenteous in mercy unto all them that call upon thee" (Psa. 86:5).

"Come now, and let us reason together, saith the Lord: though your sins be as scarlet, they shall be as white as snow; though they be red like crimson, they shall be as wool" (Isa. 1:18).

"If we confess our sins, he is faithful and just to forgive us our sins, and to cleanse us from *all unrighteousness*" (1 John 1:9).

"The blood of Jesus Christ his Son cleanseth us from *all sin*" (1 John 1:7).

What are the risks if I do not repent now?

Being ruined by sin—"*Repent*, and turn yourselves from all your transgressions; so iniquity shall not be your ruin" (Ezek. 18:30).

Suffering the vials of God's wrath—"And the fourth angel poured out his vial upon the sun; and power was given unto him to scorch men with fire. And men were scorched with great heat, and blasphemed the name of God, which hath power over these plagues: and they *repented not* to give him glory. And the fifth angel poured out his vial upon the seat of the beast; and his kingdom was full of darkness; and they gnawed their tongues for pain, and blasphemed the God of heaven because of their pains and their sores, and *repented not* of their deeds" (Rev. 16:8-11).

Dying and awakening in the torments of hell fire—"And it came to pass, that the beggar died, and was carried by the angels into Abraham's bosom: the rich man also died, and was buried; and in hell he lift up his eyes, being in torments, and seeth Abraham afar off, and Lazarus in his bosom. . . . Then he said, I pray thee therefore, father, that thou wouldest send him to my father's house: for I have five brethren; that he may testify unto them, lest they also come into this place of torment. Abraham saith unto him, They have Moses and the prophets; let them hear them. And he said, Nay, father Abraham: but if one went unto them from the dead, they will *repent.* And he said unto him, If they hear not Moses and the prophets, neither will they be persuaded, though one rose from the dead" (Luke 16:22,23,27-31).

Not entering the kingdom of heaven, but standing outside with weeping and gnashing of teeth—"From that time Jesus began to preach, and to say, *Repent*: for the kingdom of heaven is at hand" (Matt. 4:17). "There shall be weeping and gnashing of teeth, when ye shall see Abraham, and Isaac, and Jacob, and all the prophets, in the kingdom of God, and you yourselves thrust out" (Luke 13:28).

Treasuring up wrath for yourself on the Day of Judgment—"The goodness of God leadeth thee to *repentance* . . . But after thy hardness and impenitent heart treasurest up unto thyself wrath against the day of wrath and revelation of the righteous judgment of God" (Rom. 2:4,5). "And whosoever was not found written in the book of life was cast into the lake of fire" (Rev. 20:15).

What will unrepentant sinners do at the coming of Jesus?

They will blaspheme God. "And there fell upon men a great hail out of heaven, every stone about the weight of a talent (130 pounds): and men blasphemed God because of the plague of the hail; for the plague thereof was exceeding great" (Rev. 16:21).

They will be humbled and bow down. "The lofty looks of man shall be humbled, and the haughtiness of men shall be bowed down, and the Lord alone shall be exalted in that day" (Isa. 2:11). "At the name of Jesus every knee should bow, of things in heaven, and things in earth, and things under the earth; and that every tongue should confess that Jesus Christ is Lord, to the glory of God the Father" (Phil. 2:10,11).

They will cast down their idols of silver and gold. "In that day a man shall cast his idols of silver, and his idols of gold, which they made each one for himself to worship, to the moles and to the bats" (Isa. 2:20).

They will mourn and their hearts will fail them for fear. "And there shall be signs in the sun, and in the moon, and in the stars; and upon the earth distress of nations, with perplexity: the sea and the waves roaring: Men's hearts failing them for fear, and for looking after those things which are coming on the earth: for the powers of heaven shall be shaken" (Luke 21:25,26). "And then shall all the tribes of the earth mourn, and they shall see the Son of man coming in the clouds of heaven with power and great glory" (Matt. 24:30). See also Isa. 13:6-8.

They will cry to be hidden from "the face of him that sitteth on the throne." "And the kings of the earth, and the great men, and the rich men, and the chief captains, and the mighty men, and every bondman, and every free man, hid themselves in the dens and in the rocks of the mountains; and said to the mountains and rocks, Fall on us, and hide us from the face of him that sitteth on the throne, and from the wrath of the Lamb: for the great day of his wrath is come; and who shall be able to stand?" (Rev. 6:15-17).

Who will be able to stand in that day?

Those who have repented and have their sins forgiven—"If thou, Lord, shouldest mark iniquities, O Lord, who shall *stand*? But there is forgiveness with thee, that thou mayest be feared" (Psa. 130:3,4).

Those who have received the gospel of the grace of God—"Moreover, brethren, I declare unto you the gospel which I preached unto you, which also ye have received, and wherein ye stand" (1 Cor. 15:1). "This is the true grace of God wherein ye *stand*" (1 Pet. 5:12). See also Rom. 5:1,2.

Those who have clean hands, a pure heart, humility, and honesty—"Who shall ascend into the hill of the Lord? or who shall *stand* in his holy place? He that hath clean hands, and a pure heart; who hath not lifted up his soul unto vanity, nor sworn deceitfully. He shall receive the blessing from the Lord, and righteousness from the God of his salvation" (Psa. 24:3-5).

Those who belong to Jesus and depart from sin—"Nevertheless the foundation of God *standeth* sure, having this seal, The Lord knoweth them that are his. And, Let every one that nameth the name of Christ depart from iniquity" (2 Tim. 2:19). See also Psa. 1:5,6.

Those who have put on the whole armor of God—"Wherefore take unto you the whole armour of God, that ye may be able to withstand in the evil day, and having done all, to *stand. Stand* therefore, having your loins girt about with truth, and having on the breastplate of righteousness; and your feet shod with the preparation of the gospel of peace; above all, taking the shield of faith, wherewith ye shall be able to quench all the fiery darts of the wicked. And take the helmet of salvation, and the sword of the Spirit, which is the word of God: praying always with all prayer and supplication in the Spirit, and watching thereunto with all perseverance and supplication for all saints" (Eph. 6:13-18).

Those who watch and pray—Jesus said, "Watch, ye therefore, and pray always, that ye may be accounted worthy to escape all these things that shall come to pass, and to stand before the Son of man" (Luke 21:36).

Those who trust in the Lord—"Who can *stand* before his indignation? and who can abide in the fierceness of his anger? his fury is poured out like fire, and the rocks are thrown down by him. The Lord is good, a strong hold in the day of trouble; and he knoweth them that trust in him" (Nahum 1:6,7). See also Rom. 11:20; 2 Cor. 1:24.

Therefore, if you haven't repented of your sins and trusted in the Lord, do it now!

Don't neglect it until you get sick; you may never be sick.

Don't neglect it until you get more time; you may never get more time.

Don't neglect it until you get old; you may never get old.

Don't neglect it until the Spirit strives more powerfully; He may never strive again.

Don't neglect it until tomorrow; this night your soul may be required of you. Do it now! If with a repentant heart and faith toward our Lord Jesus Christ you will pray, "God be merciful to me a sinner," you will experience the joy of having all your sins forgiven and new life in Christ Jesus (Luke 18:13,14).

What will Christ's coming mean to me if I repent and believe on Him now?

If you repent and patiently continue in well doing, you will receive "glory and honour and immortality, eternal life" (Rom. 2:4,7). Indeed, it will be a glorious day for you and for all true believers when Jesus comes in His own glory, in His Father's glory, and in the glory of all His holy angels to receive His glorious Church, and to eternally reign in His glorious kingdom (Luke 9:26).

Believers "shall see the king in his beauty" (Isa. 33:17). The Bible gives us a glimpse of Christ's glory. The keepers of the tomb saw our resurrected Lord with His countenance like lightning and his raiment white as snow (Matt. 28:3). The apostle Paul described the glory of the Lord as "a light from heaven, above the brightness of the sun" (Acts 26:13). Peter, James, and John were "eyewitnesses of his majesty" (2 Pet. 1:16). They indeed had a preview of Christ's coming in glory: He was "transfigured before them: and his face did shine as the sun, and his raiment was white as the light" (Matt. 17:2).

The Bible also describes the glory of the Father. He is "glorious in holiness" (Ex. 15:11), "clothed with honour and majesty" (Psa. 104:1), and His glory is above the heavens (Psa. 113:4). The Psalmist David said, "The heavens declare the glory of God; and the firmament sheweth his handywork" (Psa. 19:1). "Blessed be the Lord God, the God of Israel, who only doeth wondrous things. And blessed be his glorious name for ever: and let the whole earth be filled with his glory" (Psa. 72:18,19).

Christ is coming in the glory of all the holy angels. How many angels are there? The Bible speaks of "ten thousand times ten thousand, and thousands of thousands" (Rev. 5:11). In other words, there is "an innumerable company of angels" (Heb. 12:22). In 2 Kings 19:35, one angel slew 185,000 of the Lord's enemies. In Revelation 18:1, the glory of one angel illuminated the whole earth. If just one angel is so powerful and glorious, how much more glorious will be "ten thousand times ten thousand, and thousands of thousands" of angels!

What will it be like to see heaven open, and to behold countless millions of glorious, holy angels "ascending and descending upon the Son of man"? (John 1:51). Words fail. They will come "with a great sound of a trumpet" and "shall gather together his elect from the four winds, from one end of heaven to the other" (Matt. 24:31).

Our glorious Savior is coming to "be glorified in his saints" (2 Thess. 1:10). At His coming true believers will:

- *Be glorified together with Christ*—"And if children, then heirs; heirs of God, and joint-heirs with Christ; if so be that we suffer with him, that we may be also glorified together. For I reckon that the sufferings of this present time are not worthy to be compared with the glory which shall be revealed in us" (Rom. 8:17,18). See also Rom. 8:30; 2 Cor. 4:17; 2 Thess. 1:10; 1 Pet. 1:7.

• *Be changed like unto His glorious body*—"Who shall change our vile body, that it may be fashioned like unto his glorious body" (Phil. 3:21). See also 1 John 3:2.

• *Be raised in glory*—"It is sown in dishonour; it is raised in glory" (1 Cor. 15:43). See also Rom. 8:21.

• *Appear with Him in glory*—"When Christ, who is our life, shall appear, then shall ye also appear with him in glory" (Col. 3:4). See also Psa. 73:24.

• *Be glad with exceeding joy when His glory shall be revealed*—"But rejoice, inasmuch as ye are partakers of Christ's sufferings; that, when his glory shall be revealed, ye may be glad also with exceeding joy" (1 Pet. 4:13).

• *Receive an eternal crown of glory*—"And when the chief Shepherd shall appear, ye shall receive a crown of glory that fadeth not away" (1 Pet. 5:4).

• *Be presented faultless before the presence of His glory*—"Now unto him that is able to keep you from falling, and to present you faultless before the presence of his glory with exceeding joy" (Jude 1:24).

• *Enter the glorious kingdom of God*—"Then shall the King say unto them on his right hand, Come, ye blessed of my Father, inherit the kingdom prepared for you from the foundation of the world" (Matt. 25:34). This eternal existence is described in part as "the holy city, [the] new Jerusalem, coming down from God out of heaven, prepared as a Bride adorned for her husband. . . . Having the *glory* of God: and her light was like unto a stone most precious, even like a jasper stone, clear as crystal. . . . And the city had no need of the sun, neither of the moon, to shine in it; for the *glory* of God did lighten it, and the Lamb is the light thereof. . . . And there shall in no wise enter into it any thing that defileth, neither whatsoever worketh abomination, or maketh a lie: but they which are written in the Lamb's book of life" (Rev. 21:2,11,23,27).

• *Inherit glory and shine with His glory forever and ever*—"The wise shall inherit glory" (Pro. 3:35). "Then shall the righteous shine forth as the sun in the kingdom of their Father" (Matt.

13:43). "And they that be wise shall shine as the brightness of the firmament; and they that turn many to righteousness as the stars for ever and ever" (Dan. 12:3).

At the Second Coming, therefore, all who have repented and believed on the Lord Jesus Christ shall behold Him coming in the clouds of heaven with power and *great glory* and shall eternally reign with Him in His *glorious*, heavenly kingdom. Oh, what a glorious day that will be!

"He which testifieth these things saith, Surely I come quickly. Amen. Even so, come, Lord Jesus" (Rev. 22:20).

Word Index

Scripture Index

About the Authors

Ken and Agnes Macdonald were involved in pastoral ministry in the United States for nearly fifteen years when God wonderfully redirected their steps. Sensing that they should seek God in all-night prayer meetings, the Macdonalds experienced a fresh work of grace in their lives, the fear of the Lord, and a renewed love for His Word. The Spirit of holiness dealt with their personal lives, causing them to repent and obey God anew. Among other things, this involved turning off their TV and getting rid of it completely.

In the midst of a thriving pastoral ministry, the Macdonalds were challenged to give up all and to answer the call of God to "Go in this thy might, . . . have not I sent thee?" (Judges 6:14). Like the reluctant Gideon, the Macdonalds needed God's confirmation. After answering with resounding clarity, God directed them according to Hebrews 13:5,6 to live by faith, telling no one their needs. They committed themselves to go where He would send them and to preach what He would give them to preach—and they have done just that.

Their ministry opportunities have spanned six continents with much of their overseas ministry being focused in Africa. Ken and Agnes travel extensively from their home base near Cleveland, Ohio.

If we may help you in knowing more about Jesus and living for Him, please feel free to write us. There will be no obligation.

Mr. and Mrs. Kenneth B. Macdonald
1298 S.O.M. Center Road #111
Mayfield Heights, Ohio 44124, U.S.A.